POLITY AND PRAXIS

A Program for American Practical Theology

Dennis P. McCann
Charles R. Strain

UNIVERSITY PRESS OF AMERICA

Lanham • New York • London

University Press of America®, Inc.
4720 Boston Way
Lanham, Maryland 20706

3 Henrietta Street
London WC2E 8LU England

Printed in the United States of America
British Cataloging in Publication Information Available

Library of Congress Cataloging-in-Publication Data

McCann, Dennis.
Polity and praxis : a program for American practical theology /
Dennis P. McCann and Charles R. Strain.
p. cm.
Reprint. Originally published: Minneapolis : Winston Press, ©1985.
Includes bibliographical references and index.
1. Theology Practical. 2. Theology—Study and teaching—United States.
3. Christian ethics—United States. 4. Christianity and politics.
I. Strain, Charles R. II. Title.
[BV3.M43 1990] 261'.1—dc20 90–36561 CIP

ISBN 0–8191–7847–0

CONTENTS

FOREWORD

We believe that *Polity and Praxis* is a distinctly different kind of book. It is neither a systematic treatise in academic theology nor an eyewitness account of the latest skirmishes in the ongoing praxis of liberation. Even so, it is inspired by passionate commitment, a commitment triggered by our growing uneasiness with the mutual incomprehension, if not downright hostility, that today separates so-called academic theologians from their brothers and sisters who reflect theologically on the praxis of the Christian basic communities. Throughout our careers we have acted in solidarity with both groups of theologians, with now relatively more emphasis on critical reflection and then relatively more on social action. Because we have attempted in various ways to be faithful to the concerns of both camps, we see the conflict between them as unnecessary and destructive of both, precisely at this moment when both are so desperately needed: the vision and commitment to religious praxis of the one and the critical rigor as well as the intellectual honesty of the other.

To begin a process of reconciliation, we offer what follows as a manual that will attempt to set the stage for all sides to debate the issue of critical reflection and religious praxis. We have deliberately avoided developing a substantively theological position here, hoping instead to provide an appropriate frame of reference in which to conduct the debate. This book, then, makes unusual demands, for it tries to explicate that frame of reference and not just lead the reader through another sympathetic discussion of the theological literature of liberation. What you are asked to judge is not another proposal for practical theology, but a program for constructing and evaluating any models of practical theology. We do intend to develop our own models of practical theology, but they are not to be confused with what we hope to accomplish in this programmatic study. For the present the pressing task is to mediate the truth of both academic and liberation theologies so that together they may lead Christianity and our American culture forward into the emerging global civilization.

We wish to thank our colleagues at De Paul University for their support for this project. In particular, Richard J. Meister, Dean of the

College of Liberal Arts and Sciences, and the College's Committee on Faculty Research and Development are to be thanked for successive Summer Grants given to Dennis McCann in 1982 and to Charles Strain in 1983, which allowed us to complete this project. We also wish to thank our friends who read all or some of the chapters that went into this book: Don Browning, John Coleman, John Dominic Crossan, Lois Livezey, Robin Lovin, and David Tracy. Those who assisted us in the typing of the manuscripts also deserve thanks: Angela Arney, Miriam Shires, Barbara Szmyd, Laima Vadeisa and Peg Zeman. Special help in graphics design was given by Dianne Hanau-Strain.

CHAPTER ONE

RELIGION AND POLITICS: THE DEMAND FOR PRACTICAL THEOLOGY

In Christ the all-comprehensiveness of the liberating process reaches its fullest sense.

(Gutierrez, 1973: 178)

The question whether objective truth can be attributed to human thinking is not a question of theory but is a practical *question. In practice man must prove the truth, that is, the reality and power, the this-sidedness of his thinking.*

(Marx and Engels, 1964: 69–70)

Religion and politics. These words do not sit well with most North Americans today. We think not of Lincoln's Second Inaugural Address pondering the inscrutable purposes of a righteous God, but of slick manipulations of public opinion by politicians compelled only by the will to power. Not Martin Luther King's dream song but the drum beats of new authoritarian moralisms echo in our mind. Most North Americans believe that little good can come of ideological conflict; still less good, when the ideology is religiously motivated. We admire a few simple souls who, with uncontestable love and little politics, intervene directly on behalf of the poor, the weak, the oppressed. Yet we despise the simple for their ignorance of the way of the world, their ineffectiveness.

Practical theologians are apt to dismiss such musings as indicative of the Babylonian Captivity of the bourgeois mind. Exiled from the polis of genuine human interaction, forgetful of their own tradition of vital religious reflection upon the ends of public life, North Americans huddle in isolation, hoping to ride out the latest firestorm of ideological conflict.

There is a truth to each of these positions: mass cynicism, the wisdom of the simple, the bold manifestoes of intellectual and religious elites. A partial truth. In his epic of the Thirty Years War, *Mother Courage and Her Children*, Bertolt Brecht dramatized the onesidedness and, therefore, the futility of each of them. (1962) The cynicism of Mother Courage, looking always for the main chance while losing life and family in dribs and drabs; the simplicity of Kattrin, her daughter, rescuing children but crushed by the war; the inanity of the Chaplain, custodian of the Word, singing the praises of the princes of war—each of these positions is derailed by the twists and turns of history. Religion and politics, however they are construed, yield only confusion.

Brecht, of course, was no cynic; his parable was designed to instigate critical reflection. How do we move beyond the terrain of confused discourse about religion and politics? How pave the way for sane ideological commitment, authentically humane praxis? A new generation of theologians, risking a recurrence of the futile confusions identified by Brecht, has committed itself to critical reflection on praxis. Led by such thinkers as Gregory Baum, Robert McAfee Brown, John Coleman, James Cone, Mary Daly, Gustavo Gutierrez, Frederick Herzog, J. B. Metz, Richard John Neuhaus, Michael Novak, Rosemary Ruether, Juan Luis Segundo and many others, this generation has rejuvenated practical theology. As in the heyday of the American Social Gospel and of Christian Realism, practical theology is once more a culturally significant and, so, a perilous undertaking. Whether this generation will succeed in developing a religious ideology that maps a route beyond Brecht's impasse, beyond the false alternatives of simple-minded activism, religious or ideological absolutism, and political cynicism is not yet clear. It is clear that any retreat from the confusions of religion and politics is impossible. The works of these theologians suggest that the potential transformation of Christian praxis through critical reflection is worth the risks involved. New models of practical theology are required by our situation, and a new generation will provide them.

We write in basic sympathy with this group of religious intellectuals and social activists, for we share their commitment both to seek justice and peace through social action and to reflect theologically on the ultimate concerns experienced in it. Yet precisely because of this sense of community, we feel entitled to scrutinize the new expressions of practical theology, to examine their new way of posing theological questions, and to criticize some of the answers they promote. We will argue that the new practical theology has a promising future only if it avoids any pretense of historical uniqueness, exclusive moral validity, and religious absoluteness. By renouncing these distortions, it will assure a proper place for religious vision in the larger world of public discourse.

We will show that the new generation of practical theologians stands in a tradition of explicitly theological reflection that goes back at least as far as the turn of the century. Like their predecessors, Ernst Troeltsch, Walter Rauschenbusch, John A. Ryan, Paul Tillich, Jacques Maritain, H. Richard and Reinhold Niebuhr, John Courtney Murray, and others, the new generation is responding to the modern historical consciousness that has worked its way into even the most conservative Christian communities. They respond to this challenge, not as a theoretical problem, but as a practical opportunity for renewing and transforming not only the traditions of these communities but also those constituting society as a public realm.

It has slowly dawned on students of this tradition that both the old and the new generations of practical theologians are involved in criticizing and reconstructing the whole range of modern ideologies, religious as well as secular. Our intention in this work is not to construct yet another ideology, but to assist practical theologians by formally clarifying the nature of this task, specifically as it emerges as an agenda for Christian communities. We hope, in short, to provide criteria for practical theology, criteria that will not prejudice the ideological questions disputed among practical theologians, but will make it possible to discuss those questions in a disciplined way and to resolve them. Whether any set of criteria can actually do this, we leave our readers to decide after they have studied our proposals.

The new forms of practical theology are most promising when they are most dialectical, that is, when they engage older traditions of religious reflection in a way that extends as it transforms their fundamental intentions. We believe that the dialectic can be extended still further by going beyond present attempts to transform practical theology. Four of these attempts at "going beyond" will serve to situate our fundamental intentions in this book *vis-`a-vis* both older and newer traditions of practical theology.

A. BEYOND THE CLERICAL PARADIGM

The new practical theologies are not an attack upon the clergy, or upon the seminaries and divinity schools that nurtured them. They do, however, stand in sharp contrast to what some may remember as the practical theology of the past. According to Edward Farley and John E. Burkhart, the old practical theology consisted of those specifically professional studies that qualified a seminarian for leadership in the Christian community. Usually it included such things as homiletics and canon law, and, in more recent times, pastoral counseling and parish management. Unlike the other genres of theological education, practical theology taught the techniques necessary for mastering the role of the priest or minister. It could not have been other than narrowly ecclesiastical in its focus. (Cf. Farley, 1983; Burkhart, 1983)

To go beyond the clerical paradigm does not mean to make a complete break with this tradition. The new practical theologies are still concerned with leadership, but the focus of that leadership has been profoundly transformed. Shifting from the preservation of the religious community to the articulation of its worldly mission, the new practical theologies seek to carry out that mission not in sublime isolation but in collaboration with other institutions working toward the common good. Not only clerics but members of base communities voicing their prophetic witness as well as educated Christians critically fulfilling their professional responsibilities are the potential leaders addressed by practical theology. The whole question of religious leadership must be recast in this broader historical and societal context.

Practical theology as discourse about the religious foundations of the *res publica*, nevertheless, does not eliminate traditional concerns with pastoral care, religious education, and the like. Flourishing within subsidiary genres related to practical theology, these concerns accord with the religious community's worldly mission. Don Browning, for example, has shown how a theology of pastoral care, operating within this framework, can become a normative, that is, religious-ethical, reflection upon the human life cycle. (1983: 189, 191–195) While we will restrict ourselves to defining the sort of framework that practical theologies construct and how they should go about it, the work of people like Browning is indispensable for reshaping the many tasks traditionally associated with practical theological education.

One striking example of how getting beyond the clerical paradigm informs the new practical theologies is evident in Gustavo Gutierrez's influential work, *A Theology of Liberation* (1973). Gutierrez repudiates the traditional differentiation of clerical and lay roles in Catholic social action movements. The residual hierarchical character of all such differentiations undermines the effectiveness of Christian participation in the struggle for liberation. Gutierrez's sense of this practical failure becomes the point of departure for an ideological critique of the dualistic theology of pre-Vatican II Catholicism, which supported such a differentiation. To go beyond the clerical paradigm, in this case, means to test every ecclesiastical discipline and theological assumption by the concrete experience of Christian witness in the world. If this test suggests that the Vatican's restriction on the clergy's involvement in "politics" unwittingly favors the status quo, then so much the worse for this particular standard of clerical professionalism.

While we agree with Gutierrez that ideological critique may be the only way to renew a genuinely Christian ministry, we believe that he and many others still have not gone far enough. A residue of sacralism still lingers in the approach of the new generation of practical theologians, and reinforces the clerical paradigm even as it seeks to get beyond it. To the extent that their program of "critical reflection on praxis" merely substitutes a sacred norm of "orthopraxis" for the repudiated "orthodoxy," it perpetuates the claims of religious absoluteness that heretofore have marred clerical involvement in politics, however well-intended. Getting beyond the clerical paradigm, in our view, involves not just shifting the focus of concern from leadership in the community to leadership in society at large but, even more so, renouncing the pretense of sacred authority in politics. Christian social activists may have a distinctive agenda for social change, but they can claim no "hermeneutic privilege" on the basis of their desire to give authentic Christian witness in the world. Nor can they claim a special competence in articulating a normative vision of social reality purely on the grounds of their solidarity with the oppressed.

To suggest otherwise is unwittingly to exploit the notion of solidarity for reasons that have little to do with solidarity itself. Privileged claims all too commonly license the intellectual equivalent of guerrilla warfare. While practical theology must be refined in the crucible of ideological criticism and reconstruction, we believe that these ideological tasks are best carried out when no privilege is sought or accepted, when all competing theologies of praxis are subject to scrutiny according to the norms and procedures of public discourse.

B. BEYOND CULTURAL ESTRANGEMENT

By insisting on a broader understanding of Christian witness, the new generation of practical theologians has done more than undermine the inherited clerical paradigm. It has also triggered a sea-change in the cultural assumptions governing theological education. A generation ago, theological education, whether in the university or in the seminary, Catholic or Protestant, was overtly universalist while covertly and provincially European. In his illuminating little book, *Hope Against Hope: Moltmann to Merton in One Theological Decade* (1976), Walter Capps recalls that when he began his teaching career in the early 1960's the one thing his students wanted to know was whether he considered himself a Barthian or a disciple of Tillich. No local options, apparently, were considered. For serious theology could be voiced only in an alien tongue. Socialized into an intellectual milieu alien from their own, American theologians usually went into exile, often spiritually but sometimes physically, by studying in Europe, in order to establish their credibility.

The new generation of practical theologians has put an end to this exile and called all spiritual expatriates home. José Comblin spoke not just for Latin Americans when he observed that "any Latin American who has studied in Europe has to undergo detoxification before he can begin to act." (Cf. Assmann, 1976: 56) This detoxification, however, requires more than just studying the local options instead of the

European classics. For cultural estrangement is experienced not just as exile but also as oppression. Detoxification thus involves confronting the contagions of racism, sexism, and the like that continue to keep North Americans in a state of estrangement from themselves. More than just attuning theological education to indigenous voices, it requires ideological critique and reconstruction based on one's own developing experience of Christian social action.

While we agree with the need to overcome cultural estrangement in both its forms, we suggest that practical theologians still rely too frequently on models alien to the North American experience. Were Walter Capps to begin his teaching career today, the burning question might be whether he was more influenced by Metz's German political theology or by Gutierrez's Latin American liberation theology. But the process of detoxification, once begun, admits no pre-established limits. Getting beyond cultural estrangement requires us to go further in facilitating a genuinely open dialogue in which North American Christians can question themselves in light of political and liberation theologies while recognizing that neither is sufficiently adapted to the North American reality.

We are optimistic about this possibility, largely on account of John A. Coleman's recent work, *An American Strategic Theology* (1982). Immersed in this dialogue, Coleman outlines an agenda for criticizing and reconstructing various aspects of the North American and Catholic traditions and their bearing on Christianity's "worldly mission" today. In order to clarify the religious vision informing this mission, Coleman turns not to the Europeans and the Latin Americans, but to Orestes Brownson, John A. Ryan, and John Courtney Murray, three North American Catholic precursors of the new practical theology. Coleman's work demonstrates that detoxification can proceed without substituting one form of cultural estrangement for another.

Our program for renewing practical theology will further the work begun by Coleman in two ways. First, we will allow the North American experience of religious and cultural pluralism an active voice in the reshaping of the theology of praxis. Second, we will approach this same North American tradition systematically, through a generic analysis of practical theology. Repeatedly we will turn for illustration to those practical theologians who have consistently favored the local option—the John Winthrops and the Reinhold Niebuhrs, the Martin Luther Kings, and the Rosemary Radford Ruethers.

C. BEYOND PRIVATIZATION

Another mark distinguishing the new practical theologies from the old is their sophistication about the theory-ladenness of experience. Although the appeal to concrete experience allows them leverage against the clerical paradigm and cultural estrangement, they usually do not consider experience as an absolute. Experience itself can be distorted and, as a result, judgments regarding the authenticity of experience often depend upon the adequacy and appropriateness of the theories which interpret it. Today practical theologians share a consensus on many points regarding these theories: they must highlight the social dimension of experience; they must provide an adequate account of the ideological struggles in which we find ourselves; and, what may amount to the same thing, they must enhance the practical theologian's capacity for socially relevant self-criticism. The role of critical social theory in practical theology is evident in a common struggle to overcome the privatization of Christian life.

Within such critical social theory, privatization appears as the ambiguous result of secularization. Secularization, the gradual eclipse of organized religion in modern societies, means the collapse of "Christendom" as a concrete historical ideal and the separation of Church and State, with all its social, political, and ethical consequences. According to the theory of privatization, these consequences are as negative as they are positive. While the eclipse may suggest a graceful renunciation of the arrogance of power, it may also portend a blind acquiescence to a public world shadowed from any moral authority whatsoever. Privatization thus means living a kind of moral and religious schizophrenia, in which one's personal "inwardness" continues to respond to the conventions of Christian piety, while one's outward behavior in various social roles displays no discernible difference from that of nonbelievers. When, in light of critical social theory, practical theologians denounce the privatization of Christianity, they are calling attention to the fact that secularization contains a threat to Christianity's worldly mission every bit as serious as that previously posed by Christendom's disastrous experiments with theocracy.

The struggle against privatization, of course, is virtually synonymous with the work of J. B. Metz. Along with his countryman, Jürgen Moltmann, Metz was the first of the new practical theologians to use critical social theory to define the phenomenon of privatization, not simply as an indication of the failure of evangelization, but as a cultural process undermining all moral and religious traditions in advanced industrial societies. (Cf. Metz, 1969: 107–55; Moltmann, 1967: 304–338) This theoretical perspective enabled Metz to establish his "new political theology," not as another apologetic for the traditional prerogatives of Christianity in public life, but as an attempt to redefine the role of the church in a secularized society as "an institution of socially critical freedom." Parallel to Bultmann's program of demythologization, Metz envisioned a "deprivatization" of Christian witness in which the church would criticize political power in all its manifestations. (Metz, 1969: 117–19, 134)

There has been considerable debate about whether Metz's understanding of the purely critical, negative role of the church in public life is adequate to the task of deprivatization, whether it limits arbitrarily the scope of Christian social action. (Cf. Segundo, 1979: 247) Metz fails to question the assumption that society is a monolithic whole, the object of uniform processes of social change. As a result, religious and cultural pluralism tends to be obscured, not just as a fact but also as a value. Even if the church could become an "institution of socially critical freedom," it alone cannot guarantee the moral foundations of society. If totalitarianism is an ever present possibility in all modern societies, it can only be resisted by adhering to an ideal of public discourse that transcends all the particular communities within a pluralistic culture. Such an ideal calls all of them to mediate their particular social agendas in an ongoing process of mutual criticism directed toward a good to be specified in common. While theologies of praxis seek to overcome privatization and so give shape to the public sphere, the experience of religious and cultural pluralism calls for a new kind of public discourse which alters fundamentally the nature of deprivatization strategies.

D. BEYOND POLITICIZATION

A number of practical theologians have focused upon a concern parallel to deprivatization, namely, the need to avoid an equally ambiguous politicization of the gospel message. These theologians have recognized that not all concern for Christian spirituality counts as evidence of phony "spiritualization," that there are distortions—both religious and psychological—latent in the dynamics of privatization and deprivatization. By failing to acknowledge this problem, the new practical theology risks substituting a merely political paradigm for the clerical paradigm, risks overcoming the cultural estrangement evident in middle class Christianity by embracing an equally alien sacralization of public life. Practical theology, in short, risks shortchanging the promise of liberation by allowing the critique of bourgeois "inwardness" to foreclose the range of authentic modes of ultimate transformation operative in religious communities.

Clearly we are not siding with reactionaries like Edward L. Norman who use the problem of politicization to dismiss the new practical theology out of hand. (1979) We turn instead to sympathetic critics, like Charles Davis, who explore the relationship of Christian mysticism and social action in the context of comparative religious history. In Davis's analysis getting beyond politicization means recognizing the fundamental difference between authentic religious interiority and an alienated modern subjectivity. The limits to deprivatization, therefore, are disclosed as soon as practical theologians admit that Christianity's worldly mission includes witnessing to "a differentiation of consciousness, which was first achieved religiously when the individual self was constituted in relation to God . . . as an interior world over against the external world." (Davis, 1980: 176) Davis thus seeks to overcome the equally unacceptable tendencies of privatization and politicization by insisting that the experience of interiority, ultimately grounded religiously, is a precondition for genuine political interaction just as political relationships are central to the full emergence of the self. (Ibid.: 178)

It is possible to go beyond even Davis's promising insights. His proposal to open the new practical theology to creative dialogue with the field of comparative religious history encourages us to examine Christianity's worldly mission in terms of the fundamental category of religious praxis. We insist, and we suspect that Davis would agree, that this mission is not to be understood simply by striking a healthier balance between "the interior self" and "the public sphere" of social action. As comparative study of the world's religions indicates, religious praxis always represents a broader range of activities than that envisioned by the modern dichotomy of public and private life. Frederick J. Streng, for example, lists four traditional modes of religious praxis, each of which is effectively present to some extent in any particular community's history of religiousness. Over and above "the mystical element in religion" recognized by Davis, Streng differentiates a "prophetic," a "sacramental," and an "ethical" mode. (Cf. Streng, Lloyd, and Allen, 1973: 9–10) In so doing, Streng puts the lie to transformational fundamentalism: there is more than one path up a mountain, and the paths frequently crisscross. While we do not mean to endorse Streng's categories as exhaustively defining religious praxis, we do wish to point out that once Davis's suggestion for placing the new practical theology in the context of comparative religious history is adopted, the question of religious pluralism becomes obvious. Getting beyond politicization will mean achieving a deeper appreciation for the plurality of authentic ways of being religious than either the new generation of practical theologians or its critics have demonstrated so far.

E. A NEW PROGRAM FOR PRACTICAL THEOLOGY

We intend to take a consistently dialectical stance towards the substantive contributions of the new generation of practical theologians. In these first few pages we have emphasized the basic affirmation underlying and supporting the criticisms that we will make throughout this book. Who can be surprised at the presence of confusions and distortions in the works of these religious thinkers? If Brecht's parable truly evokes the modern situation, confusions and distortions of both religion and politics are our particular fate. No one escapes them in a single leap.

We do not offer another substantive practical theology which claims to leap where others have stumbled. This book presents a *program* for doing practical theology. As such, it outlines a series of small, but coordinated steps which can be taken by practical theologians in order to move beyond the difficulties that we have just examined. Our analysis is formal. The positions that we take have to do with the procedures not the content of practical theology. We hope that this work will be read as a handbook, a user's manual for the examination and construction of practical theologies. We have illustrated our analysis of the various elements of the genre of practical theology by discussing small chunks of substantive models, largely drawn from the North American tradition.

It is the burden of this work as a whole to show what it means for practical theology to carry out its ideological tasks as a form of public discourse. We can, however, anticipate the itinerary just enough to give our readers a roadmap through what at times will be a complex argument. Our basic strategy in this book is to combine two different approaches often found separately in disciplinary literature: an examination of both the logic of inquiry and a genre analysis. The logic of inquiry approach usually sets out the conditions under which some form of theoretical discourse is possible: what the nature of the task undertaken is; what the major conceptual obstacles that stand in its way are; how these obstacles may be overcome. It usually proceeds deductively on a formal level. Genre analysis, by contrast, is empirical and historical. It presupposes the existence of a certain body of literature, and seeks to determine certain family resemblances in form and content. It proceeds by drawing inductively a composite picture of the underlying structure of a given form of discourse from an analysis of a wealth of fragmentary realizations. We believe that, while each of these approaches is necessary, neither alone is sufficient to establish the criteria operative in a form of public discourse like practical theology.

We do not believe that our criteriological map of the genre of practical theology amounts to a recipe for definitiveness. To think so would merely be to substitute one set of absolutist pretensions for another. As we hope to make clear throughout our presentation, to conceive of our task as one of model construction already presupposes that any particular model of practical theology is perspectivally limited in various ways. We are not advising the new generation of practical theologians to stop what they are doing in order to take up our agenda of theoretical reflection. Instead, as we hope our generic analysis makes clear, we are mapping operations that are already ongoing in their works, so that these operations might be carried out more effectively. Ours is not a substantive alternative but a formal conceptual grid against which to locate and better understand the whole range of substantive perspectives currently available in practical theology.

By providing the ground rules for public discourse, this work can clarify the terms on which practical theologians take up their task. Overcoming the distortions of religion and politics depends upon the intelligent discourse of many such theologians and the intelligent praxis of many more committed Christians.

CHAPTER TWO

PARADIGM VERSUS GENRE: THE NATURE OF PRACTICAL THEOLOGY

The writer is not defined by the use of specialized tools which parade literature . . . but by the power of surprising by some formal device, a particular collusion of man with nature, i.e., a meaning: and in this "surprise" it is form which keeps watch, which instructs, which knows, which thinks, which "commits."

(Barthes, 1972: 177–78)

Valid interpretation is always governed by a valid inference about genre.

(Hirsch, 1967: 113)

According to the literary critic, Tzvetan Todorov, there are two basic questions which one can ask about a given type of written work: (a) Why does this type exist? and (b) What is this type? (1975: 157–58) Chapter One briefly addressed Todorov's first question. Its answer, however succinct, is presupposed and consciously defended in all that follows in this book: Praxis is not blind activism. It is action generated by communities self-consciously constituted through public discourse. Religiously grounded praxis, to be specific, requires religious discourse designed to create a community committed to a process of ultimate transformation. Because this process includes the public sphere, it must make its case through rational arguments refined in a crucible of critical but committed reflection and addressed to all who participate in that public arena. Practical Theology is the result.

In the face to face interaction of the ancient *polis* where participation was restricted to the nonslave and nonfemale householder, oral discourse generally sufficed to perpetuate the praxis of the community. (Cf. Arendt, 1958: 24–31) In those modern societies where participation is reduced to the strategies and tactics of popular plebiscite, electronic mass media suffice to mobilize masses who never become nor are meant to become politically conscious publics. But in modern societies where political action is premised upon the free participation of all the citizens, a "culture of critical discourse" has traditionally served as the catalyst for creating genuine publics. Such a culture, in part, is the product of the written word which has a singular propensity for creating models of social order which can be subject to critical analysis. (Cf. Gouldner, 1976: 39–43, 167–70) Public discourse appropriate to praxis, in such a culture, thus usually becomes written discourse. Insofar as it, too, is situated in such a culture, practical theology develops as a form of written discourse.

Todorov's second question—What is the type?—is the major concern of this book. We will argue, first, that practical theology can be characterized neither as a new paradigm for theological discourse in general nor as a particular functional specialization. Instead, we propose to define it as a specific genre within the field of written theological discourse. Second, we will attempt to place practical theology in relationship to other types of public discourse, both religious and secular. Third, we will argue that the process of model-construction, already evident in other forms of critical reflection, can overcome deficiencies endemic to practical theologies as well as other genres of ideological discourse. Subsequently, we will study in detail each of the structural elements of this genre of theological reflection.

A. NEITHER PARADIGM NOR FUNCTIONAL SPECIALIZATION

Our first obstacle in defining this genre, ironically enough, stems from the excessive claims made by many proponents of the new practical theology. In their view practical theology *displaces* all other forms of theological discourse. Typically, they understand their preferred model of practical theology, say, liberation theology, as a fundamental challenge to the assumptions, methods, and forms of Western, academic, Christian theology. (Harrison, 1975: 254)

> There has . . . been a break of some magnitude in the tradition of theology. We may describe this break as the move to

> "political theology"—provided we understand that phrase in a particular way. Political theology as understood here is a new style of theology, a new way of doing theology, a new method or dimension that affects theology as a whole. It is not a part of theology, but theology in its entirety done politically . . . .
> (Davis, 1980: 2–3)

However promising in and of itself, this sense of a formal, epistemological, and methodological break with traditional ways of theological reflection (Hennelly, 1979: 23, 33–35, 51) has misled some into making absolute claims for their own paradigms of practical theology. Juan Luis Segundo, for one, argues that liberation theology is "the one standpoint indicated by Christian sources as the authentic, privileged one for the right understanding of divine revelation in Jesus Christ." (1974: 105)

While such claims may incite controversy, neither have they been warranted nor can they be justified. First, any claim to a privileged position for understanding the Christian witness undermines the claim that theirs is a new paradigm for the theological enterprise. For the concepts of paradigm and paradigm shift presuppose an explicit acknowledgment of the epistemological relativity involved in the historical evolution of any discipline. Segundo's sense of a uniquely valid standpoint violates this chastened awareness of the limits of fundamental construals of reality. (Kuhn, 1970: 94, 105, 111–35, 206) Second, such a suggestion is difficult to warrant theologically. Christian theologians have long recognized that their acknowledgment of human finitude includes an awareness of the finitude of the human mind. Moreover, to act upon Segundo's assumptions would mean to reduce radically the legitimate variety of theological works ranging from autobiographies to tracts for the times. (Cf. Ruland, 1978) Exclusive claims constrict the meanings projected in religious life and praxis to a narrow set of themes. (Gustafson, 1975: 136–38)

Even if the claims made by a Segundo are unwarranted, we still confront the typical assumption that this paradigm shift has occurred only recently. Such a view is historically myopic. Throughout this book we will argue that a dialectic of theory and praxis has been carried on by numerous practical theologians in the nineteenth and twentieth centuries who created such distinct models as the Social Gospel, Integral Humanism, and Christian Realism. Contemporary efforts represent not so much a new way of doing theology as a heightened awareness of the exigencies of *one* mode of theological discourse characteristic of the modern era. Viewing practical theology in this context, we must object to the presumption that one type of theological discourse suffices as the exclusive paradigm for doing theology. Such presumption does not just distort the history and character of practical theology; it also saps the creative vitality of the entire theological enterprise.

Another obstacle to defining practical theology as a genre involves the concept of functional specialization. This concept, as developed by Bernard Lonergan, correctly views the theological enterprise as a complex *process* comprised of interdependent sets of related operations requiring a division of labor. "Functional specialization distinguishes and separates successive stages in the process from data to results." (Lonergan, 1972: 125–26) This theory has the advantage of grasping theology as a unified enterprise that coordinates a multiplicity of approaches. The distribution of tasks, the diversity of methods and the division of goals among the various specializations called for in Lonergan's theory, of course, would curb the "one-sided totalitarian ambitions" of those who make absolute claims for practical theology. (Ibid.: 136–38)

In Lonergan's schema, as developed in *Method in Theology*, practical theology would belong to the eighth and final functional specialization—communications.

> To communicate the Christian message is to lead another to share in one's cognitive, constitutive, effective meaning . . . . Through communication there is constituted community and, conversely, community constitutes and perfects itself through communication. Accordingly the Christian church is a process of self-constitution . . . . Further, the church is . . . an outgoing process. It exists not just for itself but for mankind. Its aim is the realization of the Kingdom of God not only within its own organization but in the whole of human society and not only in the after life but also in this life.
>
> (Lonergan, 1972: 362–64)

To his credit, Lonergan's understanding of the authentic self as a process of self-transcendence through conversion and his essentially transformative theory of truth as developed in *Insight* do provide the basis for an understanding of theology grounded fundamentally in cognitive praxis. (Lamb, 1982: 116–43) Nevertheless, Alfred Hennelly correctly notes Lonergan's misunderstanding of the distinctive character of practical theology. In the scheme of functional specialization, communications remains the vaguely defined afterthought that it has been in most reflections upon the theological enterprise. Lonergan overlooks the degree to which practical theologians employ several functional specializations and combine them to create a distinct type of theological discourse. (Hennelly, 1979: 13–14) While communications is intrinsic to the constitution of the community, practical theologians stress the degree to which practical theology, as critical reflection upon the praxis of a religious community, is constitutive of theology as such. Finally, while Lonergan's theory enables us to appreciate the diversity of contributions to the *work* of theology, it does not help us to grasp the formal integrity of specific *works* of theology.

B. THEOLOGICAL GENRES

David Tracy and Schubert Ogden provide alternatives to the positions of a Segundo and a Lonergan. Both argue that theology is a single discipline with three major subdisciplines. In Tracy's case the three subdisciplines are Foundational, Systematic and Practical theology: in Ogden's, Historical, Systematic and Practical.[1] Ogden sees each subdiscipline as differentiated yet related to the others by the distinct logic of its inquiry. Thus Historical Theology focuses on the question "What has the Christian witness of faith already been as decisive for human existence?" Systematic Theology: "What is the Christian witness of faith as decisive for human existence?" Practical Theology: "What should the Christian witness of faith now become as decisive for human existence?" (Ogden, 1972: 27–28, 30, 32) If we add Tracy's entry, Foundational Theology, we can construct a fourth question: "What are the conditions of possibility for any witness of faith as decisive for human existence?"

Tracy's approach has the additional merit of analyzing the four subdisciplines both in terms of their authors' ethical or belief stance and in terms of the distinct publics which they address. Nevertheless, when he analyzes the characteristics of the works themselves, he does so in terms of such general and pervasive factors as modes of argumentation and operative theories of truth. (Tracy, 1981: 54–58, 60–79)

Like Lonergan's concept of functional specialization, both Ogden's and Tracy's theories of subdisciplines focus attention upon theology as a collaborative process. Moreover, the concepts of distinct governing questions, modes of argument and theories of truth, nurture pluralism in the *doing* of theology. Nevertheless, however insightful Tracy's suggestion that theology as public discourse is differentiated according to the publics that it serves, his own analyses in *The Analogical Imagination* indicate that there is a missing, mediating link between the analyses of distinct modes of inquiry and the recognition of intended audiences: the work itself as a formal communicative structure or genre.[2]

Guided by E. D. Hirsch's maxim, "Valid interpretation is always governed by a valid inference about genre" (1967: 113), we hope to recover that missing link. By combining attention to the *form* of theological works and their implied audiences with analysis of their logic of inquiry we hope to disclose their complex intentionalities as genres of public discourse. "The dynamics of form is at the same time a dynamics of thought . . . . Content and form . . . are 'generated' together. The theological content itself is produced in harmony with the rule of the corresponding literary genre." (Ricoeur, 1973a: 136) Attention to form thus should also lead to the derivation of publicly-binding criteria for the construction and evaluation of different types of theological discourse. Following Ricoeur, we insist that not only valid interpretation but fruitful construction and right judgment also depend upon an appropriation of generic structures.

Clearly genres are more than classificatory devices. They are culturally generated media through which disparate groups within a linguistic community share meanings. Genres place writers and readers in a common context by establishing patterns of meaning-expectation which trigger communication. (Buss, 1979: 10) They are, at once, the codes which must be internalized if the writer is to produce a work of a certain type and the rules of language games which must be followed by the reader if understanding is to occur. Furthermore, genres, like any cultural media, have a life history. They arise out of the communicative praxis of a community and they die when their structures no longer facilitate symbolic interaction. (Fowler, 1971)

We propose, therefore, to view the theological enterprise as a discipline which, in the current historical epoch, generates works within four major *genres*—Foundational, Systematic, Historical, and Practical Theology—and numerous subordinate genres. In the particular case of Practical Theology, recent history discloses a highly fluid, interactive genre. Around its distinct focal concern—to reflect critically and to shape the praxis of a religious community—practical theology organizes elements drawn from the other three major theological genres. To be more precise: Within the structure of practical theology, revised aspects and procedures of Foundational, Historical, and Systematic theology appear *as functional specializations*. It will be our task to show that, true to the character of any genuine genre, these elements are not arbitrary. They exist in necessary relationship to one another. (Cf. Todorov, 1975: 75)

While these structural elements appear to be perennial aspects of Christian theology, the particular fusion of these elements which we call the genre of practical theology is *not* a universal phenomenon in the history of Western theological discourse. We have already hinted that practical theology emerges historically as a form of theological discourse uniquely responsive to the rise of modern ideologies. Its fate as a genre is tied to the continued centrality of ideologies for mediating praxis through "a culture of critical discourse." In view of this distinctive history, let us take a closer look at this kinship of practical theologies with peculiarly modern forms of public discourse.

C. IDEOLOGICAL GENRES

Assuming that for our purposes it is not necessary to map the entire realm of public discourse, we will follow Todorov's strategy of definition through juxtaposition: "A genre is always defined in relation to the genres adjacent to it" (1975: 27). Genres are fluid; they interpenetrate. But by comparing and contrasting neighboring forms of practical discourse we can determine the frontier regions where one genre is transposed into another. By delineating the frontiers of practical theology we can secure a preliminary conception of this genre. (Cf. Hirsch, 1967: 74–76) This will set the stage for a further consideration of its constitutive elements.

We see practical theologies as positioned between two types of public discourse characteristic of the modern era. The first type expresses a religious interpretation of historical change. The name given to this genre by American religious historians is "the Jeremiad." The second type represents a secular orientation to historical transformation. We refer here to modern ideologies. So our preliminary conception of practical theology views it as that genre of practical discourse which shares the traits of both religious Jeremiads and secular ideologies yet distinguishes itself from both.

Consider first this classic example of the American Jeremiad:

> Thus stands the cause between God and vs, wee are entered into Covenant with him for this worke . . . . Wee haue professed to enterprise these Accions vpon these and these ends, wee haue herevpon besought him of favor and blessing: Now if the Lord shall please to heare vs, and bring vs in peace to the place wee desire, than hath hee ratified this Covenant and sealed our Commission, [and] will expect a strickt performance of the Articles contained in it, but if wee shall neglect the observacion of these Articles which are the ends wee haue propounded, and dissembling with our God, shall fall to embrace this present world and prosecute our carnall intencions seekeing greate things for our selues and our posterity, the Lord will surely breake out in wrathe against vs be revenged of such a periured people and make vs knowe the price of the breache of such a Covenant.

> For wee must Consider that wee shall be as a Citty vpon a Hill, the eies of all people are vppon vs; soe that if wee shall deale falsely with our god in this worke we haue vndertaken and soe cause him to withdrawe his present help from vs, we shall be

> made a story and a by-word through the world . . . ; wee shall shame the faces of many of gods worthy seruaunts, and cause theire prayers to be turned into Cursses vpon vs till wee be consumed out of the good land whether wee are goeing. Beloued there is now sett before vs life, and good, deathe and euill in that wee are Commaunded this day to loue the Lord our God, and loue one another to walke in his wayes and to keepe . . . the Articles of our Covenant with him . . . that the Lord our God may blesse vs in the land whether wee goe to possesse it . . . :
>
> Therefore lett vs choose life . . . .
>
> (Miller and Johnson, 1963: 198–99)

On board the Arbella in the middle of the Atlantic Ocean John Winthrop charged his small band of Puritan followers with a grand errand. By so doing he also created, argues Sacvan Bercovitch, the charter document for a new genre of religious discourse—the American Jeremiad. (1978: 3–4) Modifying earlier work by Perry Miller, Bercovitch insists that the Jeremiad was a staple of the North American religious imagination from the very beginning. (Ibid.: 4, 6) He defines the genre as "a ritual designed to join social criticism to spiritual renewal, public to private identity, the shifting 'signs of the times' to certain traditional metaphors, themes, and symbols." (Ibid.: xi) An ancient formula adapted to meet the needs of a modern situation (Ibid.: 6), the Jeremiad has been perpetuated and enriched through such writings and declamations as abolitionist and temperance sermons, Frederick Douglass's Fourth of July speech, Lincoln's second inaugural address, Martin Luther King's "Letter from the Birmingham Jail," and the speeches of Malcolm X. (Cf. Cherry, 1971)

1. *As a City upon the Hill. . . .* Both Miller and Bercovitch agree that the key to the genre is the notion of an Errand. (Miller, 1956: 1–15) A people have been elected to reconstruct self and society, private lives and public affairs, after a divinely revealed pattern. The Jeremiad above all orients a collectivity to the field of historical action as the locus of its encounter with God. To be religious is to be committed to a form of social praxis. Implicit in this understanding of history is the sense that we are required to create a *novus ordo*

seclorum, a new order of the ages. Bercovitch nicely captures the peculiar modernity of this American Jeremiad:

> The European Jeremiad developed within a static hierarchical order; the lessons it taught, about historical recurrences and the vanity of human wishes, amounted to a massive ritual reinforcement of tradition. Its function was to make social practice conform to a completed and perfected social ideal. The American Puritan Jeremiad was the ritual of a culture on an errand—which is to say, a culture based on a faith in process. Substituting theology for hierarchy, it discarded the old world ideal of stasis for a New World vision of the future.
>
> (Bercovitch, 1978: 23)

2. *Thus stands the cause between God and us. . . .* If the Jeremiad orients a people to history as progressive development, it places that development under transcendent judgment. The Puritans and subsequent social activists in America excelled in interpreting current events in light of the Errand myth. History is no amorphous field, no *tabula rasa*. Events invariably fall into place, into divinely revealed patterns of promise, judgment, and fulfillment. The Jeremiad is an expression, Bercovitch argues, of the figural or typological imagination applied to public as well as private history. Sacred and secular history here are utterly fused. (1978: 14–15, 39–40) Later crises in the history of the United States of America would invariably be interpreted through the same religious figures: Wilderness, Exodus, New Canaan. (Ibid.: 93–131; cf. Cherry, 1971: 67–81, 93–105, 162–76) The figurations of the Jeremiad formed history, conducted its current. (Cf. Frye, 1957: 327)

3. *If we deal falsely. . . .* We have mentioned that American leaders adapted the rhetorical strategy of the Jeremiad to interpret historical crises. Bercovitch goes further. He argues that the genre is designed to foment a sense of perpetual crisis. (1978: 23, 62, 178) The Puritans raised lamentation over the malaise of American civic life to a high art. These lamentations, however, were no counsel to despair, but a "mode of rhetoric . . . a strategy for prodding the community forward," (Ibid.: 61) in the hope of overcoming the discrepancy between its professed ideals and its daily experience.

4. *Therefore choose life . . . .* The genre then is essentially geared towards praxis. Even the bleakest analysis of America's fallen state points to a narrow defile which leads toward an alternative future. So Michael Wigglesworth, after citing the many reasons for "God's Controversy with New England," could end his Jeremiad by saying:

> Oh dear New England: dearest land to me;
> which unto God has hitherto been dear,
> and mayest be still more dear than formerlie,
> If to his voice thou will incline thine ear.
>
> (Cherry, 1971: 54)

Seize the Day! That was the ultimate message of the Jeremiad.

While some of the similarities linking practical theologies and the Jeremiad are obvious, others require further comment. Like the Jeremiad, practical theologies generally:

(1) view history as the locus of salvation and as an arena within which human action makes a crucial difference;

(2) fuse sacred and secular history, or, more precisely, call that distinction into question; (cf. Gutierrez, 1973: 153)

(3) relate the course of history to transcendent reality. McCann has argued that the single most important issue for the construction and evaluation of practical theologies is "the nature of religious transcendence and its role in Christian social action"; (1981a: 4)

(4) employ a figural imagination in interpreting the "signs of the times," the undivided drama of the self's and world's redemption. Witness Gutierrez's claim: "The Exodus experience is paradigmatic. It remains vital and contemporary due to similar historical experiences which the People of God undergo"; (1973: 159)

(5) create a sense of historical crisis. Strain has argued that virtually every example of the Social Gospel practical theology focused upon a dual crisis: a religious crisis affecting the destiny of the church exacerbated by a larger social crisis—a turning of the ages; (1978: 529)

(6) seek to stimulate praxis by using an appropriate rhetorical strategy. The central role of rhetorical modes in practical theology, as we shall see, has been a source of much consternation for theologians

who employ standards appropriate to systematic theology to evaluate this very different genre.

Practical theologies, nevertheless, differ from Jeremiads in one respect, as formal as it is crucial. They transcend the level of the mythopoeic imagination by mediating it with the norms and procedures of critical reflection. Critical reflection here includes explicit development of theological positions, critical theories of society, ideology-critique and, in most cases, critical historiography. They seek not merely to persuade but to convince. Indeed, this formal commitment to providing publicly scrutable reasons links practical theologies to their other neighbor—secular ideologies. Let us turn, then, to this second set of family resemblances.

"Ideologies are proscribed—excepting our own." (Girnus, 1973: 483) This ironic aphorism expresses clearly the self-deluding character of much of what passes for critical reflection on ideology. When the term was invented in the eighteenth century by Destutt de Tracy, it was used in a positive sense to describe a break with the authoritarian past, with its inherited prejudices and absolute norms, and a turn toward a public life shaped by rationally grounded principles. Napoleon, however, gave the term "ideologue" its pejorative connotation when he attacked the followers of Destutt de Tracy for criticizing his imperial strategems. Their ideology was proscribed; Napoleon's was concealed. (Lichtheim, 1967: 7–10; Seliger, 1977: 14–16)

By polarizing ideology and science, Karl Marx reinforced this pejorative meaning. In his own critical reflections, however, Marx vacillated between considering ideology as purely false consciousness and as a distorted reflection of the real interests of the dominant social class. Thus, on the one hand, ideology was for him a symbolic inversion of reality epitomized in the relationship of the religious consciousness to its illusory object, while on the other hand, it was a deliberate mystification, functioning to legitimate the power of one class over another. Marx remained unaware that his theory of ideology as false consciousness logically required a theory of the positive functioning of consciousness in society and, as a result, he failed to consider the role that consciousness would play in the future society. (Ricoeur, 1974: 330–31, 337; Gouldner, 1976: 15, 28) Later when Marx's vacillation yielded to "scientific" clarity, such difficulties were easily dismissed.

Ideology became the equivalent of false consciousness. (Seliger, 1977: 30–33, 35–36)

Reflecting on the sorry history of ideologically inspired political movements of the left and the right in the later nineteenth and early twentieth centuries, Karl Mannheim first defined the self-defeating paradox involved in ideological combat. "No longer . . . [is it] . . . possible for one point of view and interpretation to assail all others as ideological without itself being placed in the position of having to meet that challenge." (Mannheim, 1936: 70–74) Critics advocating rival ideologies, in other words, fail to realize that their criticisms participate in a dialectical process that Hegel named "determinate negation." The very act of criticism creates a new standpoint. The exposure of one form of consciousness as false simultaneously generates a new and concrete world view. (Hegel, 1977: 50–51, 55–56) Mannheim, alas, ignored the implications of his own theory when he sought to provide an objective vantage point for his "free floating intellectuals" outside the arena of ideological criticism. (Seliger, 1977: 8; cf. Mannheim, 1936: 153–64)

Mannheim's legacy, nevertheless, has not been entirely fruitless. Increasingly aware of the paradox involved in the purely pejorative view, social theorists have redefined ideology positively as the condition of possibility for historical action by a modern collectivity. Ideologies are both the distillate of a group's experiment with history and the formulas under which the experiment proceeds. (Girnus, 1973: 483–85) Despite their own misconstrual of the nature of ideology, Marx and Engels' pamphlet, *The Communist Manifesto*, stands as a classic illustration of the positive structure of ideologies. We will use a selection from this classic, just as we used John Winthrop's inaugural sermon, to frame our own analysis of the genre of ideological discourse and its family resemblances to practical theology.

Listen once more to the call to action issued by Marx and Engels:

> The history of all hitherto existing society is the history of class struggles . . . . The modern bourgeois society that has sprouted from the ruins of feudal society has not done away with

class antagonisms. It has but established new classes, new conditions of oppression, new forms of struggle in place of the old ones . . . .

The bourgeoisie . . . has resolved personal work into exchange value and, in place of the numberless indefeasible chartered freedoms, has set up that single unconscionable freedom—free trade . . . . The bourgeoisie cannot exist without constantly revolutionizing the instruments of production, and thereby the relations of production, and with them the whole relation of society. All that is solid melts into air . . . .

In proportion as the bourgeoisie, i.e., capital is developed, in the same proportion is the proletariat, the modern working class developed. . . . These laborers, who must sell themselves piecemeal, are a commodity. . . . But with the development of industry the proletariat not only increases in number; it becomes concentrated in greater masses, its strength grows, and it feels that strength more. . . . What the bourgeoisie, therefore, produces, above all is its own gravediggers. Its fall and the victory of the proletariat are equally inevitable.

The communists . . . are on the one hand, practically the most advanced and resolute section of the working-class parties of every country . . . , on the other hand, theoretically, they have over the great mass of the proletariat the advantage of clearly understanding the line of march, the conditions, and the ultimate general results of the proletarian movement. . . .

We communists have been reproached with the desire of abolishing the right of personally acquiring property as the fruit of a man's labor, which property is alleged to be the groundwork of all personal freedom, activity, and independence. . . . But don't wrangle with us so long as you apply, to our intended abolition of bourgeois property, the standard of your bourgeois notions of freedom, culture, law, etc. Your very ideas are but the outgrowth of the conditions of your bourgeois production and

> bourgeois property. . . . In the place of the old bourgeois society, with its classes and class antagonisms we shall have an association in which the free development of each is the condition for the free development of all. . . . The proletarians have nothing to lose but their chains. They have a world to win. Workingmen of all countries, Unite.
>
> (Marx and Engels, 1959: 7–10, 14, 16, 20–21, 24, 29, 41)

1. *All that is solid melts into air. . . .* Ideologies are fundamentally modern forms of practical discourse. As Clifford Geertz has suggested, "precisely at the point at which a political system begins to free itself from the immediate governance of received tradition . . . formal ideologies tend to emerge and take hold." Given the loss of orientation that accompanies this process of emancipation, ideologies enable us to act purposefully in "otherwise incomprehensible social situations." Specifically, they provide, in Geertz's words, "maps of problematic social reality and matrices for the creation of collective conscience." (Geertz, 1973a: 219–20) Gouldner elaborates this thesis by linking the rise of ideologies to the appearance of publics shaped by the power of mass communications media. A public as opposed to a caste or a kinship structure is constituted by shared ideas and interests. (1976: 93–96, 100) This point had already been grasped by social theorists in the late nineteenth century who recognized that mediating theories play a crucial role in transforming the public as an anonymous mass into the public as a social movement. (Strain, 1978: 537–38) Ideologies, in short, are consciously created works designed to achieve this goal. (Cf. Ellul, 1973: 342, 345)

As such, ideologies differ in one important respect from the Jeremiad. They cannot rest content with evoking and enforcing mythic patterns.

> Ideology . . . entailed the emergence of a new mode of political discourse; discourse that sought action but did not merely seek it by invoking authority or tradition, or by emotive rhetoric alone. It was discourse predicated on the ideal of grounding political action in secular and rational theory. A fundamental

> rule of the grammar of all modern ideology tacit [sic] or explicitly affirmed, was the principle of the *unity of theory and practice* mediated by rational discourse.
>
> (Gouldner, 1976: 30)

This commitment to providing "publicly scrutable evidence" within a "rhetoric of rationality," in principle, is as antithetical to the language of propaganda as it is subversive of the mythopoeic imagination. (Ibid.: 30, 33, 38–39)

2. *The history of all hitherto existing society. . . .* To provide the public with a suitably grounded map, ideologies commonly work along two coordinates, one termed diachronic, the other synchronic. Like the Jeremiad, ideologies focus upon the crises of the present moment but they place this moment within a philosophical interpretation of history's total movement. In other words, they supplement a figural sense of the drama of history with a synthetic theory of historical development.

3. . . . *has resolved personal worth into exchange value.* Along its synchronic axis an ideology typically provides a theory of the human essence and its historical deformations.

4. . . . *the whole relation of society.* But in order to foster collective action, the human essence or self must be displayed within a network of social relations. Ideologies thus typically go beyond figural images of the self in society to develop a critical social theory. (Ellul, 1973: 340–41; Gouldner, 1976: 201)

5. *The free development of each . . . the free development of all. . . .* Ideologies do not halt with the present. Extrapolating from their explanations of the present crisis, these maps retrieve alternative pasts and project alternative futures. Especially in their representations of the future, ideologies share with the Jeremiad a belief in the possibility of a *novus ordo seclorum.* (Bailyn, 1967: 80–86, 137–38, 140–41) As a complement to their analyses of the deformations of the human essence, ideologies thus provide normative images of the human good. Nevertheless, as Paul Ricoeur concludes, "this representation of the social whole . . . is necessarily schematic. The task of an ideology is to provide a model not a detailed set of policies." (1974: 332)

6. *On the one hand, practically . . . on the other hand, theoretically.* Because, as Clifford Geertz suggests, ideologies provide "matrices for the creation of the collective conscience," the unity of theory and practice which Gouldner describes, if it is to be anything more than a utopian dream, must emerge directly from the activity of generating such matrices. By the same token, neither can the theoretical aspect of an ideology be sublated. Apart from the mediation of ideas the activity, the *practice* of a group can never become a form of *praxis.*

7. . . . *Nothing to lose but their chains.* Geared towards action, ideologies frankly represent particular interests as intrinsically connected to the common good. But they are not a mere reflex of class interests. (Ricoeur, 1974: 332) They are the forge in which particular interests are joined with generalizable ideals, with visions of the common good. Ideologies are, therefore, committed to a dialectic of interests which provide the motive for action, and ideals, which invariably enlarge the original scope of those limited interests. (Gouldner, 1976: 218–23)

8. *Workingmen of all countries, Unite!* . . . Like the Jeremiad, ideologies call upon their publics to "Seize the Day!" The use of rhetorical devices is a structural aspect of any ideology. If ideologies seek not merely to persuade but to convince, the reverse is no less true. To mold the collective conscience is both to shape it and to engage it irrevocably.

9. *We . . . have been reproached.* . . . Two final aspects of all ideologies deserve mention. Because they arose simultaneously with the collapse of traditional societies, ideologies always find themselves pitted against a number of rivals. Ideology, in Gouldner's terms "is always in some part a *counter*-discourse. . . . "(Ibid.: 280)

10. *Your very ideas are but the outgrowth.* . . . Counterdiscourse manifests itself as both apology and critique. As apology, an ideology argues for its particular fusion of interests and ideals. As critique, an ideology unmasks the distortions of the common good concealed by competing ideologies. (Ibid.: 213–14, 282–83) Moreover, both as apology and as critique, an ideology is committed simultaneously to public discourse and to action as the necessary consequence of public discourse.

The recognition that this form of criticism is an element constitutive of the very structure of ideologies brings us back to the problem of ideology as false consciousness. Although the possibility of false consciousness logically requires understanding ideology as map and as matrix, it would be sheer folly to allow this point to blind us to the problem altogether. (Geuss, 1981: 46) Gouldner, in fact, suggests that *every* ideology tends to conceal the extent to which the particular interests which it expresses are *not* synonymous with the common good.

> Ideology, then, is a contradictory thing. It is pushed towards rationality by the interest on which it is grounded, but is limited in this rationality by that same interest. . . . Ideology is thus characterized by its *inhibition* about addressing the question of its own *grounding*, and thus by self-imposed restrictions on its own reflexivity.
>
> (1976: 45–46; cf. 214)

This lack of self-critical reflection is a pathology endemic to the genre. It is an example of false consciousness in virtue of an *epistemic* flaw. If an ideology fails to exhibit awareness of its linguistic status as a symbolic construction of social reality, it is false for epistemic reasons. This can occur, for example, when an ideology treats the culturally relative values which it advocates as "natural." (Geuss, 1981: 13–14) If an ideology frustrates the internal dialectic through which ideals overcome initially limited interests, here again the ideology is false for epistemic reasons. (Gouldner, 1976: 289–92) This did occur in the case of the North American colonists who employed the concept of slavery in analyzing their relationships with Great Britain but refused to heed the claims of a few that logic required the extension of this analysis to the issue of chattel slavery. (Bailyn, 1967: 241–46)

Raymond Geuss adds to these epistemic perversions of ideology two other sources of false consciousness. An ideology can be a form of false consciousness when it functions to legitimate surplus repression or an unnecessarily asymmetrical distribution of power. Ideology here is false for *functional* reasons. The difficulty, however, is to determine for a given society what constitutes *surplus* repression and *unnecessary* domination. (Geuss, 1981: 15–19) Here, too, we must look for signs of a dialectic of ideal and interest that works within the limiting conditions and functional imperatives characteristic of society at the given moment. This functional criterion applies not only to established powers but to revolutionary movements as well. The latter can also foster surplus repression in the form of a violence unwarranted by their ideals but strategically related to the consolidation of power by an interested elite.

An ideology is false in virtue of its genesis if its power depends upon self-delusion. An ideology is not false simply because it originates with a certain class or from dubious motives. Geuss rejects as vulgar Marxism, for example, the notion that an ideology is false simply because it is a product of the bourgeoisie. An ideology is *genetically* false only when participants could not acknowledge the true sources of their beliefs and still act upon them. If Nietzsche's theory of the origins of Christianity in resentment were correct, either a Christian would have to repress all awareness of these origins or would have to cease being a Christian. Christianity's normative basis in a doctrine of love requires it to proscribe consciously acting on the basis of resentment. While epistemic, functional and genetic reasons can be given for criticizing an ideology as a form of false consciousness, an adequate critical theory will synthesize all three modes. (Geuss, 1981: 19–22, 43–44) At *this* stage of our argument, however, we need only recognize that ideology is not a form of false consciousness *by definition* but in virtue of unwarranted claims to truth or deformations of its structure and purposes. Later we will advance our own criteria for distinguishing the forms of false consciousness typically encountered in practical theology.

To return to our original argument: Practical theologies are generically similar to secular ideologies. Strain has already argued this case regarding key works representing two models of practical theology: Liberation Theology and the North American Social Gospel. (1977, 1978) Rather than repeat these analyses or present examples from other models of practical theology we will simply assert here the structural similarities that later chapters will analyze in detail. Practical theologies exhibit the same unity of theory and practice, the same intent not merely to provoke action but to ground it in publicly available, rational discourse as ideologies do. They operate at the same schematic level, for example, in providing normative images of the self as located within a network of social relations. In their theologies of history they deal with the genesis of crisis and generate visions of an alternative future. They mediate their retrieval of narrative images of the human good with critical social theories and criticisms of the ideological deformations of theological discourse. Finally in their effort not merely to define crisis but to precipitate it, they employ a variety of rhetorical strategies.

In our judgment they differ from secular ideologies in only one respect, but it is the crucial one: They seek to unite each of these structural elements explicitly with an overriding vision of transcendent or Ultimate Reality. Apart from such a vision and its transformative impact upon every aspect of ideological discourse, there is no such thing as practical theology.[3]

D. BUILDING MODELS OF PRACTICAL THEOLOGY

If practical theologies are generically similar to ideologies, they may also share similar deficiencies. We fail to be convinced that an injection of faith in Ultimate Reality automatically immunizes them against these deficiencies. In fact, the facility with which practical theologians unmask the pretensions of *rival* models of practical theology merely confirms the tendency to self delusion that Girnus captured in his ironic aphorism. "[Practical theologies] are proscribed—excepting our own." Indeed, this rush to ideological criticism suggests that this genre, too, is faced with a crisis of pluralism and relativism similar to the one that Mannheim detected within the field of ideological discourse. (Cf. Reinhold Niebuhr on the Social Gospel of Liberal Protestantism, 1939: 542–46; and Rubem Alves, in turn, on Christian Realism, 1973: 173–76)

We propose to meet this crisis by insisting that any given example of practical theology must be regarded as simply a *model* within a larger genre. Why models of practical theology? Model-theory allows us to establish the perspectival limits and possibilities of practical theological discourse. Moreover, this theoretical advantage is complemented by two interrelated practical considerations: (1) Genuine political life in a pluralistic society, as we have already noted, presupposes a commitment to an arena of unfettered discourse among a variety of overlapping publics. Political absolutism, by proscribing a priori all positions "excepting our own," destroys this public arena. It subverts political *discourse*. Ideological relativism, on the other hand, is equally subversive. By viewing the choice between conflicting perspectives as purely arbitrary, it renders rational participation absurd. Political life in a pluralistic society thus must adopt a stance that transcends this false polarity. (2) Moreover, ideological discourse of its nature also risks subverting the public arena. It does so as a result of the various ways in which critical reflexivity may be impaired. These epistemic, functional, and genetic disorders, as we've already argued, make it easy to overestimate the universality of one's particular perspective. On the other hand ideological neutrality is neither possible nor desirable within the public realm. How then does our application of model-theory to practical theology provide an antidote to the pathologies of public discourse exhibited by secular and religious ideologies?

1. *Models are perspectival.* They do not present literal descriptions of reality but view it from a certain angle. (Barbour, 1974: 7, 32–34, 49, 52–53) A commitment to interpreting practical theologies as models presupposes that no single model provides an all-inclusive vision of the social whole. From the vantage point of model-theory, absolute claims are symptoms of impaired critical reflexivity. But all perspectives are not equally valid. Some are more inclusive and more sharply focused than others.

Perspectivism implies pluralism. Because no model can make absolute and exclusive claims for itself, many models will be generated. As the physicist Niels Bohr put it, "a complete elucidation of one and the same object may require diverse points of view which defy a unique description." (Barbour, 1974: 75) Applying such perspectivism to the issue at hand, we can readily see why any given genre must have a history. Not only do new exemplars of the genre appear but through constant modification new *kinds* of exemplars. (Fowler, 1971: 207) Just as the gothic romance, the *Bildungsroman*, and science fiction evolved within the genre of the novel so numerous models of practical theology have also appeared. In the Americas alone the history of practical theology testifies to the various works of the Social Gospel movement, Christian Realism, and Liberation Theology.

2. *Models are formally constructed.* A model as opposed to a myth is a self-conscious creation. In its execution of a particular theological task, it signifies a marked degree of coherence and coordination among its structural elements. (Barbour, 1974: 27) Obviously each expression of a genre need not contain every structural element. But it is certainly possible to abstract a coherent set of elements from many examples. (Fowler, 1971: 202; cf. McCann, 1981a: 7) We are suggesting by our very use of the term "model" that instances of practical theology which do formally coordinate these elements are, all other factors being equal, better than those which do not.

3. *Models*, as common practice in the sciences demonstrates, *are subject to evaluation by the relevant community of inquirers*. In the case of practical theologies neither a religious community engaged in praxis nor a group of professional theologians alone are exclusively qualified to make these judgments; only a cluster of overlapping publics. Moreover, different parts of the structure of practical theologies are subject to validation by different communities of inquiry. Chapter Four will argue, for example, that competence for the work of historical reconstruction which is part of a critical hermeneutic will be determined by one group—professional historians—whereas the intention to retrieve a *usable* past can only be validated by a community of praxis whose horizon of meaning has been actually transformed under the impact of the historical reconstruction.

Pluralism does not lead to relativism when competing models can be weighed by appropriate criteria. These criteria need not be imposed from without. They can be determined, we hope to show, by a careful assessment of the formal elements of the genre, and then applied to any model by anyone who understands the structure of the genre, who can appreciate its mode of discourse. Public discourse in which such an assessment occurs cannot exclude members of a given race, sex, or class if it is to remain genuinely public. Certainly in the case of practical theology the resulting criteria will be practical as well as theoretical but they are still to be determined by analyzing the structural elements of the genre and not by the immediate requirements of any particular political struggle.[4] Later we will argue, for example, that in *some* cases the current cry for "orthopraxis" unwittingly subjects practical theologies to substantive norms which have not been determined by public discourse among *all* qualified participants. These extrinsic norms arbitrarily predetermine the course of public debate about the nature and tasks of practical theology.

If practical theologies are, like ideologies, forms of public discourse, committed to providing "publicly scrutable evidence," if the genre itself yields appropriate criteria for evaluating its models, then truth in this case arises only through the complex operation of evaluation and judgment that Bernard Lonergan calls "dialectic." (1972: 235–66) A clash of competing models is inevitable. Both models as a whole as well as the execution of various structural elements must be weighed and compared. McCann's earlier attempt (1981a) to compare the model of Christian Realism with the model of Liberation Theology was an exercise in dialectic in Lonergan's sense of the term. In this work, however, we hope to show where and how such an operation may be carried out for any model of practical theology.

Let us summarize the argument of this chapter: Practical theology is a distinct genre of theological discourse. As such, it is neither a new paradigm for the whole discipline nor merely a functional specialization. Around its focal concern—to reflect critically upon and to shape the praxis of a religious community—it revises the work of the other major theological genres (Foundational, Historical, and Systematic theology) and reorganizes their procedures as functional specializations within its own unique structure. We achieved a preliminary conception of the structure of this genre by comparing it to the most closely related forms of public discourse—the religious Jeremiad and secular ideologies. Finally we argued that the genre in its historical development has given rise to a number of distinct models, all of which are subject to genre-based criteria. In a context of ideological and theological pluralism, faced with pathological expressions of the genre, public adjudication based upon generic criteria is the way to determine degrees of relative adequacy among competing models of practical theology.

NOTES

1. It is not relevant to our task to adjudicate the differences between Ogden and Tracy regarding what are the three subdisciplines. Combining the two thinkers, we will focus on all four: Foundational, Historical, Systematic, and Practical Theology.
2. David Tracy himself recognizes the validity of this proposition. As soon as he begins to study the "subdiscipline" of systematic theology as a hermeneutical enterprise, he introduces the category of genre as the key for unlocking the religious classics which systematic theology seeks to interpret. (1981: 126–29)
3. Because Juan Luis Segundo has been the foremost exponent of a positive view of the role of ideological discourse within theology it is helpful to distinguish our position from his. We agree with Segundo that all forms of theological discourse contain ideological implications. We do not agree with such a broad definition of ideology that virtually all forms of theological discourse become syntheses of faith and ideology. (Segundo, 1976: 7, 9, 97–124) Just as an ideology is a specific form of practical discourse, so also only one genre of theological discourse is constructed in formal similarity to ideological works.
4. We agree with David Tracy that some criteria are common to all theological genres. (1981: 58–61) The real question, however, is what specific form do they take when applied to the genre of practical theology?

CHAPTER THREE

THEORY AND PRAXIS: THE FOUNDATIONS OF PRACTICAL THEOLOGY

The materialist doctrine that men are products of circumstances and upbringing, and that, therefore, changed men are products of other circumstances and changed upbringing, forgets that it is men that change circumstances and that the educator himself needs educating . . . . The coincidence of the changing of circumstances and of human activity can be conceived and rationally understood only as revolutionizing practice.

(Marx and Engels, 1964: 70)

Practical fundamental theology is opposed to a non-dialectical subordination of praxis to theory . . . . In it, great emphasis is placed on the intelligible force of praxis itself, in the sense of a dialectical tension between theory and praxis.

(Metz, 1980: 50)

If practical theology is a genre of modern theology in which many different models are possible, then the criteria for evaluating these models must be derived from the nature of the genre itself. As the previous chapter suggested, this genre is a form of religious ideology. Defining practical theology in this way, however, at first may seem fruitless. All theologies, whatever their conceptual form, carry ideological implications, for all theologies shape religious communities. What is so special, then, about practical theology?

Practical theology, like other modern ideologies, carries out this task formally and intentionally. The problematic of ideology and social change becomes practical theology's distinctive and explicit focus. Practical theologians in one way or another, therefore, must appropriate the dialectic of theory and praxis central to this problematic, and set it to work in the service of religious communities seeking to understand and implement their worldly mission. Without this explicit focus, both the critical and constructive possibilities latent in the term, "religious ideology," may not be realized.

The dialectic of theory and praxis, however, must be explained and not merely acknowledged. For the epistemological breakthrough that it represents has engendered various conflicts of interpretation. This chapter, therefore, will clarify the dialectic of theory and praxis as it relates to the need to formulate criteria for practical theology. We will proceed in four steps: first, a survey of the current debate over the meaning of "the primacy of praxis," concluding in an argument for a dialectic of theory and praxis that rules out both orthodoxy and orthopraxis; second, a search for an alternative to both orthodoxy and orthopraxis based on Jürgen Habermas's attempt to resolve a similar impasse in Marxism; third, a reconstructed notion of "critical reflection on praxis" designed to ensure practical theology's operation as a form of public discourse; and finally, a discussion of religious praxis as the context in which this dialectic generates models of practical theology.

A. NEITHER ORTHODOXY NOR ORTHOPRAXIS

By all accounts the recent interest in "orthopraxis" is directly related to the decline of "orthodoxy." Chesterton to the contrary notwithstanding, orthodoxy no longer appeals to theologians. Instead, it has been shunted aside like a senile but still tyrannical relative, more embarrassing than awe inspiring. The irony is that orthodoxy itself is now regarded as unorthodox. No one recently has made this point more persuasively than Charles Davis:

> Religion when maintained as an orthodoxy claims a permanent self-identity, remaining unscathed by social and practical changes. It involves some purely theoretical center of reference to serve in an abstract speculative way as a norm of identity. There are indeed conflicting orthodoxies, but the differences are conceived as basically theoretical. The presupposition of orthodoxy is the contemplative conception of knowledge, according to which knowledge is the result of the disinterested viewing of reality by individuals. Orthodoxy is that contemplative

conception applied to religious truth.

(Davis, 1980: 130)

Davis's analysis suggests that a religious community's attempt to immunize its traditional form of life against historical change is practically vicious and theoretically absurd. The artificial exclusion of theory from the flux of experience betrays the deformed modernity of orthodoxy and illuminates its alienation from anything authentically traditional. While the eclipse of orthodoxy has been observed from a variety of modern perspectives, Davis's has the distinct merit of explaining it in terms of the dialectic of theory and praxis. In light of that epistemological breakthrough, he will brook no halfhearted compromises that would abort the dialectic.

Orthopraxis, ironically, is one of the half-hearted compromises that Davis rejects. (1980: 9) While the term conveys the intention of radically transforming theology in some sort of methodological inversion of orthodoxy, orthopraxis can fulfill this intention only if theology abandons the primacy of theory and acknowledges the primacy of praxis. Too often, however, this new primacy merely perpetuates the old one in a new form. Sacral authority, as we suggested, is simply transferred from doctrines to political strategies and tactics. The claim of religious absoluteness persists. Moreover, confusion abounds concerning precisely what this radical transformation entails. Let us examine, then, three different versions of the primacy of praxis. Each in its own way confirms the thesis that orthopraxis in principle is no more acceptable than orthodoxy as a foundation for practical theology.

The first of these features is the concept of orthopraxis as it was first formulated by J. B. Metz. (Cf. Davis, 1980: 182, n.4) In order to accomplish the "deprivatization" of Christian witness, Metz founded his "new political theology" on the primacy of praxis. What this meant for him was a shift of methodological horizons "toward Kant's teaching about the primacy of practical reason and the dialectics of theory and praxis in Marxism." (Metz, 1980: 53) While he now regards his earlier attempt to define the relationship "between Church and societal publicness" (Metz, 1969: 111) as still too wedded to abstract Kantian categories, his new emphasis on "social praxis" in solidarity with the oppressed seeks to maintain its distance from the praxis of Marxist dialectics. To accomplish this purpose Metz offers no formal theory of praxis suitable for a range of practical theologies but proposes a substantive Christian alternative of his own.

Orthopraxis or the primacy of social praxis in "Christian praxis," Metz defines in terms of three hermeneutic assumptions. The first of these is succinctly formulated: "Christian praxis remains ethically determined." (1980: 56) In other words, Christian social praxis must never lead to "an abstract or violent negation of the individual." Second, Metz stipulates that such praxis is "determined by an excess of historical determinations that are the non-inferred function of the prevailing social totality." (Ibid.) The "excess" determinations referred to here are the "subversive memories" of "utopian" communities, primarily but not exclusively religious or Christian in their orientation. Contrary to classical Marxism, Metz insists that these utopian aspirations cannot be seen as "a reflection or reproduction of the contemporary factors determining society and economics." Christian social praxis, therefore, is always mediated through a hermeneutic of "subversive memories" embedded in Christian narratives. The third stipulation considers "the pathic structure of praxis." (Metz, 1980: 57) In light of its distinctive perspective on the meaning of human suffering, Christian praxis does not view humanity "one-sidedly as a subject exerting control over nature and human history." (Ibid.: 58) Here, too, the limiting function of a hermeneutic of Christian narrative is evident.

In each "determination" Metz is to be commended for attempting to define a substantively Christian approach to social praxis. What remains unclear is not *whether* any practical theology requires a critical theological hermeneutic with a practical intent, but *how* such a hermeneutic is to be conceived in a manner consistent with the primacy of praxis. Since Metz's hermeneutic assumptions do not provide the necessary arguments, we fear that they will only make it possible for orthodoxy to perpetuate itself in a new guise.

This suspicion is confirmed by Metz's latest discussion of "orthopraxis." For he typically defines it as "the price of orthodoxy." (Metz, 1980: 138–145) The problem remains not so much Metz's practical intention—which is a sincere attempt at Christian witness

—but his theoretical warrants for it. Seeking to offer sympathetic criticism of the notion of "a Church of the people" developed by some Latin American liberation theologians, Metz sees orthopraxis as neither a "question of applied Christianity" nor a social praxis "subjecting all Christian praxis to the compulsive interpretations of society based purely on the satisfactions of its own needs." (Metz, 1980: 144) Orthopraxis, in other words, is neither a nondialectical exercise in practical apologetics nor an unqualified legitimation of a Marxist version of the dialectic of theory and praxis. It is "the price of orthodoxy" inasmuch as Christian praxis must overcome whatever "inhuman circumstances" prevent the oppressed from becoming "the Church in the full sense of the word, the people of God, and the subject of a new history with God." (Ibid.: 142)

Orthodoxy is not called into question here; but the people's capacity to embrace it as a form of life is. "Is it still known that to have right faith can make men free and happy? If that knowledge still exists can any price be too high?" (Metz, 1980: 144) Metz's rhetoric betrays him here. Orthodoxy still functions as the "purely theoretical center of reference," his protestations to the contrary notwithstanding. It governs his determination of the limits to social praxis in Christian praxis. It is not rejected as an alternative to orthopraxis, but is reaffirmed as a "norm of identity" for it. Davis rightfully criticizes Metz's orthopraxis as a new language covering a traditional outlook. (Davis, 1980: 9)

Davis's critique of any "half-hearted and inconsistent acceptance of the primacy of practice" is hardly applicable to practical theologians, like Juan Luis Segundo. Without always referring to the term, Segundo offers a distinction between orthopraxis (cf. Segundo, 1976: 32) and "heteropraxis" (Segundo, 1979: 245) as absolute as the distinction between orthodoxy and heresy was for his predecessors. The decision to struggle for "socialism" in Latin America is a *crux theologica.* This struggle is the only appropriate form of Christian praxis, based on a proper understanding of "the authentic historical functionality of the gospel message." (Ibid.) This functional approach to orthopraxis insists that "not one single dogma can be studied with any other final criterion than its impact on praxis," which, for him, means determining "a positive or negative relationship between dogma and socialism." (Segundo, 1979; 250)

Remarkably, such orthopraxis is both fallible and absolute. Invoking the example of Jesus' own practice of "imprudently absolutizing" acts of liberation as salvation (Segundo, 1979: 255), Segundo insists not only on the ambiguity of all political choices but also on the necessity of absolutizing them:

> The eschatological aspect is simply Christian theology's *way* or manner of accepting absolute commitments. The stress placed on the eschatological aspect depends on a proper, constantly reconsidered evaluation of the *Kairos,* of the opportunity for liberation at a given moment.
>
> (Segundo, 1979: 256)

Segundo makes the political meaning of this eschatological function explicit, insisting that "the sensitivity of the left is an intrinsic element of any Christian theology." (Ibid.: 257)

Our objection to Segundo's orthopraxis is not that it is socialist. Nor is it that his position cannot be reconciled with Metz's substantive understanding of Christian praxis. The problem, rather, lies in Segundo's functionalist misunderstanding of the dialectic of theory and praxis. His absolutizing of socialist praxis is the functional equivalent of orthodoxy. While his "hermeneutic circle" imposes no substantive "determinations" on orthopraxis, it does perpetuate orthodoxy's mistake of making exclusivist claims for itself. All other options are forms of "heteropraxis." A process of absolutizing determined by the historical demands of revolutionary movements short-circuits any genuine dialectic of theory and praxis. Yet apart from such a dialectic, religious praxis is held hostage to the political strategies and tactics of whatever group has been empowered to define the functional equivalent of orthodoxy. So, Segundo's boldly functionalist orthopraxis is just as unacceptable as Metz's half-hearted compromise with orthodoxy.

Our third example of orthopraxis tacitly recognizes the problems evident in the previous two. Matthew Lamb's "reflectively dialectical orthopraxis" is a methodological proposal which seeks to synthesize both Metz's theological conservatism and Segundo's political radicalism. Insisting that Christian "agapic" praxis requires some form of "noetic praxis" if it is to be truly dialectical, Lamb uses Bernard Lonergan's recent writings in order to develop a kind of "radical cognitive therapy." (Lamb, 1982: 85) His intent is to promote "the basic liberation of human subjects" by grounding praxis in the Lonerganian conversions—intellectual, moral, and religious—characteristic of the self-transcending subject. In this regard Lamb clearly offers a genuine dialectic of theory and praxis. Problems arise, however, when Lamb sets Lonergan's transcendental imperatives—"Be Attentive, Be Intelligent, Be Reasonable, Be Responsible, Be Loving" (Ibid.: 138)—in motion "to thematize value conflicts within the heuristic of discerning values and disvalues, which is capable of distinguishing genuine historical progress toward freedom and humanization from dehumanizing decline." (Ibid.: 137) In attempting to understand Lamb's orthopraxis, everything depends, we believe, on what he means by "the heuristic of discerning values and disvalues."

Actually prior commitment to orthodoxy, and not critical reflection on "agapic praxis" mediates Lamb's heuristic use of Lonergan's formal imperatives. Agapic praxis is presupposed and not defended, in Lamb's analysis, as the expression of basic Christian commitment. Whether that commitment accords with Lonergan's formal imperatives is never even asked. Critical social theory is not allowed to subject such commitments to dialectical reflection; rather, it is used to promote the values inherent in those commitments. (Ibid.: 138) Even if it were possible to accept without criticism agapic praxis as a *norma normans non normata,* we would still have problems with Lamb's tying it to Nicene orthodoxy as the heuristic principle governing authentic orthopraxis. "The exploitations of class, race, and sex within Christianity have resulted from failures to live up to orthopraxis expressed in Christological orthodoxy." (Ibid.: 141) Whether or not Lamb happens to be onto something promising is irrelevant here; his "heuristic" is suspect because orthodoxy is merely presupposed and not subject to scrutiny in public discourse.[1]

So, "reflectively dialectical orthopraxis" is a misnomer. If it is genuinely "reflectively dialectical," its "praxis" can be "ortho" only in the formal sense that it conforms to the transcendental imperatives explicit in Lonergan and implicit in every other thinker worthy of the name. If it is meant to be more than that—and surely it is, given Lamb's attempt to legitimate the agenda of liberation theologies by linking them with Lonergan's own theological conservatism—it must be challenged as not really "reflectively dialectical." Lamb's foundational work on the nature of "noetic praxis," however impressive its theoretical sophistication, fails to fulfill its promise because it fails to overcome the residue of orthodoxy in its own heuristic model. As long as orthopraxis preempts a truly dialectical unfolding of "noetic praxis," critical reflection will provide nothing more than an apologetic for orthodoxy. But why should the eclipse of "noetic praxis" be paid as "the price of orthodoxy"?

The preceding survey suggests not only the bewildering complexity of the discussion of Christian praxis, but also the impasse we have reached in our search for criteria for practical theology. The case against orthodoxy as a "norm of identity" is clear: any profound insight into the dialectic of theory and praxis renders it untenable. The case against orthopraxis should now be equally clear.

Let us turn therefore to the task of beginning anew with the dialectic of theory and praxis. Where can we find an adequate understanding of it? How can it still be foundational for practical theology, if neither orthodoxy nor orthopraxis can be validated by it? To explore these questions further, we propose to derive a few lessons from Jürgen Habermas's understanding of the dialectic because his work represents an analogous attempt to overcome both orthodoxy and orthopraxis in his own tradition, namely, Marxism.

B. CRITICAL THEORY ON PRAXIS

The orthopraxis against which Habermas has struggled is the Marxist-Leninist view of the Communist Party as a revolutionary vanguard. The orthodoxy that stands behind it is the Positivistic understanding of Marxism enshrined in the Stalinist ideology of "Diamat." Working within the neoMarxist tradition of the Frankfurt School (Max Horkheimer, Theodor Adorno, Walter Benjamin, and Herbert Marcuse), Habermas has tried to clarify the nature of the dialectic of theory and praxis, so that critical social theory might claim truly scientific status, and thus might offer relevant suggestions regarding the kind of social policies required to overcome the crisis of advanced industrial societies.

What makes Habermas and the Frankfurt School interesting is, unlike other Western social philosophers who have regarded Soviet theory and praxis as sufficient reason to totally discredit Marxism, they have interpreted this historical development as an aberration in the Marxist tradition that can be corrected. The Frankfurt School's program of "negative dialectics" provides a form of radical cognitive therapy for Marxist intellectuals and activists seeking to overcome the totalitarianism implicit in this aberration. Habermas's distinctive contribution is a reconstruction of this program, for the sake of addressing the global agenda of justice and peace that emerged as the legacy of World War II.

In order to liberate Marxism from the distortions of orthopraxis and orthodoxy, Habermas returns to Aristotle and Kant. Aristotle's definition of praxis makes distinctions that render any orthodoxy about praxis suspect. Kant's critique of practical reason does the same for any possible future orthopraxis.

Aristotle defines praxis as one category of human action: the cooperative interaction of the citizens to achieve the political common good. It is distinguished from "poeisis," the category of human action in which the material conditions of life are reproduced. This, of course, represents the classical distinction between doing and making. (Lobkowicz, 1967: 9) Aristotle's unique contribution to the discussion, however, lies in the realm of theory. By insisting that in neither of these categories does thought achieve the status of true knowledge *(episteme),* Aristotle *in principle* renders any orthodoxy about praxis impossible. Nevertheless, his conception of the relationship between thinking and acting remains classical inasmuch as acting is still hierarchically subordinated to thinking. His own reflections on praxis *(phronesis),* however useful to later thinkers, do not transcend the limits of the Greek polis.

Kant's practical philosophy makes an equally significant, if equally limited, contribution. When viewed historically, Kant's work reflects the difference between the aristocratic Greek polis and the liberal modern state. The political pursuit of the common good is now transformed into the modern citizen's struggle for self-determination within the law. Nevertheless, Kant's reflections on the nature of praxis see it no longer as simply the category of public affairs, but as the self-constituting realm where the "noumenal" causality of Freedom is exercised. Praxis becomes an imperative to maximize the possibility of "perfect autonomy" for all citizens. (Lobkowicz, 1967: 134–5) Kant's redefinition implies two things: (1) Praxis is no longer simply a category of public affairs but also a norm for them. (2) Praxis is now dialectically related to its own theory, and no longer just the embodiment of *phronesis*. Praxis thus depends on understanding the "noumenal" reality of Freedom, which is known only in its exercise. By thus ascribing to praxis "a cognitive value which transcends the limits of what traditionally was called 'practical knowledge'" (Ibid.: 124), Kant *in principle* renders any orthopraxis impossible. For any attempt to impose an orthopraxis is bound to run afoul of the autonomous moral self. The Kantian practical imperative, *"sapere aude,"* is just as alien to orthopraxis as it is to orthodoxy.

Marx's version of the dialectic of theory and praxis is a "determinate negation" of both Kant and Aristotle. The "perfect autonomy" envisioned in Kant's praxis had already been undermined by Hegel's critique of the distinction between noumena and phenomena. If Freedom can no longer be regarded as some mysterious noumenal reality, praxis once again must be grounded concretely in the phenomena of social life. While Marx presupposes Hegel's critique of Kant, he criticizes Hegel's *Philosophy of Right* as a legitimation of the Prussian status quo. (Cf. Marx, 1977)

Marx's praxis thus liberates the actual content of Kant's ideal of Freedom by unleashing its power as a revolutionary negation of the social status quo. Since even a revolutionary praxis must be grounded historically, Marx interprets the modern industrial proletariat as the bearer of the imperative. Praxis, in other words, remains the category of public affairs; but its normative implications are no longer noumenal and therefore abstractly universal, but historically identified with the revolutionary struggle of an actual social class.

Ironically, Marx's vision of revolutionary social praxis may have overcome Aristotle, Kant, and Hegel, only by reopening in concrete historical terms the problem of orthodoxy and orthopraxis that they had resolved, if only in principle. Habermas's distinctive contribution to the Marxist discussion of the proletariat as the historic bearer of the concrete promise of Enlightenment confirms this suspicion. For it is in this discussion that Habermas most pointedly rejects both Marxist-Leninist orthopraxis and Stalinist orthodoxy. The issue is joined in his critical remarks on Georg Lukacs's essay, *"Methodisches zur Organizationsfrage."* (Habermas, 1973b: 34; cf. Lukacs, 1971: 295–342)

Habermas criticizes Lukacs as a defender of an "instrumental" view of Communist Party praxis which inevitably reduces Marxist theory to a "science of apologetics." (Habermas, 1973: 36) Activists like Lenin found out the hard way that the subjective "spontaneities" of real working class people do not always correspond to the objective "necessities" of "proletarian class consciousness." If the proletariat remains ensnared by bourgeois ideology, Lenin and Lukacs argued, "then the Party as the embodiment of class consciousness must act representatively for the masses, and not allow itself to be made dependent on their spontaneity." (Ibid.: 35) Furthermore, the risk of ideological self-delusion is so insidious that an "iron discipline" is required within the Communist Party itself. (Lukacs, 1971: 339) Even within this embodiment of "proletarian class consciousness," social praxis must be directed "solely with a view to the imperatives of the conduct of the political struggle." (Habermas, 1973: 34) Ideological conformity is imposed any time the reigning orthopraxis is challenged. Stalinist orthodoxy codified both the form and the content of this "iron discipline." Thus when Lenin and Stalin allowed "organizational questions" to predetermine the development of "proletarian class consciousness," Communist Party ideology ceased to be a form of public discourse.

In opposition to Lenin and the apologetics of Lukacs, Habermas argued that the promised "organization of Enlightenment" remains spurious until social praxis permits "all the participants . . . the opportunity to know what they are doing." (Habermas, 1973: 37) Unless the primacy of praxis includes a recognition of the relative autonomy of theoretical reflection, such participants will be unable to "form a common will discursively." (Ibid.) The dialectic of theory and praxis remains a sham so long as social praxis preempts a formal commitment to the procedures of public discourse.

The concrete implications of Habermas's critique became apparent as he wrestled with the so-called Student Revolt of the late 1960s. At issue was whether, in an advanced industrial society, students might function in the role that Marx had originally assigned to the proletariat. If the working class had been coopted through the success of trade unionism, might not some other class—more sophisticated in its resistance to the self-delusions of bourgeois ideology—take up the proletarian task? While Habermas at first was cautiously optimistic, later on when demonstrations at German universities became violent, he warned students against "using the university for pseudo-revolutionary adventures." (Habermas, 1970: 46) Instead of comforting themselves with some romantic fantasy regarding a new proletariat, he counseled neoMarxists to create an institutional framework in which advanced industrial societies could be understood and, if necessary, transformed. University reform was to help establish this framework by democratizing all decisionmaking processes, thereby maximizing the possibilities of genuine consensus. (Ibid.: 46–8)

Having been forced by the logic of events to clarify the ambiguity of social praxis in Marxism, Habermas ends up reaffirming the integrity of critical reflection in all forms of human interaction. Since the legitimacy of the competing social systems—capitalism vs. socialism—must therefore be regarded as neither determined in advance through some dialectical *tour de force* (orthodoxy) nor dictated from below through some *fait accompli* of pseudo-revolutionary activism (orthopraxis), Habermas inevitably has undermined the distinctive basis for Marxist social revolution. (Habermas, 1970: 48–9) In its place he discerns a "quasi-transcendental . . . emancipatory interest" operative in the deep structures of human interaction and discourse as such. (Habermas, 1971a: 308f) What remains of social praxis, in short, is "a partisanship on behalf of reason" strikingly reminiscent of Kant. Yet unlike Kant, Habermas understands with the help of Hegel and Marx that such partisanship has only as much integrity as "the truth-dependent mode of socialization" that constitutes it historically. (Habermas, 1975: 142) Social praxis remains normative, but the norm is no longer exclusively realized in the struggle of any particular social class. Rather, it is transcendentally presupposed in the struggle of all persons and groups to see and say what is true, to do what is right, and above all, to remain truthful to themselves and to their fellows.

C. CRITICAL THEORY ON CRITICAL THEORY

If praxis, once detached from the material interests of any particular social class, now refers to the struggle to sustain "a truth-dependent mode of socialization" in all public institutions, critical theory necessarily becomes a theory of public discourse. Habermas saw this consequence more clearly than any other representative of the Frankfurt School, and has made it the agenda of his research and reflection. At the center of this agenda is Habermas's reformulation of the dialectic of theory and praxis in terms of a theory of communicative competence. Here practical theology can learn the most from its formal and procedural analogues in critical theory.

There are two major criteriological problems addressed by Habermas's theory of communicative competence: (1) What is authentic public discourse? (2) How is public discourse to be related to the dialectic of theory and praxis so that it remains authentically dialectical. If these questions are answered formally and procedurally, and not by invoking values embedded in any particular tradition, then the criteria of public discourse so derived *in principle* would govern "critical reflection on praxis" in any tradition, including those of religious communities. Habermas's critical theory is most relevant to rethinking the foundations of practical theology precisely when it is most rigorously formal and procedural. When it is less than rigorous, that is, when it unwittingly reflects the substantive values embedded in its own tradition of Marxist social praxis, it ceases to be formal and becomes only another ideology. As such, it must confront rival secular and religious ideologies by redeeming its substantive claims in public discourse. It is not necessary, however, to stage this confrontation prior to using Habermas's critical theory to gain insight into how practical theology may qualify as a form of public discourse.

The point of departure for Habermas's theory of communicative competence is his attempt to determine what phenomena give evidence of the emancipatory interest operative in all human thinking and acting. True to the spirit of the Frankfurt School, he proceeds negatively. The experience of "systematically distorted communication" indirectly discloses the common human interest in emancipating ourselves from this aberration. To judge any given failure to communicate as an instance of systematic distortion is to enter into a distinct way of knowing that already implies our intent to overcome it. "Systematically distorted communication" thus becomes the object of both psychoanalytic therapy and revolutionary social praxis. While it is common practice in the Frankfurt School to link the legacies of Freud and Marx, it is unique to Habermas to seek formally and procedurally for criteria distinguishing these cures from the disease.

Systematically distorted communication is a deformation of the internal structures of language and action that blocks the paths to personal maturity and public responsibility. Because human interaction is so thoroughly shaped by language, any distortions in the organization of work or the distribution of power get reflected in the structures of human communication. That any given individual or institution is in bondage to such a disorder may often be recognized intuitively from the symptoms of alienation that accompany it: the pointless suffering that is the lot of neurotic personalities and the socially oppressed. Correct diagnosis, however, requires more than human solidarity with the victims of suffering. For some forms of alienation are so deeply rooted that they no longer produce pain; and by the same token, not all suffering—however acutely experienced—is conclusive evidence of alienation. Thus, if it is to be diagnosed accurately, "systematically distorted communication" requires explicit contrast with a theoretical model of "normal" communication. If such a model can be constructed, it will provide criteria that should be useful in determining whether the patient must be referred to a psychotherapist or whether society must submit to social revolution.

Such a model, if it is to be more than another fruitless exercise in question-begging, cannot be based on common sense. For in situations of crisis, common sense itself is not exempt from suspicion as a form of systematically distorted communication. Besides, the model must reconstruct the deep structures of any successful communication. It will, in short, reflect the formal features of Habermas's "truth-dependent mode of socialization."

While there are other resources that he could have used, Habermas in fact constructs his model from the theory of "speech acts" outlined by J. L. Austin and developed by John Searle.[2] If communicative competence is defined formally as the capacity of any speaker/hearer to enter into normal human interaction and discourse, the theory of speech acts defines the criteria by which this competence as such is recognized. While Austin and Searle largely confine themselves to an explication of the deep structures common to all human utterances, Habermas uses their work to show how speech acts formally raise "universal validity claims." If his inferences are correct, he will have established the foundations for a theory of public discourse independent of any particular community's tradition and its distinctive agenda for social praxis. Habermas's basic intent, then, is to ground the emancipatory interest in the human will to communicate as such.

The theory of speech acts is based on "the double structure" common to all human utterances. Any successful communication can be analyzed both in terms of its "propositional content" ("locutionary act") and its "illocutionary force." Habermas interprets illocutionary force as referring to *"the level of intersubjectivity* on which speaker and hearer, through illocutionary acts, establish the relations that permit them to come to an understanding with one another." (Habermas, 1979: 42) Thus any successfully communicated proposition, for example, "This pen is blue," or "Honesty is the best policy," or "On the road again, can't wait to be on the road again," always is accompanied by an illocutionary act—whether tacit or explicit—that defines the force of the claim being made and its testability. Hence, (I tell you that) "this pen is blue"; (My advice to you is that) "honesty is the best policy"; (I want you to know my secret wish to be) "on the road again." This double structure might be dismissed as trivial, were it not for the fact that it demonstrates the universal basis in language for making and testing intersubjective "validity claims" concerning the adequacy of our assertions, the appropriateness of our advice, and the authenticity of our intentions.

Following Austin and Searle's work on "illocutionary" verbs, Habermas specifies four categories as defining the "cognitively testable expectations" raised in speech acts: communicative, constative, regulative, and representative. (Habermas, 1971b: 111–12; Cf. 1979: 68) While the first category of utterance, communicative, concerns the intelligibility of language as such, the other three, insofar as they concern what is communicated, provide the basis for the three kinds of validity claims actually made in utterances. "Constative" refers to the speaker's cognitive disposition toward the predicate. "Regulative" formulates the speaker's response to various action-guides. "Representative" serves to convey the personal attitude of the speaker. Each of these, in turn, defines a set of mutual expectations that together constitute the norms of communicative competence.

Competence in the "constative" dimension requires the successful mastery of the distinction between what is fact and what is fiction, in other words, a recognition of the difference between the private world of personal discernment and the public world of intersubjectively testable ideas. (Habermas, 1971b: 113) If, for example, I *assert* that this pen is blue, you understand that it is not the color everyone calls red; and if there is any dispute about it, we can settle it by taking a good look at the pen or by getting our eyes examined. Competence in the "regulative" dimension is based on the capacity to acknowledge valid rules and their ethical justification. If, for example, I *recommend* honesty as the best policy, you understand me to say that everyone ought to be fair in their dealings with others; and if there is any dispute about it, we can argue the merits of this maxim over against any alternative. Competence in the "representative" dimension depends on knowing the difference between the speaker's true self and his or her various roles and poses. If I *disclose* to you my secret wanderlust, you normally don't expect me to lie about it, nor would you expect me to fake it just to please you; if you come to suspect my truthfulness or sincerity, you may either try to confront me or stop talking to me altogether. Normal communication occurs when speakers/hearers operate successfully in all three dimensions.

Habermas's theory of communicative competence does more than just differentiate three categories of communicative interaction. By explaining how these categories also give rise to discourse and the formal procedures appropriate to it, Habermas clarifies the distinctive role of theory in the dialectic of theory and praxis. Misunderstandings normally occurring in the course of communicative interaction inevitably generate discourse. So long as these misunderstandings remain normal, they raise questions concerning the validity claims so far taken for granted. Explicitly theoretical discourse, however, is opened up in a set of operations that deliberately, albeit provisionally, withdraw from the immediacy of communicative interaction. Taken as a whole, these constitute what Habermas calls the "ideal-speech situation." They consist in (1) a suspension of the immediate pressures of action, thus setting aside all motives but a readiness to reason together as well as all *ad hominem* arguments however sophisticated, and (2) a suspension of the *prima facie* claims of common sense, thus setting aside all substantive prejudgments that might jeopardize an open discussion of the adequacy of contested assertions or the appropriateness of disputed recommendations. The authenticity of those asserting and recommending them continues to be presupposed, for the ideal-speech situation also involves (1) an expectation of intentionality: the speaker/hearers proceed deliberately and all their intentions can be verbalized, and (2) an expectation of legitimacy: the speaker/hearers proceed only according to justifiable norms. (Habermas, 1971b: 119) Habermas admits that these operations are never fully realized even in authentically public discourse. For this model of ideal communication is both warped by external contingent influences and hindered by the finite structures of actual communication. (Ibid.: 137) Despite its acknowledged "counterfactuality," the ideal speech situation does represent the formal procedural norm of discourse, implicit in the questioning process initiated by speech acts.

Let us illustrate the move to theoretical discourse by returning to our three examples. Suppose that relevant questions remain even after we've tried the most obvious ways of confirming that this pen is blue. Even though we may or may not have reached agreement on the immediate question, the process of seeking agreement may pique our curiosity as to why it is that such assertions can be validated by taking a good look while others may not. By searching for valid criteria to settle the first question, we are already engaged in a form of epistemological discourse whose integrity depends on our ability to distance ourselves from our stake in the questions that gave rise to it. Similarly, suppose that our discussion of honesty's normative claim is not exhausted by appeals to, say, the Kantian categorical imperative. It is not hard to imagine the logic of our initially practical question very quickly taking us to the heights of metaethical abstraction, where we now ponder the question, "Why be moral at all?" Here, too, the search for valid criteria is self-defeating unless ethical discourse is allowed to proceed provisionally, independent of the immediate pressures of action and the impressive plausibilities of common sense.

This model of the relationship between communicative interaction and discourse does not, of course, rule out theoretical reflection on the criteria of authenticity. My attempt at self-disclosure may lead you to suspect that my wanderlust is symptomatic of, say, my inability to resolve a midlife crisis or my bondage to the escape mechanisms built into the bourgeois ideology. In either case, you may be challenging what Habermas refers to as "the presumption of seriousness," that is, my readiness to live up to the commitments made in my speech acts, taken as a whole. (Habermas, 1971b: 132) Furthermore, if you're really determined to challenge my authenticity, your suspicions may lead you to interpret my lack of seriousness as evidence of my entrapment in the web of systematically distorted communication. Once you've entertained this possibility, you will no longer converse with me in an ideal speech situation but will appeal to an appropriate form of "counter-discourse," say, psychoanalysis or the critique of ideologies. These forms of discourse are designed to explore epistemic, functional, and genetic distortions corresponding to the various categories of speech acts with their distinct validity claims. In Habermas's view, a burden of proof remains upon any group or person that would raise the question of authenticity to the level of "counter-discourse" involved in psychoanalysis or the critique of ideologies. The various models of critical theory, in other words, are neither exempt from the relevant criteria of cognitive adequacy and ethical appropriateness, nor are they hermeneutically privileged in relation to the criteria of authenticity. They, too, can only be validated according to the norms and procedures of communicative competence.

In light of the theory of communicative competence, the function of truth in the dialectic of theory and praxis can now be clarified. Truth becomes a genuine "consensus" among successful communicators participating in the ideal speech situation, rather than a "correspondence" between an anonymous mind and reality *(adaequatio rei ad intellectum)*. Such consensus must be defined multidimensionally, that is, according to the logic of the various categories of speech acts: constative speech acts raise claims concerning what is fact and fiction in our beliefs *(adequacy)*; regulative, concerning what is reasonable and unreasonable in the routines, rituals, and moral rules by which we govern our lives *(appropriateness)*; and representative, concerning what is genuine and what is fake in ourselves and in our actions, in others, and in the institutions within which we dwell *(authenticity)*.[3] While each of these, as we have seen, requires different procedures of validation, together they establish the difference between "a 'true' (real) and a 'false' (deceptive) consensus." (Habermas, 1971b: 114)

In general, then, truth lies in judgment. Each category of speech act requires a distinct kind of judgment. Competence in judgment, however, is based ultimately on successful appeal to the hypothetical accord of all other competent judges. This implies that truth is not definitive and absolute, but tentative and relative to a consensus that in principle remains open to revision. It also implies that truth is not so relative as to be without rational justification. Both of these claims are satisfied when public discourse is governed by "the peculiarly forceless force of better arguments." (Ibid.: 137)

We believe that Habermas's "consensus" theory of truth not only provides an adequate explanation of the norms of public discourse but also formally defines the status of public discourse within the "truth-dependent mode of socialization." Consensus is the regulative ideal of those who recognize the perspectival character of all ideological models and who, therefore, consciously seek the enlargement of horizons which occurs in public discourse. Habermas's strictly formal understanding of the dialectic of theory and praxis thus may serve as the source of procedural criteria for evaluating any community's attempt to realize that ideal in its distinctive way of life. It is clear, for example, that any social praxis informed by the truth-dependent mode of socialization will have to promote the maximum feasible participation of the oppressed in their own liberation. The movement, in other words, will have to be democratic in its internal organization as well as in its aspirations for social change. The same thing needs to be said about any Christian community seeking to develop its religious praxis within this dialectic of theory and praxis. (cf. Davis, 1967; Küng, 1968) Habermas, of course, does not tell us how to conceive of religious praxis as a truth-dependent mode of socialization. All he has done, as this and the previous section have argued, is demonstrate both its necessity and its possibility within his own tradition of Marxist theory and praxis. We are convinced that his effort is quite enough to provide practical theology a number of illuminating analogies and fruitful suggestions to help shape any further analysis of this genre.

These can be specified in contrast to the relatively inadequate foundations for practical theology provided by Metz, Segundo, and Lamb:

1. Habermas's theory of communicative competence gives specific meaning to the term *public discourse.* As a form of public discourse any ideology must adhere to certain procedural criteria. Metz's hermeneutic determinations of Christian praxis cannot operate at this level of generality. Consequently it is hard to see how they could represent a foundational understanding of the dialectic of theory and praxis.

2. By stipulating that any authentic praxis must entail a truth-dependent mode of socialization, Habermas preserves the integrity of the theoretical moment of the dialectic of theory and praxis. In the non-coercive atmosphere of the ideal speech situation, however imperfectly achieved in any instance of discourse, the validation of any ideology according to the general norms of adequacy, appropriateness and authenticity heeds only the force of better argument. This position contrasts sharply with Segundo's functionalist criterion of orthopraxis. As the same time Habermas's understanding of praxis as a truth-dependent mode of socialization can be viewed as a self-critical liberation of praxis from its own deformation within a tradition enforcing both orthodoxy and orthopraxis. That Christian

practical theologians may claim immunity from such deformations where Marxist ideologists cannot seems utterly unwarranted.

3. The recognition that different speech acts raise different kinds of claims upon our powers of judgment allows Habermas to break with a purely contemplative theory of truth. Unlike Lamb, Habermas does not see a dichotomy between disclosure and transformation. Nor does he view "transformative praxis as the control of both theory and empirical technique." (Lamb, 1982: 106–107) Instead, Habermas's understanding of consensual validation maintains the integrity of the theoretical moment of the dialectic as it acknowledges the perspectival limitations of any ideological model. Yet the criterion of appropriateness also allows praxis its proper force within the dialectic. Satisfying the criterion of authenticity, with its recognition that systematic distortions of communication can infect any ideology, forecloses the uncritical acceptance of substantive beliefs and values as foundational principles. Any tradition can enforce systematically distorted communication even through its highest ideals. Neither Lamb's "noetic praxis" nor any other promising foundation principle, then, must be held captive to the self-deluding ideologies of orthodoxy or orthopraxis.

Habermas's formal dialectic of theory and praxis, by analogy, thus allows us to clarify our disagreement with Metz, Segundo, and Lamb and to outline a constructive alternative. Whatever else it does for religious praxis, the truth-dependent mode of socialization puts the lie to orthopraxis; similarly, the norms of public discourse rule out any formally orthodox model of practical theology.

D. RELIGIOUS PRAXIS: THE FOUNDATION FOR PRACTICAL THEOLOGY

We only begin to pay the price of critical reflection by suggesting that whatever else practical theology does, it must conform to the procedures of public discourse. We have not yet identified the distinctive type of social praxis for which practical theology seeks to be an appropriate form of critical reflection. In order to make explicit what is already implicit in our argument to this point, we will specify this praxis categorically as "religious praxis." For it, and not the procedural norms of theory and praxis in general, constitutes the glowing core of practical theology.

Let us examine two definitions of religion in our attempt to establish the category of religious praxis. The generic character of these definitions contrasts with Metz's largely *ad hoc* description of "Christian praxis" which, as we have seen, begs the question of criteria for *any* religious praxis as such. The first of these definitions is the work of a cultural anthropologist, Clifford Geertz:

> A religion is: (1) a system of symbols which acts to (2) establish powerful, pervasive and long-lasting moods and motivations in men by (3) formulating conceptions of a general order of existence and (4) clothing these conceptions with such an aura of factuality that (5) the motivations seem uniquely realistic.
>
> (Geertz, 1973b: 90)

Geertz's widely accepted definition of religion is useful in several respects. First, it enables us to see religion as oriented primarily to the cultural system, as a public not a private act. "Cultural acts, the construction, apprehension, and utilization of symbolic forms are social events like any other; they are as public as marriage and as observable as agriculture." (Geetz, 1973b: 91) Second, by pointing out religion's "unique realism," Geertz shows that such cultural activity can never be purely instrumental. It is never simply a means to a predetermined end, but a dialectical process that expresses as well as shapes reality. Third, by emphasizing both the "moods and motivations" and the "the aura of factuality" that accompanies them, Geertz suggests that this dialectical process of itself involves seeking and maintaining a dynamic unity of theory and praxis. Finally, with his attention to "conceptions of a general order of existence" he corroborates our assumption that religious praxis correlates visions of ultimate order with models for social action. Geertz's attempt to define religion within a cultural system may seem to belabor the obvious. The point, however, is that religious praxis, viewed in isolation, tends to degenerate into either instrumental action or abstract thought, both of which are "dysfunctional" in terms of religion's role in the cultural system as a whole.

Such a stress on the symbolic and not the political character of religious praxis may disappoint those practical theologians who wish to emphasize its transformative possibilities. While insisting on the cultural dynamics of religious praxis, we, too, intend to recognize its politically transformative character. Religion, indeed, is more appropriately thought of as a verb than as a noun. Our second definition, taken from Frederick Streng, restores the proper balance here: Religion is "a means of ultimate transformation." (Streng, Lloyd, and Allen, 1973: 6–12) This definition is useful for distinguishing not the category of religion as such, for which Geertz remains more adequate, but religious *praxis*. Religious praxis is distinct among all other forms of cultural activity insofar as it intends an ultimate transformation. In Streng's usage the term *ultimate* enfolds several layers of meaning. It refers to a transformation not only of individual psyches, and social structures, but of the totality of worldly being, inclusive of human and other forms of life. It also refers to that transformation which occurs in the creative interaction of this totality with Ultimate Reality. (Ibid.) If practical theology reflects upon religious praxis, it focuses upon those symbolically constituted actions which intend and express this dual meaning of ultimate transformation.[4]

Streng insists that there are multiple modes of ultimate transformation exhibited in the praxis of various religious communities. Traditions cohere not by isolating one mode as right (orthodoxy/orthopraxis) but by correlating and synthesizing multiple modes—sacramental, mystical, prophetic, ethical—into distinct and limited forms of life. (Streng, Lloyd, and Allen, 1973: 9–10) Any given mode of transformation, however, can lose its self-transcending focus on the Ultimate. As we suggested earlier, one of the purposes of practical theology as a form of critical reflection is to guard against this loss of focus.

There are two initial objections to linking this understanding of religious praxis as the core of practical theology with Habermas's theory of communicative competence. First, Habermas's view of the dialectic of theory and praxis, according to some of its critics, either presupposes a glowing "utopian" core of its own, or in its formalism rules out any critical reflection on matters of substance. In short, Habermas either imposes a covert hermeneutic of the specifically

Western and rationalistic tradition of Enlightment or he rejects historical hermeneutics altogether. (McCarthy, 1982; Gadamer, 197) In either case, religion and religious forms of praxis become confined, in the terminology of some critical theorists, to the realm of the "paleosymbolic." (Gouldner, 1976: 210–228) Second, Habermas himself dismisses communal forms of life and action grounded in mythic worldviews as representative of a stage of evolution outstripped *in principle,* if not in actuality. (Habermas, 1979: 154) The "God" witnessed to in political theologies, he believes, can never refer to anything more than a "communicative structure." (Habermas, 1975: 121)

The first objection may be set aside by noting Habermas's reply to his critics. He denies that his critical theory projects a specific form of life. The formalism of his quasi-universals "does indeed have a utopian content, but it does not *sketch out* a utopia." (Habermas, 1982: 251, 261–2) While the theory of communicative competence serves to identify certain formal conditions and structures of the good life, one cannot infer "an idea of the good life from the formal concept of reason with which the decentered understanding of the world in the modern age has left us." The historical mediation of the formal "ethic of discourse" and the substantive "practice of life"—that is, the mediation between the formal conditions for praxis as a truth-dependent mode of socialization, and the social routines and rituals, the ethical expectations, and cultural patterns, that make up a community's way of life—is necessary to constitute a concrete horizon for actual praxis. Historical mediation must not be short-circuited. Actual praxis is always substantive. (Ibid.: 250–63)

Habermas's admissions thus restore the missing link between praxis and critical hermeneutics without entailing "a wholesale renunciation of theoretical and critical distanciation in favor of hermeneutic participation." (McCarthy, 1982: 78) Implicit here is the point of departure for our subsequent reconstruction of critical hermeneutics. For the moment, however, we need only note that Habermas's view of the substantive character of actual praxis removes any *prima facie* obstacle to recognizing authentically religious forms of praxis.

The second objection, however, requires us to use Habermas against Habermas. As a distinctive form of praxis, religious praxis must reflect the truth-dependent mode of socialization which Habermas has shown to be characteristic of any authentic praxis. To claim that a certain set of human actions constitutes a praxis is to commit its agents to public discourse about the norms governing that action and about their theoretical warrants. Practical theology as a mode of public discourse is the attempt to fulfill these formal conditions for authentic religious praxis. If religious praxis is the ground of practical theology, a practical theology in some stage of development is necessary for religiously grounded practices to be considered as praxis. But whether *all things considered,* we are entitled to speak of an authentically religious form of praxis depends upon arguments seeking to establish religion's distinctive claims as a dimension of human life. Definitive reply to Habermas's own substantive judgment on religious praxis and the possibility of practical theology, that is, whether the one is paleosymbolic and the other an anachronistic misreading of merely a communicative structure, is not the specific task of practical theology but of foundational theology. While foundational theology develops concepts generated in the philosophy of religion in order to clarify the irreducible validity of religious existence, practical theology, in turn, borrows definitions of religion validated by foundational theology in order to give specific meaning to the nature of religious praxis. Nevertheless, because of their centrality to the very enterprise of theology, we will assess their claims at a later point.

Let us conclude by emphasizing the point of these preliminary remarks. To be blunt: practical theology is *not* critical reflection on praxis, but critical reflection on specifically religious praxis, that is, symbolically constituted action geared toward ultimate transformation. While religious praxis is not confined to the religious community, because both the community and its activity are aspects of a form of life, religious praxis is embedded within the history of specific traditions. Once again the trajectory of this analysis of the dialectic of theory and praxis leads to the point where we must clarify the role of hermeneutics in practical theology. The "glowing core" of practical theology turns out to be more like a comet with its tail extending back through space and time.

NOTES

1. By ruling out any model of orthodoxy in practical theology, we are not eliminating the possibility of a substantively conservative practical theology, that is, one that is fundamentally positive in its attitude toward the inherited theological traditions of the Christian communities. What distinguishes the two, of course, is the way in which the appeal to tradition is made. If tradition unfolds as a "truth-dependent mode of socialization," in principle it can no longer claim to be orthodox.
2. Instead of relying on Austin and Searle, Matthew Lamb suggests a synthesis of Lonergan and Habermas. (cf. Lamb, 1982: 85) This is a very promising suggestion: it could very well turn out that Lonergan's "radical cognitive therapy" is the ultimate disciplinary matrix for "sublating" the work of Habermas, Kohlberg, and Karl-Otto Apel. Nevertheless, for reasons that are implicit in our argument as a whole, we do not find it necessary to wait for this suggestion to bear fruit before proceeding to use Habermas to understand the dialectic of theory and praxis.
3. Our description of the criterion of "authenticity" is consistent with, but emphatically goes beyond, what Habermas actually says about *Wahrhaftigkeit*. We believe that our description has the advantage of clarifying the basis in a theory of communicative competence for the kind of personal soul-searching, formal therapy, and ultimately social criticism, that in modern times have converged in the disciplines of psychoanalysis and the critique of ideologies. While our threefold distinction between criteria of adequacy, appropriateness, and authenticity, clearly emerges from the three basic categories of speech-acts, it does make for a different set of criteria for theological discourse than those offered by other authors. The advantages of adopting our threefold criteria can only be seen by examining the way in which they help to focus the generic analysis developed in the following chapters.
4. Just as it might be objected that all theology carries ideological implications, it might be argued here that all theologies reflect upon religious praxis as we have defined it. In a certain sense this is true but all

theologies do not express themselves through the generic conventions of ideological discourse. An investigation of the logic of inquiry of practical theology must be complemented by a generic analysis. In terms of its logic of inquiry, however, practical theology has a real stake in interpretations of religion which underline its character as a transformative process and its power to shape a culture.

CHAPTER FOUR

MEMORY AND EXPECTATION: THE CRITICAL HERMENEUTIC OF PRACTICAL THEOLOGY

Liberation movements have no stake in a mythological history which falsifies the past. . . . We search history anxiously, trying to understand the sources of its massive failure. We look for signs of hope that a new beginning is possible.

(Ruether, 1975: xii)

Only the courage of an act combines the past and the future, by so emphasizing the historically grasped essence of a cultural complex for the present, that the future arises out of the essence in a manner demanded by the present and yet at the same time exhausting the depth of the historical impluse. But if in this sense the definition of essence is an act, then it is no longer merely a judgment about history but it is itself a piece of history.

(Troeltsch, 1971: 161)

Praxis is not *techne*. It is not determined by purely instrumental calculations nor governed by the norm of efficiency alone. All genuine praxis is symbolically constituted, and, consequently mediated by interpretive schema which represent the common good. (McCarthy, 1978: 69–73, 151–52, 156) If we define hermeneutics as the reflective appropriation of traditions claiming to represent such interpretive schema, clearly it is a necessary dimension to critical reflection on praxis. (Cf. Misgeld, 1976: 168–69) Otherwise stated, hermeneutics is an element in the structure by which any ideology is constructed to shape a concrete praxis. Apart from the retrieval of some cultural heritage, the thrust towards some future emancipation lacks all direction because the emancipatory ideal remains purely abstract. (Ricoeur, 1981: 96–97)

What is true of praxis in general is true a fortiori of religious praxis. Both as religious and as praxis, religious praxis is substantive, a determinate negation of certain modes of being human, and the presentation of an alternative mode of being human involving some process of ultimate transformation. Indeed, transformative action cannot qualify as religious unless it is mediated by a worldview and an ethos explicitly relating human activity to Ultimate Reality. Religious praxis requires, in short, a hermeneutic of religious tradition.

In actual practice historians of religion interested in emancipation and practical theologians have demonstrated the importance of a critical hermeneutic for defining religious praxis. J. B. Metz, in particular, has enriched our sense of the emancipatory potential of memory. Following Herbert Marcuse, Metz suggests that "remembering . . . is a way of relieving oneself from the given facts, a way of mediation that can momentarily at least break through the omnipresent power of the given facts." (Metz, 1980: 193) The dangerous memory of a history of suffering and of freedom shatters unquestioning submissiveness to the past even as it performs a utopian function. "The restoration of the capacity to remember goes hand in hand with the restoration of the knowing content of the imagination and . . . in this way the *recherche du temps perdu* becomes a vehicle for liberation." (Metz, 1980: 100–18, 193)

What Metz expresses in theoretical terms feminist religious historians like Eleanor McLaughlin and Black practical theologians like James Cone express concretely. In each case the writer cuts beneath the encrusted layers of "official" tradition to recover alternative forms of Christian life and praxis. The "usable" past that McLaughlin (1975) captures turns out to be a subterranean history of female spirituality. For James Cone the alternative tradition is the history of suffering, longing, and struggling of Black Christians crystallized in uniquely Black forms of religious expression.

> Black Theology must uncover the structures and forms of black experience, because the categories of interpretation must arise out of the thought forms of the black experience itself. What are we to make of the moan and the shout and the call to get on board the gospel train? What must we say about the song,

> the sermon, the prayer, and the freeing of the Spirit when the people gather for worship . . . ?
>
> (1975: 5–7, 17–19)

Although indicative of a keen awareness of the role of hermeneutics, Cone's description of his "categories of interpretation" raises some disturbing questions. Are practical theologians simply to project their own theological commitments as norms for retrieving and censoring the past? Is the critical hermeneutic of a practical theology a special hermeneutic exempt from the canons of evidence, selection, and judgment which govern other forms of historical inquiry? In other words, by what criteria do categories of interpretation emerge out of the rich and often conflicting variety of practical perspectives we call the Christian tradition?

Elisabeth Schüssler Fiorenza has provided one particularly bold answer to these questions. Her starting point is to repudiate conventional types of hermeneutics for concealing advocacy positions behind unquestioned norms of interpretation. The "doctrinal paradigm" of hermeneutics is governed, in her view, by a commitment to orthodoxy; the "historical-critical paradigm," with its claim to value-neutrality, by an "objectivist scientific worldview," and the "hermeneutical-contextual paradigm," with its recognition of pluralism in Christian thought and praxis, by a neo-orthodox form of consent to the "continuation" of tradition. (1981: 96–99)[1]

In contrast to these hermeneutic paradigms with their concealed norms, Schüssler Fiorenza offers her "feminist interpretive paradigm of emancipatory praxis." While this method accepts the historical-critical method and the contextual approach of earlier paradigms, it rejects both value neutrality and a "hermeneutics of consent." "Scripture and tradition are not only a source of truth but also of untruth, repression, and domination." (Ibid.: 106) By insisting on the need to qualify hermeneutics with the critique of ideology, Schüssler Fiorenza assumes that the Scriptures alone cannot provide the norm for discerning between truth and untruth, between that aspect of the tradition which liberates and that which oppresses. "The personally and politically reflected experience of oppression and liberation must become the criterion of 'appropriateness' for biblical interpretation." (Ibid.: 106–7, 109–10)

Most of Schüssler Fiorenza's criticisms of rival hermeneutic paradigms are warranted. As our previous discussion of the pathologies of religious and secular ideology should indicate, we also accept her basic premise that scripture and tradition themselves can be sources of systematically distorted communication. Apart from such a rationally as well as experientially grounded conviction, there would be no need to develop a *critical* hermeneutic. Nevertheless, Schüssler Fiorenza's alternative cannot be adopted. For that paradigm has a *norma normans non normata* of its own: the prior beliefs, commitments, and values of specific communities of praxis. While such a procedure is always theologically and religiously suspect, we must challenge it here as a hermeneutic analogue to the model of orthopraxis. If orthopraxis, in principle, is objectionable because it fails to establish itself as a "truth-dependent mode of socialization," the same must be said of Schüssler Fiorenza's hermeneutic criterion of appropriateness. Such a hermeneutic can never accomplish anything other than confirm a given community's pre-existent horizon of meaning. It cannot provide the basis for genuinely public discourse about the direction of praxis or the horizon of meaning within which such praxis is executed.

Our task, then, is to establish an alternative to Schüssler Fiorenza's critical hermeneutics which could contribute to practical theology as a form of public discourse. We will first stipulate the *focus* of a hermeneutic premised upon the dialectic of theory and praxis in contrast to conventional hermeneutics, and in contrast to the idealistic presuppositions of most historical theologies. Second, we will trace the steps toward a critical hermeneutic culminating in a retrieval of Ernst Troeltsch's understanding of historical development. Third, we will show how the critique of ideologies, so crucial to contemporary hermeneutics, can be subsumed under Troeltsch's notion of "immanent criticism" within any historical development. Finally, in order to illustrate our understanding of the hermeneutic process and our criteria for evaluating its products, we will present a case study analyzing the practical implications of the nineteenth century Protestant "cult of domesticity."

A. FORMS OF LIFE AND MODELS OF HISTORICAL RECONSTRUCTION

If we accept the dialectic of theory and praxis as foundational for *each* of the structural elements of a practical theology, then the task of historical reconstruction cannot focus upon the religious tradition as a history of doctrine, a progression of forms of consciousness. What is the alternative? It was Hegel's *Phenomenology,* according to Jürgen Habermas, that identified the dialectical mediation of forms of consciousness with the simultaneous rise and fall of different forms of life and praxis. As a result, the Master-Slave relationship or the Beautiful Soul must be seen not simply as modes of consciousness but as ways of projecting the self within historically developing social structures. The alteration of an entire form of life, in short, is always involved in a transformation of consciousness. (Habermas, 1971a: 17–19; Taylor, 1975: 16, 82–83, 85–88) Critical hermeneutics must focus, therefore, on a tradition's protean history of rising and dying forms of life.

Our concept of religious praxis confirms the importance of this shift from forms of consciousness to forms of life for critical hermeneutics. Religious praxis, as a means of ultimate transformation, is always embedded within the culture which it shapes. Just as it gives rise to objective structures of political and economic as well as religious life, religious praxis creates new forms of personality and of social relations, or more simply, new forms of life. A critical hermeneutic involves the dialectical mediation of these forms, the old with the new.

Classic examples of practical theology illustrate this shift of focus in hermeneutics. Reinhold Niebuhr, for example, set his critical interpretation of liberal Protestantism within a general diagnosis of the cultural contradictions of classical American liberalism as a way of life. Not simply the liberal ideology and ethos in its religious and secular variants but liberalism as a way of organizing the economic and political order was Niebuhr's focus of attention. Hermeneutics here was geared to praxis, towards the persuasive conclusion that "the great achievement[s] of liberalism cannot be maintained if liberalism is not transcended as a culture." (Niebuhr, 1939: 542–46; cf. 1979: 103–22) Gustavo Gutierrez, similarly, is not content to present his practical theology as an alternative to the ideal of development projected by Pope Paul VI's encyclical, *Populorum Progressio,* and Vatican II's *Gaudium et Spes.* He situates his critique within a Latin American cultural history showing how, more often than not, the theories of "developmentalism" *(desarrollismo)* provided cover for the practices of neo-colonialism. Here, too, Gutierrez clearly is arguing the need to transform a whole religiously supported cultural system. (1973: 33–36, 81–88)

However encouraging, these examples do not clarify the ***procedures*** for a critical hermeneutic. Nor do they stipulate the criteria by which we would judge the adequacy and appropriateness of their own or any other theologian's *work* of historical reconstruction.

The first step in our progressive clarification of the ***procedures*** of a critical hermeneutic begins with William Clebsch's *Christianity in European History.* (1979) An historian totally unconcerned with the implications of hermeneutics for praxis, Clebsch nevertheless seeks an historical reconstruction of religious forms of life. Breaking dramatically with modes of interpreting the Christian past which presuppose a continuity of Christian belief through the ages, he proposes to study the "history of religiousness." Such a history focuses, instead, upon "events initiating and signaling changes in human capabilities and aspirations, in the fundamental sensibilities of men and women, in worldviews—indeed, in the very modalities of being human." (Clebsch, 1979: 3–7) Christianity responded to such cultural crises, Clebsch argues, as occasions for spiritual transformation, for shaping new religious forms of life appropriate to new experiences of cultural order. New human identities were created through exemplary actions and actors centered upon a new image of the Christ.[2] (Ibid.: 7–8; 1974: 10)

In Clebsch's interpretation the remarkable permutations of Christian identity, the striking differences in the forms of life which human beings choose to label Christian stand forth in their utter individuality. The paired exemplars, martyrs and monks, mystics and moralists, activists and apologists, are used to dramatize a shift from the hermeneutics of dogma to the history of religious forms of life. Clebsch's approach undercuts the drive to recapture one authentic form of Christian praxis. Instead, human expressions in their cultural specificity are grasped as ineradicably plural.

In Schüssler Fiorenza's terms Clebsch rejects a "hermeneutics of consent" while wedding a contextual approach to the historical-critical method. His ruling criterion is scholarly competence in research, selection, and judgment. Clebsch thus would have his work judged by only one standard: the accuracy of his narrative reconstruction of actual forms of life. Any question of the authenticity of these forms of life and any possibility of their critical appropriation in religious praxis are simply not discussed. In short, his approach conforms to canons sanctioned by a very limited version of "the morality of historical knowledge." (Clebsch, 1979: 25–27; cf. Harvey, 1966: 38–101)

This limited version of the morality of historical knowledge, nevertheless, does reflect one norm of communicative competence. To falsify the past is to engage in systematically distorted communication. The first criterion of a critical hermeneutic, therefore, is competence as defined by a community of scholars. Having conceded this point, we must criticize this version of the morality of knowledge because it arbitrarily restricts competence to the procedures of research and selection, judgment and argumentation. It is as if the threefold criteria of truth as adequacy, appropriateness, and authenticity had been reduced to a single norm of (historical) accuracy. The act of *constructing* an historical work, however, as opposed to reconstructing the past involves a broader understanding of communicative competence in these areas.

According to Hayden White, "historiographical style represents a particular *combination* of modes of emplotment, argument, and ideological implication." (1973: 29) To move from a chronicle of events to a story which gives coherence to those events the historian must employ constructive imagination. The historian tells a story of a certain type, generally combining such narrative patterns as romance, comedy, tragedy, or irony. But reconstruction includes a moment of explanation as well as narration. To show why events happened as they have been narrated the historian appeals to some explanatory framework. Marx's mechanistic understanding of the relationship of infrastructure to suprastructure is one explanatory model; Herbert Spencer's Darwinistic and organistic explanation of social evolution is another. (White, 1973: 5–21; 1978: 46, 82–83, 92–93)

History, White claims, is always history *for* as well as history *of:* history for someone and for some purpose. (1978: 104) This suggests that the ideological implications of a historical work are not so much symptomatic of a personal bias undercutting scholarly competence as they are part of the very structure of *any* historical work. "Just as every ideology is attended by a specific idea of history and its processes, so too, I maintain, is every idea of history attended by specifically determinable ideological implications." (1973: 24) The patterns that historical narratives reconstruct, the explanations that are given for the causes of events, foreclose the range of possible actions, projects, and strategies that can be viewed as coherent. (Ibid.: 21, 24)

In matching modes of emplotment and explanatory frameworks to ideological implications, the historian creates a perspective, an angle of vision upon the field of history. Any historical work, however narrow its scope, presents a model of the historical process. (Ibid.: 29–30, 427–28) White, in other words, proposes to do for historiography what Tracy and Barbour, among others, have done for theology. Model-theory as applied to historiography means a Copernican revolution in the canons of interpretation. Those who engage in historical hermeneutics *as a mode of public discourse* will have to defend not only their reconstruction of the past but their construction of a particular model of the historical process.

If we accept White's position, then Clebsch's approach to hermeneutics becomes indefensible. Behind the veil of value-neutrality, the ideological implications of his reconstruction are concealed. His view of "the history of religiousness" as a disjunctive series of kaleidoscopic twists and turns, however, seems to promote a merely aesthetic approach to pluralism. Whatever his own convictions may be, Clebsch's work suggests that the past is merely to be savored. There is never an indication that it might compel one to choose and to act. Aestheticism, as Kierkegaard established, cuts the nerve of action. Clebsch's aesthetic approach, in turn, cuts the reader out of history.

Unfortunately, White does not provide an alternative. Adopting a self-consciously ironic attitude towards his own reconstruction, White views different, well-developed models as largely incommensurable. Where Clebsch focuses upon the relativity of religious forms of life, White stresses the relativity of the historical works that reconstruct those forms. The grounds for choosing between alternative historical models, presupposing basic competence, are ultimately personal and not subject to public argument: "We apprehend the past and the whole spectacle of history-in-general in terms of felt needs and aspirations. . . . As these felt needs and aspirations change, we adjust our conception of history-in-general accordingly." (1973: 283, 432–33)

This will not do. We did not reject Schüssler Fiorenza's version of a hermeneutic predetermined by the demands of orthopraxis in order to capitulate to Clebsch's aestheticism or White's relativism. Historical models as well as theological models are subject to criteria of relative adequacy, appropriateness and authenticity. These criteria refer to both the *procedures* and *products* of hermeneutic endeavor. Even in isolation, the criterion of scholarly competence, accepted by Clebsch and White and presupposed by practical theologians like Ruether and Schüssler Fiorenza, rules out sheer relativism. We need to go further.

B. STEPS TOWARD A CRITICAL HERMENEUTICS

A first step beyond the impasse dramatized in Clebsch's work involves a return to a classic of historical and hermeneutic reconstruction with a practical intent, H. Richard Niebuhr's *Christ and Culture* (1951). Niebuhr saw his work as a clarification and correction of Ernst Troeltsch's typological analysis of Christianity's relationship to European culture in *The Social Teachings of the Christian Churches* (1960). "Troeltsch," Niebuhr argued, "taught men to respect the multiformity and individuality of men and movements in Christian history, to be loath to force this rich variety into prefashioned, conceptual molds, and yet to seek logos in mythos, reason in history, essence in existence." (1951: xi–xii) In his own respectful scrutiny of the variety of Christian forms of life Niebuhr discovered that those forms were not incommensurable, that the fundamental dilemma involved in Christianity's relationship to culture, generated forms of life which can be typified. Despite its seemingly artificial character such a typology serves a heuristic function; it enables us to perceive resemblance even within a profusion of individual forms. (Ibid.: 40, 43–44; cf. Rupp, 1974: 13–14)

When resemblances can be shown to exist through a typological analysis, comparison becomes possible. When comparisons can be made, the relative adequacy, appropriateness and authenticity, of variations in the relationship between religion and culture can be addressed. Typological analysis, Niebuhr argued, does not foster the reduction of religious forms of life to a single orthodox, orthopraxic form; it allows for proliferation of forms within types and for overlappings between types. The careful assessment of the strengths and weaknesses of each type, in Niebuhr's view, leads to a faith decision: Since this "step cannot be taken on the plane of . . . theoretic insight and outlook, . . . [it must be] . . . attained in the movement from consideration to action, from insight to decision. (H. Richard Niebuhr, 1951: 230–33; cf. Rupp, 1974: 14)

While this emphasis upon a faith-decision reintroduces a commitment to praxis as intrinsic to the hermeneutic act, it short-circuits the dialectic of theory and praxis which Niebuhr actually develops in evaluating each of his five types. In this process of evaluation Niebuhr combines theological and ethical considerations with an element of critical social theory to expose the relative inadequacy and inappropriateness of the "Christ against culture" and "the Christ of culture" types. By the same token, he offers persuasive reasons for regarding the "Christ transformer of culture" type as the most adequate, appropriate, and authentic model relating religious praxis to cultural systems. (1951: 65–82, 101–15, 141–48, 185–89) Yet by making faith-decision the key to the choice among these competing types, Niebuhr discounts his own argument. Specifically, Niebuhr lacks a way of justifying the "theocentric relativism" which functions as his primary, and a priori theological norm for evaluating the different types. (Ibid.: xii)

To go beyond Niebuhr we must go back to Troeltsch who more than any modern thinker wrestled with the problem of transcending historical relativism and the paralysis of the practical will usually engendered by it. Troeltsch's contribution to a critical hermeneutic lies in his distinctive approach to defining the essence of Christianity. By redrafting this concept Troeltsch sought to move beyond "the diversity which history presents us to norms for our faith and for our judgments about life." (1971: 61) In order to achieve this goal Troeltsch had to strip the idealistic connotations from the notion of an essence of a tradition. The essence of a series of phenomena is no a priori concept arbitrarily imposed. Nor is it an abstract norm of identity to be grasped purely theoretically. (Cf. Davis, 1980: 130) Rather the essence of a tradition must be understood as: 1) a developmental principle, 2) a constructive act geared towards praxis, and 3) a historically derived norm for immanent criticism.

1. *Essence as a developmental principle.* The concept of development, Troeltsch argued, is intrinsic to the very notion of history itself. Not only do all historical objects exist as ineradicably individual formations of meaning and purpose but all historical individualities exist within a context of becoming. History is not one damned thing after another; it consists, instead, of bundles of interactive processes, each of which is internally unified. Historical development may be equated with neither the myth of progress nor with the scientific concept of evolution. Indeed, Troeltsch explicitly rejected the notion that history proceeds along a single axis of development. Even so, analysis of past patterns ineluctably leads the historian to ask the question of the unity of the historical process as a whole. Yet in Troeltsch's version of the concept of development, this question cannot be answered in purely theoretical terms. The comprehension of the past requires a practical determination of the course of development for the present and into the future. Without such a concept history ceases to be of interest or significance to humans immersed in present affairs. (Troeltsch, 1961: 54–63, 69–73)

The category of development allows us to see religious forms of life not only as clustered within certain types which can be compared and evaluated but also as interacting with one another along several axes to create a tradition. The essence of such a tradition, therefore, can only be ascertained by immersing oneself in the entire history of a tradition. The result of this process is not an unchanging idea but a germinative principle, reflecting the driving force of the development as a whole. To the consternation of believers in orthodoxy or orthopraxis, Troeltsch insisted that the essence can never be found completely realized in any single manifestation—not even the original classic form of life. It must be a complex principle capable of bearing oppositions and tensions within itself if it is to embrace the multiplicity of a tradition. Yet it must be sufficiently abstract to bring that multiplicity to a focus. (Troeltsch, 1977: 129–31, 142, 151–53)

Even though it seeks only to determine the essence of American Protestant Christianity, H. Richard Niebuhr's *The Kingdom of God in America* perfectly illustrates this idea of a complex principle generating itself through a series of fragmentary realizations. Having immersed himself in the processes set in motion by the Puritan errand into the wilderness, Niebuhr concluded:

> The idea of the kingdom of God had indeed been the dominant idea in American Christianity . . . but . . . it had not always meant the same thing. In the early period of American life, the foundations were laid on which we have all had to build, "kingdom of God" meant "sovereignty of God"; in the creative period of awakening and revival it meant "reign of Christ" and only in the most recent period had it come to mean "kingdom on earth." Yet it became equally apparent that these were not simply three divergent ideas, but that they were intimately related to one another, and that the idea of the kingdom of God could not be expressed in terms of one of the above.
>
> (1937: xii)

Clearly the concept of the essence of a tradition as a developmental principle is designed to meet the criterion of adequacy. Historical immersion involves all of the procedures of research, selectivity, and judgment which characterize the work of religious historians like Clebsch. But it requires something more—a power of comprehension which is not content to leave the multifarious forms of life within a tradition scattered in disarray and which grasps a complex principle of unity that is the antithesis of a lowest common denominator.

2. *Essence as constructive act geared towards praxis.* Troeltsch is quite clear that the essence of a tradition cannot be determined purely through historical investigation. It is impossible, according to

Troeltsch, to understand any development without some practical anticipation of the future: "Only the courage of an act combines the past and the future by so emphasizing the historically grasped essence of a cultural complex for the present that the future arises out of the essence in a manner demanded by the present and yet at the same time exhausting the depth of the historical impulse." (Troeltsch, 1977: 158–62) Indeed, the very act of defining the essence of a tradition gives that tradition new shape, new direction. Viewed in this light, the essence of a tradition confronts us with a live option in William James's sense: a momentous issue which forces a decision between compelling alternative visions. One cannot define the essence of a tradition without being forced to commit oneself practically to a certain future course of development. (Cf. James, 1967: 717–18) "It is no longer merely a judgment about history but it is itself a piece of history." (Troeltsch, 1977: 161)

Here, too, H. Richard Niebuhr captures what it means to formulate a tradition's essence for the sake of praxis:

> All attempts to interpret the past are indirect attempts to understand the present and its future. . . . What is true of historical interpretations in general is particularly true of attempts such as the one we are undertaking. . . . They are pilgrim's ventures on the part of those who are interested more in prospect than in retrospect but who, seeing the continuity of present with past, know that without retrospect no real prospect is possible.
>
> (1937: 1)

As a constructive act geared towards praxis, the concept of the essence embodies the criterion of authenticity proper to critical hermeneutics. No hermeneutic understanding of a tradition is possible without the religious historian's making a "pilgrim's venture" in judging that tradition's authenticity. Apart from that venture, that historically informed construal of what the essence *ought* to be, the dialectic of theory and praxis would disappear in a cloud of abstraction.

3. *Essence as a norm for immanent criticism.* Troeltsch pushes further, however, to achieve his ultimate aim of deriving non-

dogmatically a norm for the evaluation of an entire course of development. The concept of the essence is for Troeltsch just such a critical norm. By its very nature the concept of the essence stands in judgment not only regarding that which is incomplete or imperfect but also that which distorts the driving ideal. (Troeltsch, 1977: 141) But Troeltsch insists that such judgments grounded in a concept of the essence cannot be based upon extrinsic norms or personal biases.

> According to what criterion, however, is this criticism to be carried out? It is a criticism of historical formations in terms of the ideal which lies within their main driving force. It is what is commonly called an immanent criticism. To this extent it is in fact conceived purely historically; for the historical is measured by the historical, the individual formation is measured against the spirit of the whole conceived intuitively and imaginatively. (Ibid.: 142)

It could be argued that *The Kingdom of God in America* does not cohere with Troeltsch's understanding of how to apply historically derived norms critically. The book has been read as merely the standard account of the liberal Protestant Social Gospel from the perspective of Neo-orthodoxy: "A God without wrath brought men without sin into a kingdom without judgment through the ministrations of a Christ without a cross." Yet Niebuhr's intention was to challenge the Social Gospel with immanent criticism. What appalled him was any simplistic mediation of the essence of Christianity that would rob the idea of the kingdom of "its dialectical element." Such an evisceration of the essence reflected more than a loss of theological wisdom: more importantly, it represented a loss of the vision's power to generate praxis. (1937: 193, 197)

As a norm for immanent criticism, the concept of the essence of a tradition is designed to meet the criterion of appropriateness. Appropriateness can only be determined by a dialectical comparison of the whole and its parts, seeking to determine how the multiple forms of praxis which make up a tradition cohere with the tradition's driving ideal. While such a procedure can hardly be described as a "hermeneutic of consent," we must also insist that it provides an alternative to the dogmatic a priori norms of both orthodoxy and orthopraxis. (Cf.

Troeltsch, 1977: 132) The concept of an essence is, unlike Schüssler Fiorenza's criterion of appropriateness to the will of an emancipatory movement, not constrained by the finite perspectives and judgments of the present moment, however right they may appear to be. Appropriateness, as opposed to authenticity, requires critical reflection on the horizons of both past and present for the sake of future praxis.

Because it is held up to the standards of communicative competence, any rendition of the essence is open to public debate. We may examine the insightfulness and the comprehensiveness of the historical immersion which is its presupposition. We can ask whether the essence as a germinative principle is sufficiently complex to account for the various strands of a tradition yet sufficiently powerful to weave those strands into a coherent line of development. We can debate whether a given construction of the essence of a tradition represents a live option within our culture. Yet Troeltsch recognizes that the final test of any such concept is the test of action, the willingness of a community to hazard its life upon the course of development projected by the hermeneutic imagination.

We need not abandon H. Richard Niebuhr's typological construction of forms of life when we turn to Troeltsch's hermeneutic of development. The recognition that forms of life within a tradition can be grouped into types shatters any residual sense that development occurs along a single axis. Niebuhr also enables practical theologians to be precise about the crucial variable according to which their determination of the essence of a tradition will occur—namely, the relationship of religion and culture.

If we situate Niebuhr's contributions within the theoretical framework provided by Troeltsch, the critical hermeneutic of the essence of a tradition begins to require skills more like those of a gardener than those of a hunter. Rather than following a single track towards our prey, we examine the branches of a tree to discover which are dead or infected, where the leading edge of growth is occurring, and where growth is stymied. Immersion in history need not involve tracking quarry through the deep woods; more often than not, it simply calls for arranging, weeding, and pruning the main phyla of development. Niebuhr's typology makes it clear that, in part, the essence is determined by judging which type or types *dialectically* include the values of opposing types. Troeltsch's immanent criticism highlights the negative moment in such a dialectic among competing types. It measures each type by norms synthesized from all of the types. A critical hermeneutic is valid to the extent that the operations of immersion, typological construction and comparison, and immanent criticism—in short, the dialectical determination of the essence of a tradition—are carried out thoroughly and coherently with careful attention to the specifics of each operation.

C. HERMENEUTICS AND IDEOLOGY-CRITIQUE

In *After Virtue*, Alasdair MacIntyre presents a "disquieting suggestion." Suppose that through some catastrophe, of long or short duration, the operations of modern natural science should be disrupted and generations should lose a comprehension of its concepts and methods. Suppose that a still later generation should retrieve the rudiments of science, its language, and terminology without grasping their essential import. " We may describe it as a world in which the language of natural science, or parts of it at least, continues to be used but is in a general state of disorder." MacIntyre raises this spectre in order to suggest a more disturbing thesis: such a state of affairs, in fact, prevails within the world of moral discourse and practice. (MacIntyre, 1981: 1–5) Of course, like any parable, MacIntyre's formulates a limit-case. If communication and consequently practice within any sphere were absolutely and universally distorted, we would have no way of knowing it, let alone of extricating ourselves from the babble. Yet suppose that the whole operation of critical hermeneutics which we have described were simply a more artful manner of securing old illusions, that the immanent development of norms of criticism were another variation of ideological mystification. (Cf. Pannenberg, 1976: 188) For us, at least, MacIntyre's parable raises the question whether a critical hermeneutics based on a revision of Troeltsch can discern systematic distortions even within the essence of a tradition.

To confront this issue let us turn to the critical theorists who have pointed out severe shortcomings in most hermeneutic theories. Jürgen Habermas and his followers have argued three counts against modern hermeneutics as represented especially by Hans-Georg Gadamer. (1) It does not distinguish between reason and authority. Hermeneutics submits itself all too completely to the alleged "wisdom" of tradition. (2) Hermeneutics fails to take into account how the organization of labor and power within a society shapes and, therefore, may warp the mediation of forms of life. Sheer force cloaks itself with the appearance of being merely the executor of consensually derived values. (3) Hermeneutics fails to acknowledge its limits in those sectors of life where human subjects know not why they act as they do. Psychoanalysis reveals a limit-situation where patients are unable to own their own behavior or to penetrate their own systematically distorted communication. (Habermas, 1971c: 132–33, 156–57; Apel, 1980: 67)

We can dismiss the first count because it simply does not apply to the operations of a critical hermeneutic in the tradition of Ernst Troeltsch. Unlike Gadamer, Troeltsch does not offer a variation on what Schüssler Fiorenza calls the "hermeneutics of consent." The second count, however, may be considered as a variation of the third, since Habermas treats distortions in the collective consciousness resulting from defects in the organization of labor and power, as analogous to the role played by neurosis in personal life. Correspondingly ideology-critique is to systematically distorted communication on the social level what psychoanalysis is to the same phenomena on the personal level. Both seek to overcome breakdowns in the hermeneutically oriented process of self or community formation. (Habermas, 1971c: 132, 136–39, 147–48, 156–57)

In the case of psychoanalysis, breakdowns are surmounted when the patient interacts with a therapist who uses an explanatory theory to unravel the psychological knots by reconstructing their genesis. While the explanatory theory is validated argumentatively by appealing to the metapsychology of psychoanalysis, it is validated practically when the patient's reflective appropriation of the insights generated by the theory actually restores his or her processes of self-formation. Here, too, ideology-critique functions analogously. This form of "depth hermeneutics" provisionally suspends the hermeneutic mediation of cultural traditions in order to confront societal breakdowns owing to systematic distortion in the communication of ideologies. With the aid of an explanatory social theory, ideology-critique promotes a process of emancipatory reflection designed to restore hermeneutic mediation as the normal means of communal formation. (Ibid: 147–49; Apel, 1980: 68–71)

We have already argued, with Hayden White, that any historical reconstruction employs, whether consciously or not, an explanatory model defining both the elements of a culture and the mode of their interaction in processes of historical change. (White, 1973: 11–21) Now we must go a step further. Precisely because a truly critical work of historical reconstruction must face the possibility of systemic distortions in the relationships of labor, power, and symbolic interaction, a critical hermeneutic will necessarily involve critical social theory. So Troeltsch's understanding of immanent criticism must be revised explicitly to include ideology-critique with its epistemic, functional, and genetic analyses of ideological deformation.

Before we outline this revision of Troeltsch's concept of immanent criticism, let us consider the objection that ideology-critique is not justified in its assumption of a privileged standpoint towards society analogous to that of the therapist's relationship to his or her patient. A number of thinkers have insisted that there are no privileged standpoints for ideology-critique, that ideology-critique itself is impossible apart from a prior commitment to some hermeneutic tradition which it surreptitiously mediates. (Gadamer, 1971: 294, 307–308; Ricoeur, 1974: 352–54; 1981: 71) Such objections raise questions about the degree to which ideology-critique itself measures up to the standard of immanent criticism.

These objections can be met if we recognize that critical social theory is itself grounded hermeneutically. For immanent criticism requires its subjects, that is, the community whose tradition is under suspicion as systematically distorted, be not entirely deluded. Otherwise, the attempted genetic reconstruction of the deformations of their form of life could not be made plausible in terms that they could internalize. Geuss makes this important clarification of the presuppositions of ideology-critique:

> *Ideologiekritik* is possible only if we can extract the very instruments of criticism from the agents' own form of consciousness—

> from their views about the good life, from the notions of freedom, truth, and rationality embedded in their normative epistemology. It is the particular insidiousness of ideology [in the pejorative sense of the term] that it turns human desires and aspirations against themselves and uses them to fuel repression. These aspirations and desires do find a kind of expression in the ideology, and, to the extent they do, the ideology is said to have a "utopian kernel" which it is the task of critical theory to set free. In describing the genesis of an ideological form of consciousness the critical theory shows how it was subjectively rational for the agents to acquire it—in what way it seemed to allow the development, expression, and satisfaction of their basic desires within the framework of their normative beliefs—but the critical theory must also show in what way the particular form of expression these needs and desires found is self destructive, how it prevented the development of some desires and frustrated the satisfaction of others.
>
> (Geuss, 1981: 87–88)

But in order to make these assessments, critical social theory must itself unfold as a form—albeit, a particularly intense form—of immanent criticism. Viewed in this light, the insertion of ideology-critique as a diagnostic element in Troeltsch's hermeneutic procedures is not an alien graft. Critical hermeneutics and critical social theory, in short, are dialectically related.

The stigma of hermeneutic privilege erroneously attached to Habermas's ideology-critique disappears as soon as we recognize that critical hermeneutics does not stand in judgment upon the past from the invulnerable heights of the present. Not only does it seek to further the development of authentic forms of life which have arisen in the past and remain live options within the present, it also seeks to work through the inherited distortions and deformations for the sake of these live options. Perhaps, not the therapist-patient relationship but rather Freud's own self-analysis more fittingly illuminates the purpose of critical hermeneutics. Past developments are subject to diagnosis *only* insofar as they contribute to or impede the processes of self and communal formation *(Bildungsprozess)*. In fact, the focus of critical hermeneutics upon live options among historic forms of life means that any critique of a given form of life from the standpoint of the essence necessarily calls forth further self-formation. "The cognitive process," in Thomas McCarthy's words, "coincides with a self-formative process." (McCarthy, 1978: 89–90) Habermas and other critical theorists are quite firm in insisting that explanatory theories must be corroborated in self-transcending praxis. (Habermas, 1971c: 156–57; Bernstein, 1976: 215–16) So the procedures for critical hermeneutics are tested finally by a practical criterion: how well they enhance the dialectically transcending processes of self and communal formation.

Several implications stem directly from our understanding of this final, practical criterion for critical hermeneutics: (1) The search for an alternative usable past, like that of James Cone or Eleanor McLaughlin, does not count as a critical hermeneutic if it merely functions to edify a particular religious group. In a critical hermeneutic the search for an alternative past requires immanent criticism in order to overcome any systemic distortions in the communication of that tradition. The alternative pasts presented by Cone or McLaughlin help to overcome the distortions endemic to a Christianity mediated solely by white, male models of religious experience. Without a fully critical hermeneutic, such systemic distortions might continue to infect female and black Christians as well as other Christians in ways that would go unrecognized. (2) In contrast to Schüssler Fiorenza, we insist that hermeneutics must transform the community's horizons of meaning, value and action, in a manner critical of *both* past *and* present. Troeltsch's dictum that the essence is never fully realized in any of its manifestations implies that no religious praxis, whether of the earliest or of the most contemporary community, can be taken as the orthopraxic norm governing the tradition as a whole. (3) Whatever our reservations about Schüssler Fiorenza's position, we formulated this criterion likewise to rule out the "hermeneutics of consent." A merely consensual as opposed to a diagnostic approach can never ferret out the systemic distortions that corrupt even the highest ideals of a tradition. To assume the contrary is to limit arbitrarily the scope of critical hermeneutics.

D. CASE STUDY: THE CULT OF DOMESTICITY AND SENTIMENTAL RELIGION

Since the critical hermeneutic that we are proposing here is so obviously a hybrid combining Troeltch's philosophy of history with Habermas's critique of ideologies, we think it necessary to test it fully in a particularly fallow field of religious historical reconstruction. In the following case we hope to show that, given the agenda that practical theologians pursue today, our proposal to focus critical hermeneutics upon the work of reconstructing the essence of a religious tradition in fact is workable, once allowance is made for the depths of immanent criticism opened up by critical social theory. Our case study begins, like much of our presentation here, with another look at the legacy of Niebuhr. Only in this instance, the one to be challenged is Reinhold Niebuhr.

In his own critique of the liberal Protestant Social Gospel, Niebuhr emphasized its alleged failure to distinguish between mutual love as the basis for a perfectionist utopianism and the genuinely Christian principle of agapic or self-sacrificing love. In historical life and praxis, he argued, agapic love is not a simple but a paradoxical possibility. Rooted in the symbol of the cross, it represents the transcendent norm which stands in judgment over every human achievement of justice and mutual love. Although paradoxically related to every Christian form of life and praxis, agapic love is for Niebuhr the hallmark of prophetic religion as the highest but never simply achievable ideal of Christianity. (1958: 532–33; 1964: 2, 68–97; 1979: 4–6, 62–83)

In not only Niebuhrian terms but those of numerous other practical theologians, self-sacrificing love thus appears to be a plausible candidate for representing the essence of Christianity. But could self-sacrificing love itself ever become an element in the deformation of Christian life and praxis, the systematically distorted norm of a self-deceiving form of life? It is just such a possibility that a number of feminist historians of American religion and culture have raised, in carrying out their hermeneutic of suspicion against what they have dubbed "the cult of domesticity."

A recurrent theme in the writings of practical theologians, the privatization of religion, provides the point of departure for this hermeneutic of suspicion. As we noted before, privatization is usually interpreted as a consequence of the ideology of bourgeois individualism. It is not described in specific terms, however, as a religious form of life fully integrated into the cultural system with its triangular relationships of labor, power, and symbolic interaction. Feminist historians of nineteenth century culture in the United States, however, have established the link between the privatization of certain dominant forms of American Protestantism and the creation of a "woman's sphere" in American culture. The link—no, the shackle—was forged in the "cult of domesticity," an unmistakably Christian form of religious life and praxis tied to the emergence of a specific cultural system.

The origins of the cult of domesticity coincide with an economic revolution in the Northeastern part of the United States. During the half century between 1780 and 1830, a commercial culture gradually supplanted the largely self-subsistent household economy typical of colonial New England. Within the older economy women produced goods essential to the household's survival, according to a gender-based division of labor. In the new commercial culture, however, married women lost their role as producers of goods. Men went to work for wages, while women remained at home. Later as the franchise was gradually extended to all white males, women's legal rights and powers deteriorated. (Cott, 1977: 3, 19–62; Douglas, 1977: 55–56, 69–70; Epstein, 1981: 29–31, 33–36, 79–80)

Women started to respond to this erosion of power and status by partially creating and partially acquiescing in the "cult of domesticity." The cult simultaneously accommodated itself to the new order while it sought to provide compensation by glorifying the new role of women. (Epstein, 1981: 7; Cott, 1977: 62, 69; Sklar, 1973: 193–94) If women's economic and political power had eroded, personal influence would take its place. As the daughter of a nineteenth century statesman wrote to her father, "You may benefit a nation, my dear Papa; I may improve the condition of a fellow-being." (Catherine Sedgwick quoted in Cott, 1977: 23) In fact, the influence of a mother upon her child and of a wife upon her husband was viewed by many proponents as a more awesome responsibility than participation in the culture's political and economic processes. (Cott, 1977: 47; Sklar, 1973: 134–135; Douglas, 1977: 80–90)

If women were to be confined to the home, the home was to become the redemptive agency within an impersonal world, to paraphrase Marx, the heart of a heartless condition.

> The central convention of domesticity was the contrast between home and world. Home was an "oasis in the desert," a "sanctuary" where "sympathy, honor, virtue are assembled," where "disinterested love is ready to sacrifice everything at the altar of affection."
>
> (Cott, 1977: 64, 97–98)

Through the use of religious metaphors the two spheres of home and work were assimilated to the traditional antitheses of the Christian community and "the world." In this way domestic values and religious values were conflated. By making the home and women the repository of traditional Christian values, nineteenth-century society could salvage a traditional value system which had become dysfunctional to the growth of a commercial culture. (Welter, 1974: 138; Cott, 1977: 65, 68, 136) Protestant ministers, themselves experiencing an erosion of power and status during this era of disestablishment, collaborated with women writers in relocating the focus of Christian life and praxis from the holy commonwealth of the Puritan community to the privacy of the middle class Protestant home. The privatization of religion, in large measure, was the result of its domestication. (Welter, 1974: 138–139; Douglas, 1977: 94–139)

Thus a bifurcation of the moral life corresponded to gender-based divisions of labor in the economic order. Power and influence in the political realm were distributed in a similar pattern. What was natural and moral for a male became unnatural and immoral for a female, and vice versa. Because the sphere of Christian values was to be the home, men in the workplace were "freed" to follow the ethos of what later became known as Social Darwinism. Because sacrificial love was taken to be the essence of Christianity, women became the designated suffering servants. (Cott, 1977: 98; Epstein, 1981: 77; Sklar, 1973: 83; Douglas, 1977: 83–85, 152–53; Welter, 1974: 140–41) In the writings of the chief proponents of this cult, women like Catherine Beecher, women's designated role was elevated to a universal ethical principle. "We now come to the *grand* law of the system in which we are placed, as it has been developed by the experience of our race, and that, in one word, is SACRIFICE!" (Beecher, 1857: 36) Yet however much she may have believed her principle to be a live option for a democratic America, formulation of this ideal remained simply part of a strategy of compensation that did not challenge the structure of nineteenth-century society.[3] (Sklar, 1973: 134–36, 157–58, 171–72, 194)

In their reconstruction of the cult of domesticity these historians demonstrate the operation of at least some of the hermeneutic principles we have discussed. We will assess their work in terms of the criteria of communicative competence (adequacy, appropriateness, and authenticity) as these are embodied in the procedures we've proposed for critical hermeneutics.

Some historians have viewed the cult of domesticity as an instance of the victimization of women by an alien ideology. Others as a case of the heroic struggle of women to turn an oppressive ideology to their own advantage. Nancy Cott rejects these alternatives and argues for an interpretation which accepts the real gains for women achieved through the cult but identifies as well its tragic limitations. (Cott, 1977: 197–201) We can see that Cott here is debating the relative adequacy of the narrative modes described by Hayden White. Which one, pathos, or romance, or tragedy, among others, is the best way of emplotting the development of the cult? She argues, in effect, for a strong qualification of the mode of romance by that of tragedy. In contrast to Cott, Ann Douglas employs an ironic mode as a means of accentuating the malignancy of self-deception permeating the cult. Given these alternatives, we can easily be persuaded that either mode, tragedy or irony, is more fitting than the oversimplifications involved in the pathetic and romantic modes. Whereas the tragic mode allows an appropriation of the utopian kernel of the cult while acknowledging its tragic limitations, the ironic mode is more fully geared to unveiling "the particular insidiousness of ideology [in the pejorative sense of the term] [in] that it turns human desires and aspirations against themselves and uses them to fuel repression." (Geuss, 1981: 87–88) Either mode allows for a complexity of presentation which is *adequate* to the ambiguous character of the cult itself.

None of these authors makes her explanatory framework explicit. While changes in modes of production and relations of production are generally seen as catalytic, it is also clear that these changes did not determine either the creation or the triumph of the "cult of domesticity." To some degree, each author tries to correlate changes in the dimensions of labor, power, and symbolic interaction. Monocausal theories of alienation and its historic vicissitudes—especially victimization theories—are rejected. The development of a religious form of life is viewed as a function of the transformation of an entire cultural system. While simplistic explanations are thus rejected, these works do not make fully explicit their comprehensive frameworks for understanding cultural interaction and social change.

The judgments that these authors make about the cult of domesticity are relatively *appropriate* because they are grounded, in varying degrees, upon immanent criticism. Crucial in most cases are their analyses of various live options expressing alternative strands of normative development within nineteenth-century America. So Catherine Beecher's paean to the cult of sacrificial love is contrasted, by one author, with the Grimke sisters' appeal to an ideology based on inalienable natural rights. Why the culture opted for the former when its own heritage implied the latter becomes a central issue. (Sklar, 1973: 113, 132–37) Margaret Fuller's romantic vision of the infinite scope of the self-reliant individual is contrasted, by another, with the sentimentalism of the cult of domesticity. (Douglas, 1977: 307–309; cf. Fuller, 1971: 96)

But Douglas carries immanent criticism still further. In labeling the cult of domesticity sentimental she seeks to identify the root of inauthenticity and, by implication, one characteristic of any malignant religious form of life.

> Sentimentalism is a complex phenomenon. It asserts that the values a society's activity denies are precisely the ones it cherishes. . . . Many nineteenth century Americans in the Northeast acted every day as if they believed that the economic expansion, urbanization, and industrialization represented the greatest good. It is to their credit that they indirectly acknowledged that the pursuit of these "masculine" goals meant

> damaging, perhaps losing, another good, one they increasingly included under the "feminine" ideal. Yet the fact remains that their regret was calculated not to interfere with their actions.
> (Douglas, 1977: 11–12)

Here immanent criticism and ideology-critique are fused. Douglas's treatment of sentimentalism should be compared with Geuss's description of ideology-critique as grounded in the discernment of unacknowledgeable internal contradictions in the consciousness and commitments of the group. Although Catherine Beecher may have been on the right track, at least in asserting the universalizability of sacrificial love, her acceptance of the concept of "woman's sphere" insured that her ideal, in principle, could not be universalized. In other words, the essential pathology of the ideology of domesticity lay in its inability to recognize the fundamental incompatibility between its universal claim for the ideal of sacrificial love and the categorical limits placed upon that love's actualization.

Douglas's interpretation can be construed as the most *authentic* of the works before us because it is most conducive to a dialectically transcending process of self and community formation. Her use of an ironic narrative mode is not calculated to condemn the past from the heights of the present. Rather, it reflects the pains of self-liberation. Douglas's own words underline her critical transformation of both past and present horizons of meaning, value, and action:

> I expected to find my fathers and my mothers; instead I discovered my fathers and my sisters. . . . The problems of the women correspond to mine with a frightening accuracy that seems to set us outside the process of history. . . .
> (1977: 10–11)

These works do not presume to construct a concept of the essence of a Christian tradition. In this sense they do not pursue the central task of critical hermeneutics, as we have defined it specifically for practical theology. Nevertheless, we can learn something about the procedures of a critical hermeneutics from the findings of these interpreters. This is especially true because the cult of domesticity stands as a *limit-case*. It provides an ultimate challenge for a critical hermeneutics seeking to reconstruct the essence of Christianity, the challenge not of an imperfection within the tradition or of an aberration from it but a deformation of what plausibly is a crucial element of the essence itself. Here dry rot occurs within the very pith of a tradition. How can a critical hermeneutics restore the integrity of Christian life and praxis in light of such a case?

1. *Essence as a developmental principle.* The historical immersion conducted for us by Douglas, and others, confirms several of Troeltsch's propositions. First, no simple notion, like that of sacrificial love, can be seen as in itself exhausting the essence of Christianity. Only a dialectical complex of norms constituting the essence can overcome the subtleties of distortion plaguing partial norms. In contrast to Reinhold Niebuhr's appeal to the principle of sacrificial love as "the pinnacle of the moral ideal," (1964, 2: 246–47) our limit-case teaches us that no single norm stands as a *norma normans non normata.* Second, as Troeltsch would have us expect, the essence of Christianity does maintain a dialectical relationship to any of its manifestations. This implies that a limit-case does not invalidate a generative principle. Resurrection of lost integrity is a distinct possibility even within the Christian tradition. This dialectical relationship also implies that any exclusive claim to embody the essence, whether the claim is made on behalf of one's own group or delegated to another, falsifies the essence.

2. *Essence as constructive act geared towards praxis.* It becomes clear from this case study of the cult of domesticity that any arbitrary limitation of the scope of religious life and praxis betrays the essence of the regulative ideal. The privatization of the Christian value system destroys it. Correlatively the formulation of the essence as a live option for the present not only *can* bring that model of religious life and praxis into a transformative relationship with the dimensions of labor and power, it *must*! Failing that, Christian influence becomes a sentimental, that is, a debased form of religious praxis.

3. *Essence as a norm for immanent criticism.* Self-deception, as the cult of domesticity demonstrates, can cloak itself in the highest ideals. Immanent criticism, consequently, *must* become ideology-critique in order to ferret out the epistemic, functional, and genetic deformations of religious and secular ideologies. Such criticism is not to be based

upon any orthopraxic norm which miraculously avoids pathological deformation but upon the dialectic of norms within the concept of the essence and upon their dialectical relationship to the variety of live options within a tradition.

We hope that this case study illustrates the utility of our criteria and that it confirms the need for a critical hermeneutics focused procedurally on reconstructing the essence of a religious tradition. Apart from such procedures and criteria the practical theologian has and can claim no privileged insight into the varieties of authentic Christianity. The experience of personal commitment and communal action may generate in the practical theologian a profound awareness of new and compelling forms of life and praxis, but only critical hermeneutics operating more or less as we have defined it can warrant labeling those new forms as Christian.

NOTES

1. We see no substantial difference between Schüssler Fiorenza's delineation of a critical hermeneutic in this essay and her lengthier treatment of it in her more recent work, *In Memory of Her: A Feminist Theological Reconstruction of Christian Origins.* (1983; cf. especially Chapters 1, 2, and 3) Indeed, Schüssler Fiorenza refers the reader to her earlier essay as a fuller treatment of the topic. (Ibid.: 36, n. 2)
2. Clebsch sees transformations of the forms of sovereignty as key to cultural change. Religious change is interpreted as a reaction to such alterations of relations of power. (1979: 7–8) Such an approach ignores the positive role of religion, elucidated by Geertz, in shaping cultural reality. It also ignores the transformations of the means of production and relations of production. Minimally a form of life can only be constituted by a correlation of the spheres of labor, power, and symbolic interaction. (Cf. Ricoeur, 1973b: 142–48)
3. This judgment is warranted despite the fact that the cult of domesticity could be used and was used to further such progressive causes as women's suffrage and protective labor laws for women and children. (Cf. Degler, 1980: 357–59)

CHAPTER FIVE

EMANCIPATION AND REDEMPTION: THE SYSTEMATIC STRUCTURES OF PRACTICAL THEOLOGY

Christianity faces ultimate issues of life which transcend all political vicissitudes and achievements. But the answer which Christian faith gives to man's ultimate perplexities and the hope which makes it possible in the very abyss of his despair, also throw light upon the immediate historical issues which he faces. It is rather the perceived wisdom of God which makes decisions in history possible.

(Reinhold Niebuhr, 1939: 545)

It is important to bear in mind that there are forms of conceptualization that are praxeological in the sense that they take their rise from an analysis of purposive rational action but that are situated at such a high level of abstraction that this fact may no longer be readily evident and may even seem implausible in the light of the formal similarities which the theoretical apparatus in which these concepts are imbedded may bear to structures of theory in the nonpraxeological sciences. If this injunction were taken seriously, . . . the result might well be to expose the immense and instructive complexity to which the simple paradigms of action that have been described here can give rise.

(Olafson, 1979: 188)

Having described the role of critical hermeneutics in practical theology, we are faced with another impasse. Why doesn't the process of historical-hermeneutic reconstruction exhaust the requirements for critical reflection on religious praxis? Why go on to articulate "systematic structures" in practical theology? Aren't these rendered redundant, once we have reconstructed the historical "essence" of Christian praxis? Doesn't success in focusing critical hermeneutics on this essence belie the hypothesis that the genre of practical theology reorganizes the structures and procedures of the other theological genres—including systematic theology—as functional specializations within it? What function remains to be attributed to systematically theological reflection if the work of historical reconstruction provides the essential norm for delineating a field of possibilities within which a community must act if they choose to define themselves as part of a religious tradition? What other role might systematically theological reflection play in our religiously constituted dialectic of theory and praxis?

The comparative novelty of our problem is worth noting. Others who have attempted methodological reflection on systematic theology seem to assume the self-evident need for systematic forms of conceptualization. Schubert Ogden's focus on understanding the Christian witness of faith for the present, and David Tracy's intention of addressing specifically the concerns of the ecclesial public, both define a moment in the process of theological inquiry. Yet neither explains why this particular moment should be elaborated in systematic conceptual form. Both seem to take for granted the existence of a form of theology whose authority rests on the weight of ecclesiastical tradition.

Practical theologians, both old and new, are even less illuminating about the role of systematic structures in their thinking. Reinhold Niebuhr's *The Nature and Destiny of Man* recasts the wisdom achieved through his own protracted struggle with religious praxis in systematic form, without ever considering why it was necessary to do so. Similarly, Gustavo Gutierrez's *A Theology of Liberation* merely assumes that the vision of "Christ the Liberator" requires "thematic" presentation. Such unreflective appropriation of inherited conceptual structures will not do, if the dialectic of theory and praxis is to be worked out fully in practical theology. Once that dialectic is grasped, we are in the novel situation of trying to explain how systematic thought can play a role without distorting practical theology once more in the direction of orthodoxy.

The fact that systematically theological reflection must always remain suspect in a dialectic of theory and praxis is not sufficient reason to ban it altogether. On the contrary, we believe that practical theology is best served by retaining this functional specialization insofar as it is required by the logic of religious praxis. We argue in this chapter, then, that critical reflection on religious praxis requires systematic reflection precisely because praxis becomes praxis only when it is informed by theoretical models *of* and *for* reality. If emancipatory praxis always includes the establishment of a "culture of critical discourse" (Cf. Gouldner, 1976: 58–64), these models will tend to be discursive, textual, and systematically abstract. Theoretical models which are highly systematic are required in modern societies for coordinated collective action in complex situations. These models Frederick Olafson calls praxeological "in the sense that they take their rise from an analysis of purposive rational action but . . . are situated at . . . a high level of abstraction." The formulation, criticism, and revision of these models will proceed with a discursive integrity of its own. Public discourse testing the validity claims of competing theoretical models will aspire to the status of a disciplined praxeology. (Olafson, 1979: 187–8) The functional specialization of systematic reflection in practical theology fulfills this "praxeological" requirement in the situation of modern Christian religious praxis.

Perhaps an analogy drawn from the discipline of economics will help establish the plausibility of our attempt to distinguish the role of systematic reflection from that of historical-hermeneutic reconstruction. Arguing a similar point, Frederick Olafson notes that economics as a science is both historically situated and praxeologically constituted. Both aspects are necessary in order to understand economic theory and praxis, even though these aspects will give rise to significantly different modes of conceptualization. (Ibid.: 188) His point is evident as soon as one considers the difference between two important works on modern economics, Louis Dumont's *From Mandeville to Marx: The Genesis and Triumph of Economic Ideology* and Paul A. Samuelson's *Economics*. Dumont's work is an example of historical-hermeneutic reconstruction; Samuelson's, of economic praxeology. Both attempt to explicate the meaning of "economic rationality." Yet Dumont seeks to reconstruct this historic essence as a cultural development with its own contextual limitations and distortions within the modern ideology of "equalitarianism." (Dumont, 1977: 3–30) Samuelson, however, more or less presupposes economic rationality as axiomatic and on its basis seeks to construct a number of quantitatively oriented theoretical models for explaining and ordering the complex patterns of exchange characteristic of the "mixed economies" of Western industrial societies. (Samuelson, 1980: 13–14) While their inquiries overlap insofar as each is concerned to establish the meaning of economic rationality, they differ insofar as their distinctive foci give rise to radically different forms of conceptualization. They appropriately operate at different levels of abstraction.

Although both levels are necessary for praxis, praxeological inquiries must thus be distinguished from critical hermeneutics insofar as they "take as their point of departure some form of rational human action as defined in terms of certain axioms about goals and the means of achieving them and proceed to construct, often by purely deductive means, a theoretical account of the immensely complex structures of interlocking agency that can develop out of this simple paradigm of action." (Olafson, 1979: 187) If Olafson's distinction is correct, we expect that the systematic structures in practical theology will show greater affinity to the kind of model building operative in Samuelson's work than to the kind of reconstructive process so brilliantly executed in Dumont's.

We hope to make good this claim by proceeding in the following manner: First, we must prepare the way for practical theologians to elaborate systematic models of and for the praxis of ultimate transformation. This will be done by meeting the challenge presented by the Marxist tradition that a religious praxeology is inadequate, inappropriate and inauthentic *in principle.* Second, we will attempt to show how any religious praxis responsive to the essence of Christianity inevitably generates two forms of systematic thought, namely, theological anthropology and theology of history. Third, we will develop a set of typological models for each of these two, which will provide criteria for determining the relative adequacy of systematic concepts operative in any given instance of practical theology. On the basis of these criteria, finally, we will try to identify the most important structural problems inhibiting the development of this dimension of practical theology today. Our argument, however, is intended only to establish the generic conventions of this functional specialization in practical theology. It is not meant as a substantive model of practical theology.

A. INTERPRETING RELIGIOUS TRANSCENDENCE

Much of the current literature in practical theology gives the impression that the liberating effect of Christian praxis in itself invalidates the Marxist critique of religion. Judging by the way many theologians have adopted the program of "critical reflection on praxis" and proceeded immediately into a critical reconstruction of the theological themes of their traditions, it is as if they had forgotten or misunderstood Marx's assertion that "the criticism of religion is the premise of all criticism." (Marx and Engels, 1964: 41) Marx's intent is to impose a praxeological perspective: If praxis emerges in a dialectic with critical theory, and the criticism of religion is the premise of all criticism, then religious praxis is a contradiction in terms and its systematic elaboration the paradigm of mystification. In other words, the Marxist critique of religion is a theoretical challenge to the adequacy, appropriateness, and authenticity of explaining and ordering Christian religious practices theologically within the framework of public discourse. However sincere their commitment to the struggle against oppression, theologians who fail to address this challenge do justice to neither the claims of Marxist theory nor the commitments of Christian religious praxis.

The praxeological problem of religious transcendence is implicit in Marx's pioneering insight into the dialectic of theory and praxis. His "Theses on Feuerbach" not only establish the priority of praxis but also assert the illusory nature of religious transcendence. For in Marx's rendering, the priority of praxis means that the "religious sentiment is itself a *social product*." (Marx and Engels, 1964: 71) Religious transcendence becomes "an epiphenomenon." (Davis, 1980: 124) Religion doesn't just perpetuate oppression; it distorts reality, and in so doing perpetuates oppression. Liberation from oppression, therefore, demands first that we give up this illusion which, in turn, will free us to struggle against the oppression that it legitimates. However liberating their intent, Christian religious practices, in Marx's account, can never become a liberating praxis so long as Christians refuse to give up the illusion that constitutes their tradition's "glowing core." Since practical theologians can never admit that this glowing core is illusory, systematically theological reflection must be dismantled in favor of a critical theory that explains religious transcendence as epiphenomenal. Then the theologian's liberating intent can be redirected in authentic social praxis. Hence, "the premise of all criticism" necessarily entails the repudiation of theology as an inadequate, inappropriate, and ultimately inauthentic form of praxeology.

If Marx's praxeological challenge is to be met, it will require us to formulate an alternative perspective for interpreting religious transcendence. Such a response, we believe, involves three things if it is to be consistent with the dialectic of theory and praxis: (1) It must proceed as an immanent critique of the Marxist tradition, showing the arbitrariness of Marx's judgment on religion. (2) It must provide a more satisfactory explanation of Marx's judgment than Marxists can provide in defending it. (3) It must reconstruct the theory of religious transcendence in such a way that communicative competence in systematically theological reflection with a practical intent becomes possible in principle. Only then can any form of systematically theological discourse claim to represent a valid praxeological perspective in which to build theoretical models for handling the problems inevitably generated by Christian praxis.

(1) The immanent critique of the Marxist perspective can be formulated as follows: Marx may be right in claiming that "the religious sentiment," like all other things human, "is itself a *social product*," but this does not necessarily mean that it is epiphenomenal, or illusory in Marx's sense of the term. Because all forms of experience and reflection generated by praxis of whatever sort qualify as social products, some further argument is needed to determine which of these social products are illusory and which ones are real. So, Marx's judgment on Christianity can only be warranted by developing some sort of critical hermeneutic capable of deconstructing the essence of Christianity as the paradigm case of false consciousness.

In asserting that "*the criticism of religion* is in the main complete" (Marx and Engels, 1964: 41), Marx simply assumes that Hegel and Feuerbach have accomplished the task of deconstruction. Marx along with Feuerbach accepted the Hegelian view of bourgeois Protestant Christianity as "the Absolute Religion." In this formulation Christianity is perceived as the highest possible realization of the religious impulse in history. For Young Hegelians, like Feuerbach and Marx, then, the successful criticism of this form of Christianity would automatically demystify all other possible manifestations of "the religious sentiment"—including any future configurations of the essence of Christianity. For Christianity had already gone beyond them all in reaching the "Absolute" stage in its own historical development. The distinctively Feuerbachian move, of course, was to expose this Absolute Religion as an illusion, an inverted form of consciousness projecting upon the heavens the ultimate aspirations of the human species (*Gattungswesen*). Marx, then, takes up Feuerbach's critique of Hegel as the point of departure for his own critical hermeneutic of Christian religious praxis.

By breaking with Feuerbach's still contemplative approach to materialism (Marx and Engels, 1964: 60–72; Davis, 1980: 124–5), Marx produces a paradigm case for developing the critique of ideologies as an explanatory mode of "counter-discourse." In terms of Geuss's categories, we can see that Marx's critique of religion explains Christianity as an epistemic, functional, and genetic deformation of the aspirations of the human species. Christian religious practice and theological discourse are systematically distorted on all three levels: epistemically, because Christianity is blind to the fact that its claims concerning religious transcendence are, like everything else, a symbolic construction of reality; functionally, because these claims historically have invested religious authority in oppressive social structures; and genetically, because Christianity cannot change the latter without admitting the former, which would precipitate its own disappearance from the stage of history. All this, it seems, is implicit in Marx's assault upon "the opium of the people." (Marx and Engels, 1964: 41f)

An immanent criticism of this paradigm case of ideology-critique will not be content to point out that Marx's early writings are merely programmatic and perhaps inconsistent with the "materialistic method" of his later works. (Cf. Davis, 1980: 125–6) The problem is not that Marx makes some rather large assumptions in his early writings on religion, but that these assumptions are unwarranted, and will remain unwarranted even if reformulated in terms of the "materialistic method." In neither his early nor his later writings is there any argument defending Hegel's historical reconstruction of bourgeois Protestant Christianity as the Absolute Religion. Yet it is hard to see why the criticism of religion is paradigmatic for all ideological criticism unless this form of Christianity embodies some sort of Absolute, albeit, an absolutely negative limit in distortion.

Equally arbitrary is Marx's assumption regarding the validity of Feuerbach's "transformative method of interpreting the alienated consciousness of religion." (Davis, 1980: 124) Feuerbach's reversal of the religious "projection" must be placed in the context of efforts by other Young Hegelians to use this paradigm for wholesale ideological criticism. Not Feuerbach and Marx alone, but the whole movement excelled in unveiling the projections hidden in the ideologies of their former friends now turned political opponents. Yet each of these critics failed to acknowledge the role of projections in his own thought, claiming instead to have accomplished a final break with all religious illusions and their ideological analogues. (Strain, 1976: 263–5, 293–6) If projection is that common, can we accept the arbitrary assertion that some projections are mere illusions whereas others disclose, like a prenatal sonargram, the embryonic but truly essential reality? If Marx suffers with Hegel from an understandable provincialism regarding the paradigmatic status of the Christianity with which he grew up, with Feuerbach he displays a touchingly youthful naivete about "the weapons of criticism," as if they can be fired without recoil. A truly critical theory of religious transcendence, seeking to avoid both provincialism and naivete, will recognize that even if we assume that all forms of religious consciousness are "social products," we are not entitled thereby to assert that they all are systematically distorted.

(2) The arbitrariness of Marx's criticism of religion suggests not only that this paradigm does not suffice to explain religion but also that it is itself in need of explanation. What is the ideological function of the criticism of religion in Marx's own thought? Is the projectionist theory of religion itself a projection; and if so, of what precisely? In light of the criticisms of Albrecht Wellmer and other neo-Marxists, we hold that Marx's animus against religious transcendence is merely one of a number of symptoms of his own projection of the "objectivistic illusion" of positivism onto the dialectic of theory and praxis.

Here, too, the epistemic, functional, and genetic deformations typical of perverse ideologies are evident: epistemically, because Marx insisted on transforming critical reflection on praxis into a "presuppositionless" science of revolution capable of making objective claims about the "necessary motor of social progress" (Wellmer, 1971: 100–101); functionally, because such a presuppositionless science allowed Marx to repress all other forms of revolutionary socialism, however authentically grounded in utopian ideals of emancipation, while institutionalizing his own leadership in the revolutionary workers' movement; and genetically, because Marx could not have admitted the truth of either of these ideological suspicions without abandoning his claim to exclusive intellectual leadership in this movement.

Marx's critique of religion, in short, is not so much a paradigm of ideological criticism as it is another example of an "illusion" projected from the requirements of his struggle to banish whatever he deemed "utopian" in revolutionary praxis. Marx's refusal to admit the utopian logic of his own praxis, and his equally uncompromising insistence on the scientific status of his critical theory lie at the root of his systematically distorted communication on the subject of religion. The sarcasm of Marx's rhetorical dismissal of those still moved by "the religious sentiment" is matched only by the bitterness of his invective against those utopian socialists most in sympathy with his desire to liberate the oppressed. Ironically, as Wellmer notes, Marx's attempt to negate the transcendence still operative in both groups "produced only a half-hearted extra-Hegelian secularization of Christian eschatology: beneath his image of the suffering proletariat there is still the authoritative power of God, which guarantees salvation." (Wellmer, 1971: 62) Bluntly stated, Marx's critique of religion not only is arbitrary but also bears explanation as "a form of negative utopianism." It is the projection of a scientistically false consciousness that cannot admit the utopian character of its own "ideal of an unalienated society." (Davis, 1980: 125)

(3) This explanation, of course, does not validate the cognitive claims made in systematically elaborated models of and for ultimate transformation. But it does establish a necessary preliminary for

taking them seriously. At least they deserve the same serious attention that utopian projections usually get from those working within a dialectic of theory and praxis. For if religious transcendence is illusory, then all other symbols of transcendence, including the various forms of utopia also are called into question. By the same token, if these utopian forms may project what is real, in whatever way that is understood, then symbols of religious transcendence may also project what is real. For all are social products; all involve some element of projection.

Far from denying that the religious sentiment in some sense is a projection, a critical theory of religious transcendence will seek to show how that projection can be constructed adequately, appropriately, and authentically, as a praxeological model. If our theory can show this, it will have refuted the suspicion that religion is an illusion in the only sense relevant to the praxeological question. By insisting on the unique and irreducible role of religious transcendence in any authentically transformative praxis, we hope to show how and why models of systematically theological reflection fulfill an indispensable praxeological function.

To get our argument off the ground, let us recall Frederick Streng's general definition of religion as a means of ultimate transformation. This definition serves to distinguish the category of religious praxis from all other forms of praxis on the basis of its explicit reference to the Ultimate. Religious praxis, in whatever tradition of communicative interaction it appears, symbolically mediates the reality of the Ultimate apprehended in the processes of transformation, in whatever way(s) the Ultimate may be apprehended. Note, however, that this definition merely establishes the category of religious praxis, and not its claim to normative validity.

The next step is taken by following foundational theologians like Langdon Gilkey who argue that religious transcendence functions as the dimension of depth necessarily and inevitably operative in any human culture. (Gilkey, 1981: 43–5) Gilkey's point is not just that religious transcendence is important enough to deserve anthropological and sociological study, but that "any community or society is held together by sharing in, expressing and devoting themselves to, something sacred and ultimate—or a sacrality and an ultimacy—that permeates their life together, holds them together, directs their common life, and makes that common life possible." (Gilkey, 1981: 19) This, evidently, is a normative as well as a descriptive claim. If Gilkey is right, religious transcendence has praxeological significance.

We must press further to determine what precisely is the praxeological significance of this sacrality or ultimacy. Surely, Gilkey is not nostalgic for the orthodoxy and orthopraxis of premodern theocracies. While "the meaning of common life," "the rules of behavior," and a "society's self-interpretation and identity," are rooted in the "religious substance" of a culture (Gilkey, 1981: 19), the praxeological problem is to model precisely how this substance transforms these symbolically constituted norms ultimately. The crucial clue, we believe, is provided by the theory of limit-situations formulated by David Tracy. (Tracy, 1975: 91–118; cf. McElwain, 1983) Without rehearsing all the details of this theory and its philosophical warrants, we can say that the religious sentiment in general expresses the common human experience of being in limit-situations, that is, "those experiences, both positive and negative, wherein *we both experience our own human limits* (limit-to) as our own as well as recognize, however haltingly, *some disclosure* of a 'limit-of' our experience." (Tracy, 1974: 292; McElwain, 1983: 25–6) Furthermore, we have no hesitation in claiming that both "limit-to" and "limit-of" experiences are ultimately transformative in Streng's sense of the term. In other words, it is the experience of religious transcendence in praxis that reconstitutes that praxis as religious praxis. Religious praxis, thus understood, symbolically mediates the ultimate limits of praxis, whatever the symbols may turn out to be, however they may be projected and apprehended. As the mediation of sacrality or ultimacy, religious praxis thus functions to define the boundary conditions of any praxis whatsoever.

The final step in our critical theory of religious transcendence is to determine how such sacrality or ultimacy may be expressed praxeologically. Recall the argument made earlier in behalf of model construction. Models are perspectival, formally constructed, and subject to evaluation by the relevant community of inquirers. Like David Tracy, we see no reason to restrict authentically human expressions of limit-situations to either the profound silence of Wittgenstein or to the limit-language of metaphor. (Tracy, 1974: 295) "Limit-concepts" are possible, provided that they can be constructed and assessed in full awareness of their limits as models. This, we believe, finally discharges any residual burden of proof resulting from Marx's projectionist theory of religion. Let us explain why.

Constructing an interrelated set of limit-concepts as a praxeological model implies that the theorists doing the modeling already recognize the element of projection operative in their constructions. Projection, at this point, merely explains how and why the model is necessarily perspectival. Since there are as many perspectives as there are theorists projecting them, we can expect a plurality of praxeological models, each open in principle to the suspicion of systematic distortion, each potentially warranted as systematically responsive to the demands of praxis. Since these sets of interrelated limit-concepts are meant to model the "limit-to" and "limit-of" character of praxis, they inevitably will be formal insofar as they articulate the religiously apprehended boundary conditions of praxis. At no point, however, can they formulate these conditions in a way that obscures their own perspectival limits. To do so would be to break the dialectic of limit experience and ordinary experience, the dialectic of limit-language and ordinary language, and the dialectic of limit-concepts and ideological concepts that constitute a practical theology. Indeed to obscure the perspectival limits of these constructed models is to regress in the direction of orthodoxy, a victim once more of the pathology of systematically distorted communication.

Systematically theological discourse, to conclude our argument, is a functional specialization in practical theology because models of interrelated sets of limit-concepts are praxeologically necessary if religious praxis is to fulfill its mediating role in social praxis intelligently. Systematically theological discourse, like all forms of model construction, finally, is subject to evaluation by the relevant community of inquirers. Otherwise it fails to qualify as public discourse. The relevant community of inquirers, however, will not consist exclusively of theologians, but may also include those critical social theorists, like Albrecht Wellmer, who recognize that transcendence, however apprehended, cannot be suppressed in the logic of emancipatory praxis. Implicit, then, in this as in each step of our argument is the thesis that such systematically theological discourse will enrich the communities' own distinctive development as truth-dependent modes of socialization.

B. ACTION AND NARRATIVE: THE ROOTS OF SYSTEMATIC REFLECTION WITH A PRACTICAL INTENT

This argument for the praxeological significance of models of religious transcendence does not tell us what kinds of systematically theological reflection are appropriate for practical theologies. Certainly practical theologies are not intended to duplicate the efforts of systematic theologies. Genre analysis can help us to discover what systematic elements are intrinsic to any praxeological model. Earlier we stressed the importance of a diachronic and synchronic element in the formal structure of ideological discourse. Ideologies map the course of human events; they seek to ground as "self-evident" certain truths about what it means to be human. So Bernard Bailyn argues that the ideological pamphleteering in America between 1760 and 1776 transcended constitutional questions to provide a "conceptualization of American life."

> Americans [came] to think of themselves as in a special category, uniquely placed by history to capitalize on, to complete and fulfill, the promise of man's existence. . . . "The liberties of mankind and the glory of human nature is in their keeping," John Adams wrote in the year of the Stamp Act. "America was designed by Providence for the theatre on which man was to make his true figure, on which science, virtue, liberty, happiness, and glory were to exist in peace."
>
> (Bailyn, 1967: 20)

Without a representation of history as the "theatre" of human fulfillment, without some image of that "true figure" which we are called upon to make, ideologies do not exist. (Cf. Ollmann, 1971: 131–35; Overend, 1975: 309–10, 313–14; Schroyer, 1973: 41–47) Nor, by analogy, do practical theologies. In the latter case, the theatre refers to the diachronic element we call "theology of history" and the true figure to the synchronic element, "theological anthropology." While generic analogies are helpful, they may leave the impression that these elements are simply adventitious. We suggest to the contrary, that these elements will necessarily emerge in any theology which seeks to mediate the transition from action to praxis. The role of narrative in effecting this transition, of course, will have to be clarified. For a number of practical theologians, among them J.B. Metz, have maintained that practical theology must be a narrative theology. (Metz, 1980: 205–18) We believe that there is a profound truth to Metz's intuition but it is a truth which needs to be subsumed within a larger perspective. Religious narratives are one moment in the transition from diffuse, religiously motivated actions to models of religious praxis. Systematically theological reflection on history and the normatively human is the other moment.

"To act in its most general sense," insists Hannah Arendt, "is to take an initiative, to begin . . . , to set something in motion. . . . " (Arendt, 1958: 157) Action flashes forth across the landscape of human relationships, altering it permanently, affecting it unpredictably, generating processes whose end cannot be foreseen. Consequently, action stands in stark contrast to the laborious processes which maintain material existence and to the fabrication of objects. Action is purposeful intervention in human affairs. (Ibid.: 9–11, 170, 207–8)

Arendt is equally insistent that action in its flashing forth is always accompanied by words and that the mode of discourse appropriate to action is narrative. Action demands narrative because narrative is the only way in which the activity of the agent can be revealed to self and to others. In it the limitless consequences of action can be contained and, therefore, internalized. "Only sheer violence is mute . . . ," and violence is rooted in the modern illusion that history is something to be made and not the consequence of human interaction. (Arendt, 1958: 25, 204)

> This realm of human affairs, strictly speaking, consists of the web of human relationships which exists wherever men live together. The disclosure of the "who" through speech, and the setting of a new beginning through action, always fall into an

> already existing web where their immediate consequences can be felt. Together they start a new process which eventually emerges as the unique life story of the newcomer, affecting uniquely the life stories of all those with whom he comes into contact. It is because of this already existing web of relationships, with its innumerable, conflicting wills and intentions, that action . . . "produces" stories with or without intention as naturally as fabrication produces tangible things.
>
> (Ibid.: 163–4)

So, selfhood emerges as the distillate of narrated actions and history appears as the compound of many narrated lives. Yet history as the web of human relationships also precedes each new flashing forth of action and each expression of that action in a new story.

Because of this historical matrix action may exhibit qualities beyond those of initiative and intervention, which Arendt assigned to it. If action, as purposeful, cuts across the web of human relationships, it also, as intentional, reorders that web. Intentionality, argues Frederick Olafson, signifies the "internal teleology" of action, that is, its power to retain its unity through the various phases of its execution. Action generates not only events but the ordering of events. Past and present are no longer disparate moments locked in blind succession. Action integrates; it creates a configuration, a patterned whole, out of a sequence. (Olafson, 1979: 22, 25, 130–31)

Narrative, suggests Olafson, is uniquely constituted to give verbal expression to the integrative character of human action. The internal teleology of action is paralleled by the teleological thrust that manifests itself within the complex context of purposes established by a narrative. Against Frank Kermode, Olafson argues that the "sense of an ending" provided by narratives is more than a pleasing fiction; it is the linguistic equivalent of an ontological trait of human action. The integrating function of action has its counterpart in the plot structures of narratives which situate patterns of interaction along normative axes, thereby giving the story a "moral ordering." (Olafson, 1979: 36, 49–52, 65–6, 137, 151–53; cf. Kermode, 1967: 39–40)

Finally, the power of action to create a unity out of a succession of events is mirrored in the "configurational operation" through which narratives provide a sense of coherence for beings fated to live *in medias res* by constituting "significant wholes out of scattered events." (Ricoeur, 1978: 183–4; Mink, 1974: 114, 117, 120–3) Action as integration, then, is necessarily accompanied by narrative exhibiting a synthetic pattern. Apart from some sort of narrative synthesis our lives, whether collective or singular, resemble—in Joan Didion's poignant description—"flash pictures in variable sequence, images with no 'meaning' beyond their temporary arrangement, not a movie but a cutting room experience." (Didion, 1979: 13)

Through narrated action, then, the paired realities of self and history emerge. If action, however, presents itself in the two modes of intervention and integration, can we not find two corresponding modes of narration? Clearly, yes. Operating beneath and, in various combinations, within the archetypal forms of emplotment, such as tragedy, comedy, and romance, are two fundamentally different modes of narration. We will call them figural and synthetic narrative modes.

Action as intervention is a flashing forth. The moment of intervention is fatefully consequential. How can a narrative capture this unpredictable initiative? It can do so by freezing the momentous and the momentary in images, in figurations which, themselves unfrozen, dance across the landscape of our memory and imagination.

While narratives contain many such images, only a few "master images" figure the whole. They provide the moral core of personal and community identity. These are the images which stick, which become more vivid with the passage of time, which shed a growing light on the whole of our experience. (Harned, 1973: 160; cf. Warren, 1946: 118–19) A genuine figural narrative assimilates such personal master images within larger cultural stories punctuated with their own master images. *Figural narratives*, then, present paradigms of human action. "Such stories and the symbolic worlds they project," as Stephen Crites puts it, "are not like monuments that men behold, but like *dwelling places*. *People live in them*, they are the moving forms, at once musical and narrative, which inform people's sense of the story of which their own lives are a part, of the moving course of their own action and experience." (Crites, 1971: 295)

Metz's description of the practical significance of dangerous memories can only refer to this work of narrative figuration. Dangerous memories embodied in narratives "break through the omnipresent power of the given facts." Such stories themselves become events, forms of action which transfigure embedded patterns of behavior. (Metz, 1980: 193–4, 207–8) The spirituals of Black slaves are a good example of this process of narrative figuration. The slaves chose alternative narrative expressions of the Christian mythos in deliberate contrast to figural narratives which would have inculcated a sense of slavish submission. They focused the dangerous memories contained within these selected figural narratives upon the full range of contemporary experience and action, from escape along the underground railroad (O Canaan, sweet Canaan / I am bound for the land of Canaan) to the Civil War (O Fader Abraham / Go down into Dixie's Land/ Tell Jeff Davis / To let my People go). (Raboteau, 1978: 246–50)

Figural narratives present *dramatic* visions of self and history. They are the linguistic basis for what Victor Turner calls "social dramas." These recurrent dramatic processes of social change enfold and steer the actions of both individuals and communities. (Turner, 1974: 151, 158–9; 1980: 153–4, 156) Action, then, is stylized, conformed to the master images of the figural narratives. Correspondingly praxis, as collective action mediated by figural narratives, itself emerges as a stylized endeavor, a carefully determined and deteminate transvaluation of the existing web of relationships. As *transvaluation*, praxis interrupts the repetitive compulsion of oppressive social dramas and initiates social dramas of hope and liberation.

Action as integration calls forth a different narrative mode. From this combination a distinct style of praxis emerges: a teleological reordering of the web of human relationships. Not the flashing forth of action across the landscape of human affairs but the geological upheavals of that landscape, the seismic waves of cumulative interaction, are brought to expression in *synthetic narratives.* Here there is no assumption of events within their master images. Rather, meaning aggregates slowly; form is discerned within fragments carefully pieced together. Synthetic narratives map historical developments the way we might survey an entire watershed. In fact, synthetic narratives tend to predominate in works of historical reconstruction where the whole is the context for understanding the parts in contrast to chronicles where events leap unmediated across the blank spaces of time. (Cf. Mink, 1981)

Synthetic narratives generate perspectives upon the self as well as upon history. Augustine's persistent interrogation of himself in the *Confessions*, his laborious tracing of the trajectory of his life, is a masterpiece of synthetic narrative. Here, the self *is* that whole, painfully pieced together, which can only be grasped in narrative form. In synthetic narratives, then, relational visions of self and history predominate. The self is a nexus in the network of relationships which we call history. Both the self and the community define themselves through altering that objective network. Praxis, as collective action mediated by synthetic narratives, becomes *objectification* in the Hegelian/Marxist sense of forging institutions which reflect the collective intentionality.

To recapitulate: action manifesting itself as both intervention and integration calls forth two corresponding modes of narrative, figural and synthetic. Finally, as collective action mediated through narratives, praxis itself takes two different forms: transvaluation and objectification. (See Figure 5.1)

Figure 5.1

ACTION	NARRATIVE MODE	PRAXIS
INTERVENTION	FIGURAL	TRANSVALUATION
INTEGRATION	SYNTHETIC	OBJECTIFICATION

So far we have operated with a truncated concept of praxis. Narratively mediated collective action alone cannot establish a form of praxis. Praxis, as we have insisted throughout our argument, requires critical reflection, that is, a dialectical relationship with theory. Recall the difference between the approach to Western economic practice of a Louis Dumont in contrast to a Paul Samuelson. In its full elaboration the dialectic of theory and praxis requires a shift from the first to the second kind of approach. To achieve the status of religious or secular praxeological models narrative visions of self and history must be *conceptually* mediated. We must move from visions of self and history to theological anthropologies and theologies of history. Metz's commitment to a narrative, political theology may express a profound insight into the nature of action, but it fails to provide a *model* for practical theology insofar as it neglects this necessary task of conceptual mediation.

It would be naive to believe that the dialectic of theory and praxis can be perfectly accomplished in all renditions of theological anthropology and theology of history. Theologians dealing with the issues of theological anthropology or theology of history will inevitably skew their reflections more towards one or the other pole of the dialectic of theory and praxis. Likewise such theologians will work from actual religious narratives which contain different combinations of the pure figural or synthetic narrative modes. Provided the dialectic of theory and praxis is not fundamentally abrogated, we can respect and cherish this variety of emphases.

To discover variety in theological models is one thing; to lose all sense of the coherence of theological anthropologies and theologies of history is another. So we suggest that the various ways that theological anthropologies and theologies of history are developed can be clustered into four broad types in each case. These four types emerge out of the particular placing of reflection along a narrative axis marked by the poles of figural and synthetic narrative and along an axis of mediation marked by the poles of theory and praxis.

Figure 5.2

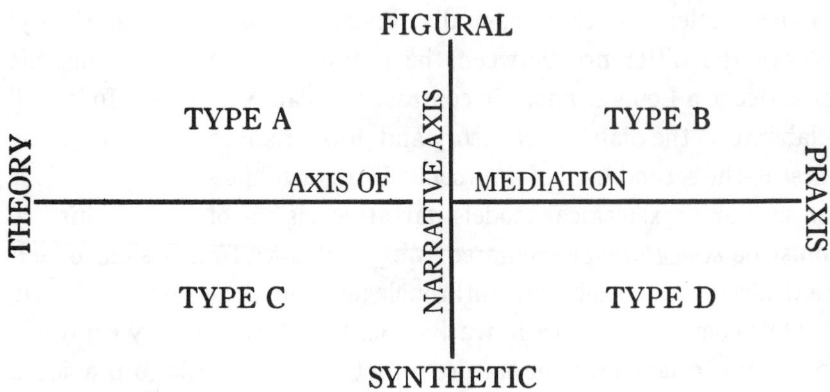

This typology has the advantage of having been constructed from the formal elements constitutive of theological anthropologies and theologies of history. But a typology is only valid if it can be shown to be both comprehensive in its scope and coherent in its demarcations. In the following sections we will use this typology, first, to bring order to the range of focal concerns represented in theological anthopologies and theologies of history, and then, to argue the relative adequacy of one of the four types in each case.

Although many practical theologians have developed theological anthropologies and theologies of history without fully being aware that the very nature of praxis demands precisely these systematic elements, these same theologians have been absolutely clear that a practical theology must correlate a secular vision of emancipation with a religious vision of redemption. J.B. Metz, more than any other practical theologian, has made us aware of the difficulties of making such a correlation. Theories of both emancipation and redemption tend to make exclusive, totalistic claims. Theories of emancipation of whatever stripe argue categorically that authentic social transformation is an autonomous process of self-liberation whose final end is utopia. Theories of redemption are equally insistent that genuine change occurs only within a theonomous process of ultimate transformation whose end is the divinely willed eschatological future. "Emancipation is not simply the immanence of redemption, nor is redemption just the transcendence of emancipation. . . . " (Metz, 1980: 122; cf. 120–121, 123–124) Metz's reservations, however, only make it imperative that practical theologians become more explicit about their correlations of emancipation and redemption.

Given the ruling character of the three related concepts, emancipation, autonomy and utopia, in the ideological frameworks of many modern societies, practical theologians would do well to reconsider H. Richard Niebuhr's classic analysis in *Christ and Culture* (1951) of the range of possible correlations between theological constructs and the dominant ideas of surrounding cultures. Using Niebuhr's typology as our basis, we may categorize the various possible correlations of emancipation and redemption within five types: (1) Redemption against emancipation, (2) redemption reduced to emancipation, (3) redemption superimposed on emancipation, (4) redemption and emancipation paradoxically related, and (5) redemption dialectically transforming emancipation. Nonetheless, the point which we want to stress now is this: whichever type a model of practical theology represents, it cannot treat the substantive issue of emancipation versus redemption without advancing some understanding of religious transcendence, some normative concept of the human, and some interpretation of historical process and destiny. Within the formal elements of theological anthropology and theology of history the substantive issue of emancipation versus redemption becomes, respectively, the issue of autonomy versus theonomy and the issue of utopia versus eschatology.

C. THEOLOGICAL ANTHROPOLOGY: FOUR TYPES

When Kant defined the meaning of the modern Enlightenment as a new moral imperative, *sapere aude*, in effect he identified the quest for autonomy with humanity's "quasi-transcendental interest" in emancipation as such. (Kant, 1963: 3–10; Habermas, 1971a: 301–17) In the name of autonomy, humanity, among other things, must set aside the restraints imposed by the Judeo-Christian myths of Creation and Fall, and embrace the ancient sophistry, now thoroughly refurbished, that "man is the measure of all things." Henceforth no sacred narrative could be invoked to understand and to justify humanity. For *sapere aude* means that whatever humanity dares to know cannot be known in an act of piety or reverential obedience.

Those who have heeded this new moral imperative have transformed our inherited perceptions of what it means to be human. Often in narrative discourse and sometimes in the form of explicitly theoretical models like those of Kant, Marx, Nietzsche, and Freud, the theory of autonomy as a struggle for individual freedom has been interpreted, criticized, and revised in terms of a variety of cultural perspectives. Common to both the narratives and the models is a basic emplotment which projects autonomy, however concretely defined, as the "internal teleology" of human aspiration and achievement. Not surprisingly, such narratives and models tell us more about the pathologies, the systematically distorted forms of communication, evident in "heteronomy" than they do about its alternative. For personal autonomy, like its societal counterpart, utopia, projects an ideal possibility: it describes a vision of human fulfillment in spite of —no, precisely because of—its absence.

The modern imperative of autonomy, of course, conflicts with the theory and practice of religious orthodoxy. For if autonomy, formally considered, postulates the self as "self-legislating will," that is, as a being whose essence can only be actualized through rational free choice, then anything external to the self that limits that actualization must necessarily be rejected as heteronomous. Understandably, the inherited norms of Judeo-Christian tradition, as institutionalized in the conventional morality and piety of the communities of faith, were indicted *en masse* as a rationally unjustified and unjustifiable restraint upon self-legislating free will. While Kant himself may have anticipated many of the theological implications of this indictment, and tried to reconstruct morality and piety in a manner responsive to it, most of the partisans of autonomy have simply ignored his case for *religion within the limits of reason alone*. Systematically theological reflection which seeks to operate within the dialectic of theory and praxis thus is faced with the challenge implicit in the modern imperative: If autonomy rightfully puts an end to the orthodox forms of religious heteronomy, does that mean that the religious sentiment itself is finished, a story no longer worth retelling as the basis for future models of authentic selfhood?

Our answer to this specific question can readily be guessed. Beyond the impasse between modern autonomy and traditional religious heteronomy stands an alternative to both, a vision of the self as "theonomous"—in which humanity's struggle for autonomy is now dialectically related to an Ultimate Reality that both limits and transforms that struggle. For theonomy, in the words of Paul Tillich, is "the substance and meaning of history" which, insofar as it remains religiously open to the Unconditional, must affirm autonomy as a finite principle of historical development. (Tillich, 1957: 45) Contemporary religious thought and action, we believe, cannot be understood apart from the premise that such a vision is pervasive in religious communities and operative in the processes by which these communities are currently revising the religious narratives and theological models by which they interpret their social praxis. *Theological anthropology is the mode of systematically theological reflection seeking to present this dialectical relationship between theonomy and autonomy.* Its practical intent is evident not only in the traces of ideological conflict that are sedimented in it, but also in its normative claim for guiding the self to authentically human fulfillment through religious praxis.

Before we attempt to map the models of theological anthropology, we must diagnose two patterns of relating theonomy and autonomy that fall short of this interpretation of the dialectic.

Autonomy versus Theonomy: While one-sided partisans for either of these visions reject our dialectic, typical of those who do so in behalf of autonomy is Kai Nielsen. His important little book, *Ethics Without God* (1973), suggests that morality itself must be emancipated from religion before an authentic "humanistic ethics" can be developed. Since all forms of the religious sentiment can only refer to a heteronomous "will of God," the claims for a distinctively theonomous view of the self are dismissed as either unintelligible or unjustifiable. Any systematically theological reflection correlating autonomy and theonomy, therefore, is praxeologically superfluous and incapable of making a contribution to public discourse.

Nielsen's defense of autonomy apart from theonomy, however, is vulnerable to criticism on similar grounds. While his "rational egoist" asserts the self-sufficiency of certain human desires and intentions, it is hard to see why these really matter, if we are left with no way to consider seriously the question of ultimacy that these desires and intentions inevitably raise. (Cf. Nielsen, 1973: 60–4) Such an outcome looks less and less like an appropriately austere vision of human fulfillment and more and more like the eclipse of vision altogether.

Theonomy versus Autonomy: The opposite mistake is made by theologians, like the young Karl Barth, who reject any correlation in order to embrace the radical transcendence of a "wholly Other" God. Such an embrace typically means an impassioned "Nein!" rejecting any "point of connection" between Christian faith and contemporary culture. Since faith must represent the crisis which affirms the will of God against the claims of humanism, the theonomous self transformed by such faith has no need to reappropriate the claims of autonomy. Were the Barthian "Nein!" to stand, practical theology, as we have been describing it, would be impossible. Yet this refusal to see any point of connection can only be sustained by insisting on the categorical uniqueness of Christian faith. In light of the generic features common to Christian faith and the "works" typical of the religious sentiment, we can only regard this refusal as a form of special pleading. Far from ensuring the integrity of theology, the Barthian "Nein!" succeeds only in removing it from the realm of public discourse. The religious silence that ensues is just as self-defeating for practical theologians as Nielsen's metaethical silence.

Theological anthropology, in short, cannot be constituted apart from some correlation between autonomy and theonomy. While such a correlation establishes the necessary subject matter for this form of systematically theological reflection, it does not explain the diversity of praxeological models within this discipline. In order to do that, let us return to our hypothesis regarding the typological patterns that arise when religious narratives are conceptually mediated in the dialectic of theory and praxis. If, as we argued in the previous section, these establish both a *narrative axis*, plotted along the continuum differentiating figural and synthetic narrative modes, and an *axis of mediation* representing the conceptual modes of theory and praxis, we have four formally distinct types: Type A, which develops the theoretical implications of figural narratives; Type B, which does the same for their practical implications; Type C, which focuses on the theoretical dimensions of synthetic narratives; and Type D, which does the same for their practical dimensions. (See Figure 5.3) While this typology need not be regarded as exhaustive, it will serve as a useful heuristic for differentiating four models expressing different dimensions of the correlation between theonomy and autonomy. It will also allow us to formulate reasons why one of the four is relatively more adequate for practical theology. The types may be characterized as follows:

Type A: Theological Anthropology as the comprehension of authentic humanism.

Type B: Theological Anthropology as a paradigm of humanity transformed.

Type C: Theological Anthropology as abstractly formalized theonomy.

Type D: Theological Anthropology as a model of responsible selfhood.

Figure 5.3 THEOLOGICAL ANTHROPOLOGY

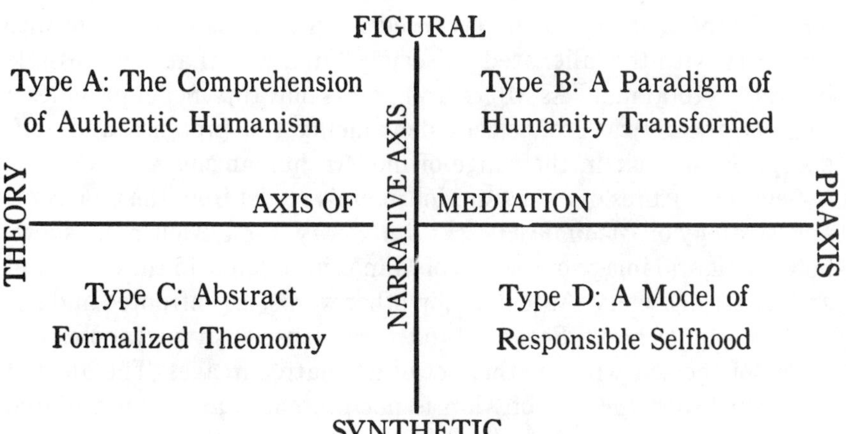

In Type A, theonomy provides a kind of religious wisdom for clarifying and ultimately transcending the various images of the autonomous self available in contemporary humanism. Formally, it is constituted by a figural use of Biblical narrative, and developed primarily as a theoretical form of systematically theological reflection. It does exhibit a practical intent, however, insofar as any theological anthropology must function as normative discourse for shaping the moods and motivations operative in religious praxis. Type A formulates the theoretical norms implicit in authentic humanism from the perspective of religious wisdom as disclosed in biblical narratives.

Jürgen Moltmann's *Man: Christian Anthropology in the Conflicts of the Present* (1974) is a good example of the limits and possibilities involved in Type A. An attempt to spell out the theoretical implications of his theology of hope for the already existing disciplines of "Christian anthropology," Moltmann's *Man* sees authentic humanism as "an anthropology of the crucified Lord: it is in relation to this 'Son of Man' that man recognizes his truth and first becomes true man." (Moltmann, 1974: 20) The self constituted in relation to "the crucified Lord," however, emerges through a series of figural juxtapositions in which the images of "man" implicit in the range of modern humanisms are confronted by various christological images. For example, the young Marx's anthropological vision of "the total man" is contrasted with "Christian hope directed . . . towards the 'new man'." (Ibid.: 57) The "new man's" superiority consists in his awareness of "the memory of the crucified Lord [which] brings him into solidarity with the 'alienated' of society" in a way that is impossible for Marx's total man. As Moltmann points out, this model provides a form of theoretical iconoclasm denouncing the pretense and self-deception implicit in the range of modern humanisms.

Several features distinguish Moltmann's model from the unacceptable strategy of *Theonomy versus Autonomy*. First, Moltmann shows how the figural image of the Son of Man is intelligible in the context of an industrial society. Autonomy, in other words, is confronted and not rejected out of hand. Second, Moltmann consciously juxtaposes one image of the self with another set of normative images. The ideal of fellowship with the Son of Man is not presented as an unmediated absolute. Consequently, as a praxeological model of the self, Moltmann's theonomous fellowship shows how religious transcendence defines Ultimate "limits-to" the modern imperative of autonomy.

Moltmann's model, unfortunately, remains figural and theoretical, exhausting itself in the dynamics of iconoclasm. Humanistic doctrines of man are examined and criticized in terms of a contrasting theological doctrine, but the praxis of fellowship remains sketchy. Moltmann's tendency to present the crucified Lord primarily in figural terms only reinforces this sketchiness. Apparently, he assumes some sort of consensus shared with his readers concerning the processes of personal formation as an *imitatio Christi.* At any rate, a more adequate praxeological model would have to examine these processes critically in light of the correlation between autonomy and theonomy.

Type B, theological anthropology as a paradigm of humanity transformed, appropriates the power of religious transcendence in order to clarify and reinforce the ultimate meaning of humanity's struggle for liberation. Formally, it, too, is constituted by a figural use of Biblical narrative, but it is developed as a form of explicitly critical reflection on praxis. In contrast to Type A, its practical intent is emphasized while its relationship to the inherited discipline of theological anthropology often remains obscure. It is less interested in elaboratng the doctrinal content of Biblical narrative than in using it to guide the processes of personal formation already operative in emancipatory praxis.

One major area of concern in Gustavo Gutierrez's *A Theology of Liberation* (1973) exhibits the limits and possibilities of Type B. In a section appropriately entitled, "Faith and the New Man," Gutierrez maps out the theological structures supportive of a "spirituality of liberation."

The figural image of "Christ the Liberator" not only represents for Gutierrez the culmination of Biblical narrative; it also gives ultimate meaning to emancipatory praxis: "In Christ the all-comprehensiveness of the liberating process reaches its fullest sense." (Gutierrez, 1973: 178) In order to reflect systematically on this image, Gutierrez establishes a series of correlations between it and the process of liberation, structured as a complex of (1) immediate social and political objectives, (2) world historical destiny, and (3) religiously transcendent aspiration. (Ibid.: 36–7) These correlations warrant a spirituality that finds "Christ in the Neighbor," specifically, that is, in solidarity with the oppressed. The power of religious transcendence, and its impact of self-actualization through "prayer, commitment, and action" (Ibid.: 204) thus are brought to bear on emancipatory praxis as the source of its "qualitative" transformation.

There is no ambiguity regarding the practical intent of Gutierrez's paradigm of humanity transformed. By correlating the modern imperative of autonomy with the theonomous meaning of salvation history, Gutierrez suggests that both emerge in one authentic image of the self, the "Christofinalized" self that discovers itself in the praxis of liberation. Nevertheless, this vision uniting autonomy and theonomy, in Gutierrez's words, "is not an identification." (Gutierrez, 1973: 177) While the praxis of liberation itself contains iconoclastic tendencies as well as constructive possibilities, their ultimate ground is discovered "only through the acceptance of the liberating gift of Christ, which surpasses all expectations." Clearly Gutierrez emphasizes the "limits-of" rather than the "limits-to" the praxis of liberation. Salvation symbolizes the complete fulfillment of processes already operative in emancipatory praxis, and not an iconoclastic restriction upon them. Theonomy is actualized within autonomy, and vice versa.

The limitations of Gutierrez's praxeological model may be inherent in Type B's tendency to interpret figural narratives too selectively according to the requirements of emancipatory praxis. While Gutierrez does not intend to equate autonomy and theonomy, he fails to show how the interaction between an autonomous human agency and a divine agency understood as theonomous is coherently conceivable. (Cf. Fierro, 1977: 236–7) Yet surely, his praxeological model of the new man requires such an explanation if it is to bear fruit in an authentically Christian spirituality of liberation. Gutierrez apparently is unaware of the difficulties that ensue when figural narratives and praxis orientations selectively reinforce each other to the exclusion of other possibilities. As theological anthropology, Gutierrez's paradigm of humanity transformed is impressive in its capacity to inspire and renew religious commitments to praxis, but inadequate in its capacity to provide theoretical clarifications of these same commitments.

Type C, theological anthropology as abstractly formalized theonomy, reconstructs the wisdom of Biblical narrative in dialogue with the classical tradition of *philosophia perennis*. Formally, it is constituted by a synthetic narrative linking both the religious and the philosophical traditions under the rubric of "Christian humanism," and the specifically philosophical quest for contemplative truth. Distinguished from Type A by its synthetic narrative basis and its recognition of the universal claims of philosophical reason, Type C's perspective on the self is emphatically theocentric. To the extent that the figure of Jesus Christ is evident in it at all, he serves not as a concrete personality for imitation but as the Logos incarnate, a symbol personifying the ideal pattern of intellectual synthesis.

Paul Tillich's *Biblical Religion and the Search for Ultimate Reality* (1955) is but one instance of this type of theological anthropology. Ostensibly an attempt to integrate the philosopher's search for an answer to "the question of being" with the theologian's attempt to understand God faithfully, Tillich's distinctive view of both tasks ensures that the focus rests on the existential self who must integrate the two or perish: "To live serenely and courageously in these tensions and to discover finally their ultimate unity in the depths of our own souls and in the depth of the divine life is the task and dignity of human thought." (Tillich, 1955: 85) What makes this a Type C praxeological model is that the narrative rehearsing the traditions of philosophy and Biblical religion highlights long term trends in Western culture and not just the figural confrontations between, say, a Socrates and a Jesus of Nazareth. Hence, Tillich tries to map out the meaning of "Biblical personalism" in creative tension with philosophical ontology. His model of the self, therefore, seeks to reconcile these by correlating faith and reason in a conception of the self as one who accepts an ultimate identity grounded in the divine *Logos*. The practical intent of Tillich's model is evident from its thoroughly existential approach to systematically theological reflection. For behind Tillich's every word stands the tacit assumption that, at the very least, the Truth shall make us free.

That this vision of the authentic self as personal participation in the divine Logos is theonomous should be obvious. What needs to be pointed out is that for all its existential intent, Tillich's model remains abstractly formal. Here, too, its limitations are those of Type C itself, where the convergence of synthetic narrative and theoretical concern tend to predispose the model toward limit-concepts that remain at too high a level of generality to make much practical difference. Whereas the limit concepts in Moltmann's model serve an iconoclastic function ("limit-to" autonomy), and in Gutierrez's, a liberating function ("limit-of" autonomy), Tillich's model provides a formal definition of both the "limit-to" and the "limit-of" autonomy, but of an autonomy abstractly understood as the ground of the strictly intellectual processes of questioning and believing. Tillich's relative advantage over Moltmann and Gutierrez in theoretical comprehensiveness thus seems to have been purchased at the price of practical relevance. For the self who has undergone the kind of spiritual integration that Tillich's model calls for would still lack the kind of practical guidance that is prominent in Moltmann's and Gutierrez's.

Type D, theological anthropology as a model of responsible selfhood, appropriates the power of religious trust in Being in order to clarify what it means to be a moral agent involved in religious praxis. Formally, it is constituted by a synthetic narrative in which the Christian ethos is seen to emerge historically in interaction with a variety of other cultural traditions, on the one hand, and an emphasis on the situation of praxis conceived as a socialization process, on the other. In contrast to the other types, the question governing Type D's correlation of autonomy and theonomy is neither "What is a human being?" (Type A), nor "What is liberation?" (Type B), nor "How must a person think and believe?" (Type C), but "Who are we becoming in the totality of our interactions?". Although the synthetic narratives from which this type emerges emphasize personal integration in a manner similar to that of Type C, they differ in that Type D's model is not a theoretical ontology of the inner person but a descriptive account of "the social self" continually being transformed in the situation of praxis. Like Type C, however, it is explicitly theocentric, although with a stronger christological perspective than that allowed by the Logos theory.

Readers will not be surprised to learn that H. Richard Niebuhr's *The Responsible Self* (1963) exemplifies Type D. Intended as a prolegomenon to Christian ethics, this seminal work executes the dialectic of theory and praxis in terms of the root metaphor of responsibility. To be responsible is to be responsive to the social context in which we live, and move, and have our being. Theonomy in this model is a religious wisdom about the Ultimate Reality that empowers the self as one among many who respond: "God is acting in all actions upon you. So respond to all actions upon you as to respond to his action." (H. Richard Niebuhr, 1963: 126) Such a vision of theonomy is always already synthesized with the modern imperative of autonomy. The responsible self, though continually acted upon by others including "the loving dynamic One," is genuinely free and must be so in order to act responsibly. (Ibid.: 173)

The theoretical coherence of this praxeological model depends on Niebuhr's appropriation of G. H. Mead's social psychology. (Ibid.: 71f) Just as all social interactions exhibit a "triadic form" that points beyond themselves to some aspect of reality, so religious transcendence experiences God as the Ultimate Reality in all social interactions. The model of responsible selfhood, in other words, affirms both our freedom and our absolute dependence, and coherently explains how these entail one another in the processes of socialization. While this model's relationship to praxis operates at a level of generality higher than that encountered in the concrete emphases of Type B, in principle Type D's notion of praxis as responsibility includes a concern for liberation. The two types differ, we believe, insofar as the figural use of Biblical narratives in an "Exodus paradigm" differs from the synthetic narrative in which the Christian ethos unfolds its distinctive—but not categorically unique—world-historical meaning. Theological anthropology, therefore, is less a call to commitment than an attempt to clarify the perspective from which the self empowered by "the Gestalt of grace" (Ibid.: 175) emerges only to converge toward "one universal ethos" of responsibility.

As a look at the specific features of his theological limit-concepts will indicate, we believe that, of the four types, Niebuhr's is the most adequate, appropriate, and authentic. As a praxeological model, the responsible self defines both "limit-to" and "limit-of" autonomy, but unlike Type C which also does this, Niebuhr's model defines these limits not just in terms of the theoretic activities of questioning and believing, but also in terms of the concrete situation of human moral agency. The "limit-to" autonomy is evident in Niebuhr's category of "the fitting." Agency is never absolute, but emergent in a field of enabling and constraining possibilities, *all* of which are ultimately disposed by the "loving dynamic One." The "limit-of" autonomy is evident in Niebuhr's theocentric interpretation of Jesus Christ as an exemplar and redeemer of "the ethos of universal responsibility." In both concepts critical correlation takes the form of synthesis rather than either critique (Type A) or legitimation (Type B), for as in Type C the limits defined presuppose autonomy for their very intelligibility.

In short, Niebuhr's praxeological model of the responsible self is more adequate theoretically because it combines both greater comprehensiveness with an explanation of what it means for the self not only to think but also to act theonomously. It is relatively more appropriate and authentic because it clarifies the ultimate nature of all possible situations of praxis while also disclosing the moral ambiguity inherent in all of them. Such ambiguity eventually must give rise to explicitly ethical reflection. The appropriateness and authenticity of this model will be realized, in other words, when its sense of ambiguity is recognized as opening up the ethical perspective necessary for guiding the religious praxis of Christian communities.

Our typological analysis of *The Responsible Self* should not be misunderstood as implying, contrary to the pluralism of models affirmed previously, that systematically theological reflection can only proceed on a Niebuhrian basis. Far from making a substantive judgment of the relative adequacy of Niebuhr's own theological perspective, we intend only to recommend it as an exhibition of the possibilities in Type D, the most promising of the four quadrants for structuring praxeological models at the level of either theological anthropology or theology of history.

In order to demonstrate the plurality of substantive models possible within Type D, let us return to Niebuhr's own typology, as elaborated in his earlier work, *Christ and Culture* (1951). Translating the types developed there, we can specify five possible models for correlating autonomy and theonomy as we did in correlating emancipation and redemption: (1) Theonomy against autonomy, (2) theonomy reduced to autonomy, (3) theonomy superimposed upon autonomy, (4) theonomy and autonomy pardoxically related, and (5) theonomy dialectically transforming autonomy. Of these five, our preliminary remarks eliminated the first two. The other three, however, are conceivable within Type D and each of these, in turn, allows for a plurality of actual positions.

So, practical theologians developing praxeological models must make, and, in fact, inevitably make a number of formal decisions regarding the presentation of a normative image of the human self. The first of these deals with the types of religious narratives which will be employed and how they will be subjected to conceptual mediation. Is Type D, theological anthropology as a model of responsible selfhood, indeed the most adequate, appropriate, and authentic representation of the practical power of religious symbols? The second decision refers to the way in which specific models of the theonomous self and of the autonomous self will be correlated. Is, as H. Richard Niebuhr intimates, a dialectical synthesis of theonomy and autonomy preferable to a paradoxical relation or a hierarchical superimposition? While decisions on these procedural issues will rule out a number of praxeological models as hopelessly inadequate, inappropriate, and inauthentic, they leave open a large but carefully defined space for the development of many different normative syntheses of theonomy and autonomy.

D. THEOLOGY OF HISTORY: FOUR TYPES

If it is true that the role of religious transcendence in personal formation can only be grasped theologically by correlating autonomy and theonomy, it is equally true that its role in social formation is best seen in terms of the range of praxeological models correlating utopia and eschatology. Earlier we stressed the disastrous consequences of trying to repress the utopian impulse within one's praxeological model. The struggle for transcendence in history inevitably generates utopian projections. Eschatologies emerge out of the same hope for the ultimate transformation of history. Whether, sharing this common ground, utopias and eschatologies can be synthesized is the first issue that we must address. Second, we must show how various theologies of history like the different theological anthropologies are formed from distinct combinations of figural and synthetic narratives with theory and praxis. Third, we will map the typical patterns by which theologies of history, in fact, correlate utopia and eschatology.

According to Paul Tillich the presence of utopian narratives and utopian thinking in modern societies is no accident of history. Utopias are the flowering of the human struggle for transcendence in history. They have ontological significance. "To be man means to have utopia, for utopia is rooted in the being of man itself. . . . To understand history, that is, to have historical consciousness and activity, we must posit utopia at the beginning and at the end." (Tillich, 1971: 167–8) While Tillich thus confirms our thesis that utopian visions are the crucible within which conceptions of the normatively human and conceptions of history are joined, he also indicates why the logic of action—as described previously in this chapter—requires such visions: "Every utopia is an anticipation of human fulfillment. . . . Without this anticipatory inventiveness innumerable possibilities in human history would have remained unrealized. Where no anticipating utopia opens up possibilities there we find a decadent present, . . . for the present can be fully alive only in tension between past and future." (Ibid.: 169) Utopian projections, in other words, are intrinsic to any praxeological model. Depending upon the narrative modes in which they are expressed, these projections make room for action both as intervention and as integration. Once such action is mediated conceptually, they also serve as the catalyst precipitating both forms of praxis: transvaluation and objectification. This, at least, is our working hypothesis in seeking to establish the practical intent of theologies of history.

The full meaning of utopia has only gradually been realized. The first genuine utopias, arising in the sixteenth century, were narratives projecting ironic contrasts to reality. They were not meant to evoke action. Only in the seventeenth century were utopias elevated to the status of theoretical models. At this point they began to include a discursive element, a reference to the underlying principles of the good society. By the end of the seventeenth century utopias had been assimilated to the newly emergent modern ideologies. In that form they were tied to universal philosophies of history and geared toward rational political action. (Manuel and Manuel, 1979: 2–5; Shklar, 1966: 107) Narrative fancy thus gave way to the projection of concrete historical possibilities.

However, the notion of utopias as fanciful projections divorced from reality lingered on, notaby in Marx's dichotomy of scientific and utopian socialism. Mannheim, to the contrary, demonstrated the power of utopias to shape a future reality and set them in opposition to ideologies conceived as the reinforcement of the established order by a ruling class. (Mannheim, 1936: 193–204) While his polarization of ideology and utopia helped set the stage for the recognition of a utopian core within Marxian "scientific" socialism, it also imposed a "manichean strait-jacket" upon the variety and complexity of modern perspectives on history, society, and politics. (Shklar, 1966: 101–2) Other thinkers, as we noted, have wriggled out of this strait-jacket by moving towards a non-pejorative, generic understanding of ideologies. We welcome the growing recognition that ideologies of every stripe contain a utopian element. (Cf. Geuss, 1981: 88) Even ideologies that legitimate the status quo are defending some vision of ultimate human fulfillment whose realization in the present needs to be examined in public discourse.

In correlating their theological visions with various modern ideologies, some practical theologians have adopted Mannheim's polarized categories. For them the process of correlation is simple: utopias—without asking which ones—are considered good; ideologies by definition are repudiated as evil. Correlation becomes more complicated, however, when we recognize that there are only ideologies, in the generic sense of the term, of bewildering variety, all of which express narrative visions of the normatively human, all of which project models of historical fulfillment containing a utopian core. Here choice is no longer trivial.

Utopia versus Eschatology: When practical theologians choose among rival ideological perspectives, they implicitly affirm the possibility of bringing eschatological vision into some sort of correlation with utopian projection. Yet that possibility has been rejected from two sides. On the one hand, numerous theorists have suggested that utopias historically have superseded eschatology; on the other hand, some theologians have argued that eschatological vision radically negates the utopian imagination. Just as the anthropological visions rooted in the doctrine of original sin have given way to modern notions of human autonomy, so, insist theorists enamored with the secularization hypothesis, utopias bear witness to a Promethean usurpation of the eschatological power of the gods. "It will probably not be contested that in our time eschatology is no longer an actively operating force in actual history. . . . Thus the main force of appealing images of the future now lies in utopian thought in the broadest sense. . . . " (Polak, 1966: 112; cf. Manuel and Manuel, 1979: 112; Shklar, 1966: 104) Only a residue of eschatology is said to remain, "like the structure of a superseded form in biological evolution."

This concept of utopia, then, takes its place among modern theories of autonomy and emancipation which are based on an a priori denial of all models of religious transcendence. What confronts us is an interrelated series of rejections dismissing the very possibility of theological correlations with each of the core elements of any praxeological model. So our argument for the praxeological significance of such models at the beginning of this chapter against the Marxist paradigm of critical theory becomes all the more important. Practical theologians cannot presuppose any elective affinity between utopian and eschatological projections.

The argument for some sort of affinity complements our previous discussion. We can present it schematically. First, the theory of the supersession of eschatology in utopian visions clearly depends on understanding secularization as the paradigm of modern historical processes. (Cf. Polak, 1966: 285–91) Yet from every conceivable angle anthropologists, historians, and phenomenologists of religion have argued that as an explanatory framework the secularization paradigm is simplistic. We are no longer Comteans; history sends forth multiple tendrils of development, not a single line of "progressive" evolution. The claims of utopian theorists are as unwarranted as the arbitrary conclusion of social theorists like Gouldner and Habermas who relegate religious discourse in general to the realm of the "paleosymbolic."

Second, theologians like Metz and Tillich insist that there are fatal limitations to the utopian visions. Even utopias envisioning human emancipation commonly repress awareness of the sufferings of finitude and the persistence of alienation. (Metz, 1980: 119–35) The ultimate response of utopian thinking in the face of the mortality of individuals, cultures, and even the human species as a whole is resignation. Similarly, the failure of utopian thinking lies not in the projection of fantastic possibilities, but in the contradiction between its vision of total alienation and its naive estimation of the capacity of humans, warped by alienation, to change the nightmare into a dream. (Tillich, 1971: 170–1) Eschatological models, precisely because they show how religious transcendence projects a hope in spite of both the suffering of finitude and the persistence of alienation, are more inclusive than their counterparts.

Third, there is a religious horizon to utopian thought, as there is a utopian core to ideological models. Moving beyond the case that has been made for the presence of ultimate concern in all political thought and action (cf. Gilkey, 1976: 36–39), we can detect an eschatological horizon in both the underlying premises of utopian models and the metaphorical extravagance of utopian discourse.

Consider Thomas Jefferson's substitution of the inalienable right to pursue happiness for the goal of attaining an otherworldly, beatific vision. Eighteenth century ideologists like Jefferson did not supersede eschatology; they merely translated it. There was no loss of ultimacy in the translation. While the principle of the greatest good for the greatest number functioned as the "limit-to" the individual's pursuit of happiness, the Newtonian vision of a finally harmonious universe operated similarly as the "limit-of" that pursuit. (Cf. Wills, 1979: 151, 240–55)

Or consider Chairman Mao. In one of Mao's final poems, a Russian bird revels in the promise of vulgar communism:

There'll be plenty to eat
Potatoes piping hot,
Beef-filled goulash.

His vision earns him only the contempt of the Chinese bird:

> Stop your windy nonsense!
> Look you, the world is being turned upside down.

Authentic utopia, Peking-style, resounds with eschatological fulfillment:

> We can clasp the moon in the ninth heaven
> and seize turtles deep down in the five seas.
> We'll return amid triumphant song and laughter.
> Nothing is hard in this world
> If you dare to scale the heights.
> (as cited in Manuel and Manuel, 1979: 804)

Poetic extravagance? Or an insight into the fundamental intentionality of utopian discourse? We opt for the latter interpretation: in utopian discourse social change, however prosaic, takes place within a horizon of ultimacy. In light of the ultimate questions and hopes articulated wittingly or not in utopias, the eschatological residue should more accurately be described as the magnetic field within which utopias operate. Eschatological hope, to vary the image, discloses the expanding universe within which the utopian imagination constructs its multiple galaxies.

Eschatology versus Utopia: Theological models which construe eschatology either in purely otherworldly terms or only as a *via negativa* also repudiate the possibility of a genuine correlation between eschatology and utopia. The "eschatological proviso" formulated by some European practical theologians, for example, has been criticized for maintaining a purely negative relationship between eschatology and utopia. Latin American practical theologians in particular reject such an understanding of eschatology because it severs the link between the Kingdom of God and the utopian projects of human history, leaving destiny exclusively in the hands of a God who creates the millennial future *ex nihilo*. In Segundo's estimation such a purely critical eschatology, while initially liberating, ultimately stifles hope and the will to struggle. (Segundo, 1976: 144–148) Given the intrinsic connection between action and utopian projections that we have insisted upon earlier, Segundo's contention rings true. To repeat: practical theologies are religious ideologies. If religious ideologies are to sustain praxis, a utopian element is essential. A purely negative correlation between eschatology and utopia aborts practical theology's commitment to provide concrete models for praxis. Second, if the eschatological proviso is a purely formal, critical principle which dissolves the utopian pretensions of all ideologies without dialectically generating new models with their own unpretentious yet unmistakably utopian elements, then it becomes extremely difficult if not impossible to credit practical theologies based on such a principle as modes of public discourse. Public discourse does not allow anyone to lay sole claim upon some "Archimedes' point" of criticism nor can those committed to public discourse long endure anyone who refuses the risks of creatively projecting new human possibilities.

Theology of history, then, is the mode of systematically theological reflection seeking to present the dialectical relationship between eschatology and utopia. Furthermore, if we recall the diagram already developed, we see that various models do so through different combinations of figural and synthetic narratives and different articulations of the dialectic of theory and praxis. Arising from the intersection of the *narrative axis* and the *axis of mediation* are four types of theology of history, each with its own set of issues and concerns, each with a distinctive contribution to make to practical theology. (See Figure 5.4) These four types are:

Type A: Theology of History as comprehension of authentic historicity.

Type B: Theology of History as paradigm of transformation.

Type C: Theology of History as theodicy.

Type D: Theology of History as cultural synthesis.

Figure 5.4 THEOLOGY OF HISTORY

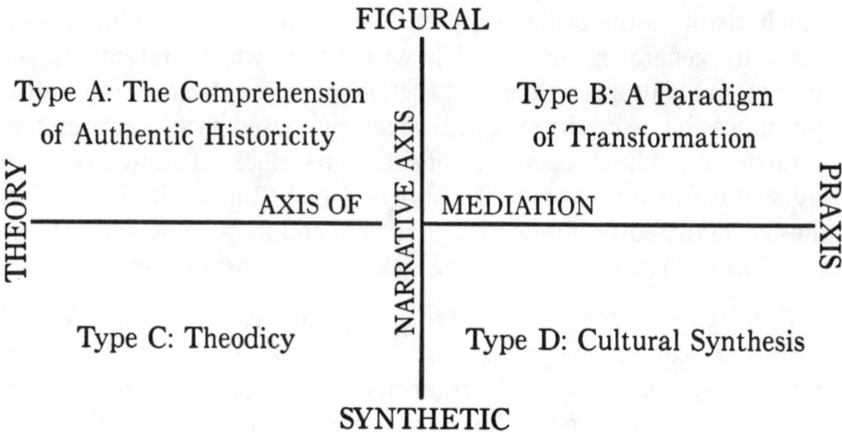

Type A, theology of history as comprehension of authentic historicity, correlates an ontological analysis of the structures of historical existence with religious, figural narratives. Because this type remains at the level of formal analysis of the possibilities and limits of finite temporality and makes only an iconic presentation of authentic fulfillment in history, its practical intent is limited to establishing the theoretical conditions of possibility for praxis conceived as a transvaluation of the existing web of historical relationships. Inasmuch as Type A understands the eschatological reality as kairos, it envisions a new authentic mode of historicity, one in which action undistorted by self-love and the will-to-power in the moment of kairos flows freely, contagiously outwards. The figural narratives symbolize such an eschatological historicity as rebirth. Eschatologies based on this symbol function as the counterparts of utopian visions of human society freed of alienation. Marx himself provides an image of this utopian possibility when he looks forward to a future of permanent kairos when it will be possible "to do one thing today and another tomorrow, to hunt in the morning, fish in the afternoon, rear cattle in the evening, [and] criticize after dinner. . . . " (Marx and Engels, 1947: 22) Emerging from both the religious symbol and utopian figure is a model of historicity as existential freedom.

One creative rendition of Type A comes, interestingly enough, from a systematic theologian turned practical theologian, John B. Cobb. Cobb's earlier work, *The Structure of Christian Existence* (1967), illustrates the practical implications of Type A, its limits and possibilities. There he views human history as a process of evolutionary emergence. Moments of kairos witness the creation of new structures of existence. While a structure of existence includes both conscious and unconscious elements, its emergence depends upon the access to new dimensions of self-understanding. (Cobb, 1967: 16–19) These breakthroughs, particularly at advanced stages of development, depend upon the actions of certain "axial" figures. (Ibid.: 52–59) Although Cobb does not discuss the role of narrative, figural narratives could be interpreted as the emergence stories of these axial figures and as the dramatization of their structures of existence. The praxeological significance of Cobb's view of history is clarified in his chapter on Christian love. Each structure of existence has a mode of action implicit in it insofar as each structure modifies thoroughly and in distinctive fashion a whole set of human virtues. (Ibid.: 125–36) In other words, structures of existence *transvalue* modes of action.

The strength of Type A models of the theology of history lies in their presentation of certain religiously based structures as intrinsic to utopian or eschatological fulfillment. Historical fulfillment does not ride in on silver clouds; it arises from ultimately transformed human action. When Marx and Engels argue that the free development of each is the condition for the free development of all, they are implicitly providing a norm for judging what constitutes an authentically world-transforming praxis. Likewise, in Cobb's model Christian love, as an eschatological structure of existence, mediates the "limit-to" and "limit-of" such a utopian norm of existential freedom. Beyond this concern for authenticity, these models acknowledge the criterion of appropriateness to the degree that they claim to grasp the practical implications of religious figural narratives for human existence. But they rarely deal with the issues of adequacy: their models provide little theoretical insight into the ambiguous and complex unfolding of history itself.

Insofar as it fails to illuminate the actual process of development, Type A's model of authentic historicity may seem indistinguishable from theological anthropology. Nevertheless, precisely because it does recognize the need to explain the structures of existence in their historical development, Cobb's model really is a theology of history. This, at least, is a move in the right direction. Most practical theologians, however, prefer not to stress the self-understanding of axial figures so much as the power of action in giving rise to these new structures. Figural narratives as the expression of dangerous memories retain the originating power of those actions, the power to set in motion countervailing forces within the drama of history. Consequently, most practical theologians develop their theologies of history as paradigms of transformation, Type B.

The issue placed in center stage by Type B is eschatological liberation. Eschatological reality breaks in upon human history thereby defining the "limit-to" and "limit-of" our human projects. Frequently Type B theologies of history convey eschatological liberation through the figural narrative of Exodus. While praxeological models of history as a process of Exodus may match the dramatic intensity of Marx's dialectical utopian model, they see the crisis of history and its resolution ultimately in religious terms. So, Gustavo Gutierrez, in light of his interpretation of the "Exodus paradigm," can speak of history as "Christo-finalized." (Gutierrez, 1973: 153) Jürgen Moltmann, for his part, expands the drama of Exodus into an analysis of the interlocking, vicious circles of historical alienation, each of which is overcome by an appropriate form of liberation. The same drama of liberation overcoming alienation is danced out on each of the five tiers or circles: political, economic, cultural, ecological, and existential or religious. (Moltmann, 1974: 332–35)

From the vantage of Type B, praxis is largely symbolic transvaluation; it is activated by a disclosure of the dramatic movement of history itself. When related to political theory and social ethics such a praxeological model can indeed break the dominance of history's deadly repetition compulsion. (Cf. Metz, 1980: 161–3, 193–5; Cobb,

1982: 91) This demonstrated effectiveness in dramatizing the political and social intentionality of the Christian message may explain why Type B models of history are most favored by practical theologians. Once they adopt these models theologians place primary stress, therefore, on criteria of appropriateness. Secondarily, these models are accountable to criteria of authenticity. To view history as Exodus is to recognize that authentic existence can only be achieved communally and politically. The presence of liberating praxis becomes the hallmark of authentic historicity. Nevertheless, as with Type A, these models rarely strive for adequacy in their theoretical understanding of the historical process in which such praxis is activated.

John Cobb, while commenting favorably upon the development of what we are calling Type B theologies of history, simultaneously criticizes some practical theologians for failing "to wrestle with the eschatological question of ultimate meaning." (1982: 78) The enervating sense of the possible extinction of life on earth brought on by ecological and nuclear crises casts the practical theologian into an unavoidable dark night of the soul. How can one write about "the practical meaning of a theology of hope," Cobb asks, "without discussing the relevance to that practical meaning of the serious doubtfulness of human survival." (Ibid.: 118–19) Another way of putting his question would be to ask: how does the sense of religious transcendence at the core of practical theology relate to the success or failure of humanity's practical endeavors? Or what does success and failure mean when even a utopian society must admit its own mortality? To confront such questions is to recognize a "limit-to" all human projects, utopian or otherwise. "If justice and righteousness are not achieved, what then? Are we simply failures? Has God also failed? Is history simply a waste of time and effort?" (Ibid.: 80) No theology of history that evades these issues can long maintain the sense of a hoped-for coherence and meaning which makes praxis possible. The problem of theoretical adequacy to the historical process as a whole, in short, has important practical consequences.

Type C, theology of history as theodicy, seeks to confront these connsequences by making explicit the theoretical link between the vision of religious transcendence and the practical intent of theologies of history. Not all theodicies, however, exhibit the formal characteristics of Type C. Moltmann's theology of the "Crucified God" (Moltmann, 1974: 200–90), for example, represents a concerted effort to address the theodicy question. But it is not adequately developed as a Type C theology of history. This is because Moltmann, like other practical theologians, chooses to build his theology largely out of figural narratives. Only when a practical theology employs synthetic narratives in order to discern—in Hegelian terms—the rose in the cross of the present does Type C fully emerge. To be sure, the emergence of this type depends upon recognizing both the coherences and the incoherences of history. (Cf. Reinhold Niebuhr, 1953: 175–203) While there is certainly much room for disagreement among practical theologians regarding the degree to which such a synthesis can be achieved, praxis itself becomes possible only with the assertion of some degree of ultimate coherence to the historical process.

Although he has been accused of quietism, Hegel exhibited two crucial aspects of any theology of history as theodicy. First, he argued that it is possible to penetrate beneath the chaos of events, the "slaughter-bench of history," to discover a thread of meaning. (Hegel, 1953: 26–7) Apart from some such sense of *telos* gained from a provisional grasp of the whole, history becomes one damned thing after another and no intervening action, even some sort of divine intervention, amounts to anything more than a meaningless twitch. Action to be praxeologically meaningful must conform to an "internal teleology": it must form tendrils, however fragile, reaching toward future fulfillment. Second, Hegel saw that the monstrous sacrifice of the past and present to the future could not be justified, theoretically or practically, by the glory of utopian fulfillment. Only the sense that the divine reality is eschatologically present in every moment of history can create hope out of the ashes of history's perpetual holocaust. "The life of the ever-present Spirit is a cycle of stages, which, on the one hand, coexist side by side, but, on the other hand, seem to be past. The moments which Spirit seems to have left behind, it still possesses in the depth of its present." (Ibid.: 95) Without a theodicy capable of illuminating the activity of the everpresent Spirit, both eschatology and utopia become absurd.

A theology of history claiming to be a theodicy thus first and foremost subjects itself to criteria of adequacy. The eschatological vision of the whole expressed in synthetic narratives which manifest the *logos* in history must apprehend both life and death, good and evil, happiness and suffering. "Whole sight," as John Fowles puts it, "or all the rest is desolation." Of course, practical theologians will object that such comprehension can never be purely theoretical. The danger is that Type C models will simply declare that the real is the rational without ever realizing the dialectical character and the transforming power of that affirmation. So, Type C must meet the criterion of appropriateness by upholding those normative images, embedded in traditions, which negate the spurious reality of injustice. Nevertheless, while it ultimately depends upon a transformative praxis grounded in reason, Type C usually does not fully respond to the criterion of authenticity. For the "whole sight" that it promises too often reinforces the rationalist's reluctance to engage in real historical struggle.

Type D, theology of history as cultural synthesis, like Type C, emerges from synthetic narratives which provide a synoptic vision of history. Grounded in and existing for integrating action, and based on an ethic of responsibility, Type D presents models essential for praxis as objectification. (Cf. Little, 1968: 216–18) Type D is centered on the issue of eschatological fulfillment. It seeks to relate utopian projections of partial fulfillment directly to an eschatological interpretation of the Kingdom of God. Through Type D models of history practical theologies present a direct challenge and alternative to the exclusively utopian core of secular ideologies.

The classical description of the tasks of this type of theology of history was presented by Ernst Troeltsch. Only a substantive philosophy or theology of history, Troeltsch believed, could provide the norms for action in a world paralyzed by relativism. (Troeltsch, 1961: 67–69, 113–14; cf. Little, 1966: 351) His approach towards creating a cultural synthesis followed the path he laid out to determine the essence of a religious tradition. It is enlarged, however, by two critical maneuvers. (Troeltsch, 1961: 694) First, the historical immersion now proceeds within the totality of processes defining the practical theologian's own cultural context.

> So, every historically reflective age, must from its own standpoint, interpret the unity of meaning of the whole as including its own standpoint or aiming at it. . . . In any case, the historical thinker through such a construction arranges his own present and future within the totality of a human unity of meaning, and attains from the whole the direction of development, just as he must reflect further upon it from his own standpoint."
>
> (Ibid.: 71–73)

The synthetic narratives which result from this expanded historical immersion express, not the interaction of complex principles within a single tradition, but the interaction of all of the main ideological currents feeding into the practical theologian's specific cultural context. (Ibid.: 116–17, 167–68) Such a determination can only take place within the larger context provided by a periodization of universal history which juxtaposes and contrasts the various cultural contexts. (Ibid.: 700–701)

Insisting that theology of history cannot remain in the "calm region of contemplation," Troeltsch saw the need for a second maneuver: the creation of a cultural synthesis in the strict sense. Here the complicated pattern of value development discerned in the construction of a model of universal history is dialectically related to the demand for responsible action in the present crisis. No simple extrapolation of norms is possible, Troeltsch argued, because historical immersion yields conflicting lines of development. Without "a practical taking of a stand under the pressure of events," these value conflicts cannot be mediated. Values and norms abstracted from their developing traditions must be courageously refashioned and wedded to the socio-economic body of an emerging cultural system. As in the case of determining the essence of a tradition, the ultimate validity of such a cultural synthesis depends upon its practical fruitfulness. (Troeltsch, 1961: 768–72; cf. Troeltsch, 1957: 88–91, 103, 119–20; Little, 1968: 216–18; for Troeltsch's own attempt to formulate a fresh cultural synthesis, cf. McCann, 1976)

Each of these four types of theology of history has its contribution to make to a practical theology. Nevertheless, while many practical theologians opt for Type B, we think that Type D is best suited to the requirements of praxis because it is comprehensively the most adequate, appropriate, and authentic. First, the historical immersion which is a precondition to defining a cultural context is designed to meet the canons of adequacy. A cultural synthesis responsive to both eschatological hope and utopian projection must meet the test of historical immersion if it is to be solidly rooted in the multiple lines of historical development. Second, this mode is the most appropriate because it is able to integrate the results of a critical hermeneutic focusing upon value conflicts among several ideological and religious traditions. Third, it recognizes that a valid cultural synthesis depends upon the courageous and creative acts of practical theologians committed to transforming the cultural system. Authenticity means adherence to an ethic of responsibility in the effort to construct objective possibilities for cultural transformation. From this vantage point eschatology appears as the horizon of fulfillment, that is, the "limit of" specific utopian projections. Nevertheless, because cultural synthesis recognizes the clash of values within a given culture and requires a construction which resolves this conflict, eschatological projections may also function as the "limit-to" utopian models. As most fully adequate, appropriate, and authentic, theology of history as cultural synthesis offers the most concrete and complete alternative to the exclusively utopian projections of secular ideologies.

In our earlier analysis of theological anthropology we insisted that we are not canonizing H. Richard Niebuhr's *The Responsible Self.* The same holds true for Troeltsch's substantive contributions to the theology of history. It is the formal procedures of theology of history as cultural synthesis which we find most intriguing. Many different models of cultural synthesis can be constructed by following Troeltsch's procedures.

Just as the typology from *Christ and Culture* helped clarify the pluralism possible within theological anthropology, so it is equally helpful in establishing the plurality of possible correlations of eschatology and utopia in theology of history. In this case the five possible relationships would read: (1) Eschatology against utopia; (2) eschatology reduced to utopia; (3) eschatology superimposed upon utopia; (4) eschatology and utopia paradoxically related; and (5) eschatology dialectically transforming utopia. Since the first two options were eliminated by our preliminary discussion, we contend that *any* of the last three could be valid forms of a theology of history because each of these relates eschatology and utopia both positively and negatively. None of these three maintains the absolute bifurcation of divine and human action as in the eschatology against utopia model. None reduces religious transcendence to a meaningless residue, as in the eschatology reduced to utopia model. Niebuhr's typology thus enables us to wriggle out of Mannheim's "manichean strait-jacket" by requiring not only an actual cultural synthesis that is explicitly ideological but also a recognition of the kind of model of eschatology and utopia that is operative in it. Thus any theologian of history who wishes to contribute to the praxis of a religious community should be concerned with four basic questions: (1) Is Type D, in fact, the type of theology of history best suited to the requirements of praxis? (2) If so, what are the objective possibilities for cultural synthesis? (3) Which utopian vision best captures the human good intended in this cultural synthesis? (4) Which way of relating eschatology and utopia best illuminates the limits and possibilities for ultimate transformation implicit in this utopian vision?

E. THE DECENTERING OF PRACTICAL THEOLOGY

Commitment to *religious* praxis entails commitment to some theory of religious transcendence in the praxeological models of theological anthropology and theology of history. Apart from all considerations of content the various combinations of elements possible in theological anthropologies and theologies of history necessarily result in a plurality of praxeological models. If all models are perspectival, then they are also limited. There is a blind side to every perspective. Having surveyed the systematic elements of practical theologies, we must now ask the question: are there forms of blindness which tend to be endemic to all of these models? We wish to point out three problems which correspond to the elements which we have analyzed in this chapter: excessive homocentrism, lack of awareness of the pretensions of the eschatological imagination, and blindness to the limits of the praxis of liberation.

Beyond homocentrism: In its concern with human action a practical theology necessarily stresses a normative image of the human good. Without anthropological models there would be no norms to guide actions. Yet many practical theologies have translated the necessary concern with normative models for human action into an exclusive concern with *human* destiny. Beyond social and political liberation, practical theologies tend to anticipate, in Gustavo Gutierrez's terms, the creation of a "New Man." (Gutierrez, 1973: 36–7, 145–6) The coming of the Kingdom tends to be viewed not as the liberation of all creation, groaning in travail, but as the consummation of human life and history. This is what we mean by excessive homocentrism.

Process practical theologians have taken the lead in insisting that homocentrism, in Schubert Ogden's blunt words, "is both theoretically false and practically vicious." (Ogden, 1979: 108) Homocentrism, while the hallmark of most modern Western theologies, is neither an adequate understanding of the place of human life *within* nature nor an appropriate form of Christian witness to the intrinsic worth of all life. Process theologians consequently reject the notion that we must choose between a practical theology centered upon politics and one centered upon ecology. (Ibid.: 108–112; Cobb, 1982: 111–33)

The practical viciousness of homocentrism is a direct result of its theoretical falsehood. It functions as an active ingredient within compounds of alienation. The reduction of nature to the level of raw material upon which humans work their will is tied to a similar reduction of classes of human beings. (Ogden, 1979: 113; cf. McElwain, 1983: 85–87) Rosemary Ruether has developed these intuitions by analyzing the "interstructuring" of multiple forms of alienation. In Ruether's judgment, sexism and ecological destructiveness have been correlated theoretically with dualistic forms of consciousness which separate spirit from matter, and "man" from "nature"; and practically, with the industrial mode of production which confined women to the home while it ravaged the earth. (Cf. Ruether, 1975: 186–214)

The dualistic separation of human destiny from the fate of the earth generates a complex structure of evil. Our purpose in pointing to this interstructuring of homocentrism with other forms of alienation is not to recommend any specific models of practical theology, such as Ogden's or Ruether's, but to point to a distorting tendency inherent in all forms of practical theology. Congenital flaws, however, can be treated. In our estimation, the treatment entails recognizing a difficult paradox: only that praxis can liberate human beings whose vision transcends the human.

Beyond the imperialism of the eschatological vision: If the necessary emphasis upon theological anthropology breeds side effects which must be treated, so does the equally necessary emphasis upon the theology of history. Millennial visions, whether eschatological or utopian, are visions of a specific end to history. But this very specificity—a quality absolutely necessary for praxis—can transform utopias into dystopias. By the very specificity of their "sense of an ending" eschatological and utopian visions tend to rule out alternatives. Thus they constrict the multiple lines of human—and nonhuman—development to a single teleology. Indeed, while it is not surprising that the notion of orthopraxis would seem to require such a single axis of development, where do we find alternatives which recognize the plurality of developmental lines, that is, practical theologies whose vision transcends the religious or ideological imperialism of Western messianisms, whether Christian or Marxist?

John Cobb points to yet another dimension to this kind of imperialism. History and politics, as commonly defined, are the province of urban communities. The drive of such "civilization" is toward industrialization. "Unconsciously, perhaps, the subsistence farmer, and even the peasant village, are assimilated to images of an unhistorical nature which serves civilization and industrialization but has no inherent reality." Ideological movements, of whatever stripe, all too commonly share the same notion of biased "development"—a kind of development which exacerbates the problems of rural societies and tears their social fabric. "All this," Cobb concludes, "because the 'reality' is 'history' and not 'nature.' " (Cobb, 1982: 120–1) If we are to get beyond this ultimate form of imperialism, again, we must confront a difficult paradox: only that praxis ultimately transforms whose model of eschatology and utopia refuses to absolutize its own vision of liberation.

Beyond liberation theology: Despite these inherent problems, the systematic elaboration of a model for religious praxis requires both a theological anthropology and a theology of history. Both of these systematic structures can be construed in a variety of ways. However, must any theology of praxis, worthy of the name, be a theology of liberation? Is liberation the goal of any genuine praxis?

Schubert Ogden has attempted to establish the limits of any theology of liberation by arguing three related theses: (1) Theology, formally considered, as reflection on the meaning and truth of the Christian witness need not be a theology of liberation. (2) While the faith operative in the New Testament may rightfully be called a praxis of love, the latter may not be construed as synonymous with liberating praxis. " '[L]iberating praxis' is a special form of something more generally called 'historical praxis'. . . . " (3) Nevertheless, theology considered in light of our current understanding of the full scope of the responsibility of being human must be conceived as a theology of liberation. (Ogden, 1981a: 131–39)

Our own position becomes clear in contrast to Ogden's. (1) Ogden does not distinguish here between the theological genres of systematic and practical theology. His first thesis is undercut because its formulation is geared toward the task of systematic theology. Our own question is whether a *practical* theology must be a liberation theology.

(2) We agree that liberating praxis is but one form of historical praxis. Liberating praxis is praxis mediated by the historically and culturally specific concepts of alienation and liberation. Such models may not be appropriate to every cultural context. Even when the immediate goal is political revolution, praxis need not be interpreted or promoted as a liberating praxis. Thomas Jefferson supported a revolutionary praxis with the moral sense theory of the Scottish Enlightenment which focused not on processes of personal or social liberation but on the imperative of the greatest good for the greatest number. (Cf. Wills, 1979: 167–258) Likewise, Gandhi adapted the Hindu tradition of *ahimsa* to a modern context through the development of the praxis of *satyagraha* without appealing to the western concepts of alienation and liberation. (Cf. Bondurant, 1958: 105–45) Moreover, the root concepts of alienation/liberation can lead to the obscuring, if not the repressing of certain historical dilemmas. These

concepts tend to reinforce what Hugh McElwain calls the Western penchant for viewing limits as purely negative, an attitude which fosters the repression of death and ecological destructiveness. (1983: 4–6) (3) In light of the cultural specificity of the model of alienation/liberation as well as its own tendencies towards distortion, we must qualify our acceptance of Ogden's third thesis. While some sort of theology of liberation may be adequate to much of the contemporary situation, we look forward to the flowering of many different models of praxis drawn from a wide range of religious and secular ideologies.

Any model has formal as well as substantive limitations. There are substantive differences between a road map of Illinois and one of Pennsylvania. But there are formal differences between a road map and a topographical map. Although the issues that we have discussed in this section are substantive, our discussion of them here was intended to delineate the formal limitations of any model of practical theology. Immanent criticism, we suggest, can be focused in ways that offset these intrinsic limits.

Our thesis is that the systematic element in practical theologies raises critical reflection on religious praxis to the formal status of a model. A model, like a crystal, is a complex balance of structural elements. The systematic elements of a practical theology complete this process of crystallization. Through the model's power to refract, action—compelled by divine command and human suffering—becomes praxis. A coherent strategy for the transvaluation of the ends of human life and the creation of more humane structures of social life emerges. At this juncture, however, we must repeat a point which was developed previously, namely, that practical theology does not exhaust the field of practical religious discourse. The model which a practical theology presents is necessary but not sufficient to the full structuring of the praxis of ultimate transformation. Even more important than the relationship of practical theology to such modes of primary religious discourse as Jeremiads is its partnership with Christian social ethics. We turn now to examine the complementarity of these two genres of secondary religious discourse geared toward praxis. This complementarity is the theme of our next chapter.

CHAPTER SIX

VISION AND CHOICE: PRACTICAL THEOLOGY AND CHRISTIAN SOCIAL ETHICS

The practical moral question in a theocentric construal of the world is . . . , "What is God enabling and requiring us to be and to do?" The most general answer is that we are to relate ourselves and all things in a manner appropriate to their relations to God.

(Gustafson, 1981: 327)

"Conscientization" is this pessah, *or passover—this passage or transition in which, within a historical praxis, the people become aware of the hope and power behind the symbols and stories of their traditional faith and begin to shape a new ethos, a new way of dwelling in the world and in history. This, surely, is a first response—from the point of view of political ethics—to the question of power. But there is . . . a second question. . . . Do we have any ethical guidelines to guide our action so far as the possibilities and costs of radical social change at a particular juncture in history are concerned?*

(Miguez-Bonino, 1983: 106)

As we argued in the previous chapter, limits can be interpreted in two ways: as boundaries and as thresholds. With the completion of our attempt to define the role of model construction in practical theology, we have reached the limit of abstract theoretical discourse in it. But this limit, it seems, stands only as a threshold opening us to the concrete demands of religious praxis. In this and the next chapter we will give an account of how to proceed from this threshold once more to the immediacy of religious praxis. From our perspective the systematic elements of practical theological discourse must be mediated ethically and rhetorically. As we will argue, without a properly rhetorical dimension practical theology will not be able to foster the development of religious praxis as a "truth-dependent mode of socialization." The burden of this chapter, however, is to explain the ethical dimension of practical theology, its possibilities and its limits.

Our analysis will proceed in four stages. First, we will observe the ambivalence about ethics that seems typical among the new generation of practical theologians by examining three Latin American liberation theologies. Second, by returning to the formal dialectic of theory and praxis, we hope to clarify the role of explicitly ethical reflection within it. Third, consistent with the mode of generic analysis spelled out previously, we will show how practical theology and Christian social ethics take up specific tasks involved in ethical reflection, as two distinct genres of public discourse. Finally, we will examine a case study of ideological conflict involving both genres, in order to show the advantages of maintaining this distinction of tasks and genres. Underlying our analysis is a single thesis: ideological criticism and reconstruction, on the one hand, and ethical reflection, on the other, are two different, but related, operations in public discourse. Insofar as practical theology maintains its focus on the former, it contributes a necessary contextual element enabling Christian social ethics to concentrate on the latter.

A. A LEGACY OF AMBIVALENCE

Hugo Assmann, a Brazilian theologian known for his trenchant formulations, distinguishes Latin American liberation theology from European political theology on the basis of the former's unique approach to ethics. In rejecting the "dualism" by which truth is defined *a priori* and then applied to practical situations (1976: 77), the Latin Americans also reject the traditional distinction between ethics and dogmatic theology. Contrary to Metz's political theology, which at that time still acknowledged a mediating role for "political ethics" (Ibid.: 120), Assmann conceives of liberation theology as an "ideology of struggle" in which the ethical dimension is coextensive with "the political choice, contained in any attempt at interpreting a historical situation." (Ibid.: 105) An all too-common experience among Latin American Christians provides the reason why liberation theology seeks to identify ethics with the whole of critical reflection on religious praxis:

> Vague "evangelical motives" (such as those proposed by Catholic Action, or found in the social teaching of the Church) are

> insufficient to secure commitment, through being too much of a preamble to action and finally leaving the militant on his own when it comes to the most difficult part: trying to put principles into practice. They are too distant from reality, speaking of commitment in a language far removed from the level of strategy and tactics, which for many means that they are not in fact speaking of commitment in any sense that they can call real.
>
> (Ibid.: 119)

Mired in its mating dance of theory and principles, political ethics inevitably undermines the ethical leap of commitment to liberation.

Arguments like Assmann's, not surprisingly, have met with equally trenchant responses from some Christian ethicists. In the course of an essay contrasting Moltmann's theology of hope with "the social ethical tradition in America," James M. Gustafson observed that the new generation of practical theologians tends to "move from theology to history or to politics without going through a stage of more careful ethical reflection—both about why certain things are judged to be bad and about what concrete proposals are necessary to make them better. . . . " (1974: 188) Elsewhere, Gustafson has expanded this line of criticism, noting that the new practical theology remains "incomplete" so long as its concern "to interpret the significance of general historical trends and movements through the use of biblical symbols, on the whole comes only to the threshold of ethics in a more limited sense." (1978: 31) Specifically, in relation to a symbol like liberation, "the principle of distributive justice is [required] . . . to give a more detailed assessment of certain circumstances, and to provide action-guiding principles." (1975: 141) Gustafson, in other words, argues that the ethical leap of commitment will be undermined unless the symbol of liberation gives rise to "ethics in a more limited sense."

Each author confronts an important problem. Assmann fears that the kind of "more careful ethical reflection" called for by Gustafson actually prevents commitment. Gustafson fears that unreflective involvement may fail to discharge "the burden of the ethical" that is a chief feature of the Christian way of life. Is there any way of initiating what Gustafson himself calls "a dialectic of disinterestedness and involvement" (1974: 33–46) that would do justice to both the new practical theology and those who sense the inadequacy of its ethical component? To pursue this possibility, let us look more closely at what three Latin American liberation theologians have done by way of ethics.

Despite the promise given in its title, Enrique Dussel's *Ethics and the Theology of Liberation* makes little advance beyond the position outlined by Assmann. Ethics, for Dussel, apparently consists in defining a fundamental political option, in terms of which he criticizes the ethos of the status quo and anticipates the ethos of a liberated society. True, Dussel goes beyond "critical hermeneutics" to make moral judgments about private property (1978: 25, 49) and the role of violence in both maintaining and overturning the rule of "the Evil One." (Ibid.: 43–6, 48) He also reconstructs the traditional three theological virtues and four cardinal moral virtues in light of the ethos of liberation. (Ibid.: 46–48) But he does not provide any explicit discussion of the principles warranting these judgments. Indeed, "moral theology"—which heretofore had provided the context for such a discussion—is dismissed as a distorted and distorting "application of dogma to praxis." (Ibid.: 155) Given his attitude toward moral theology, it is not surprising that Dussel fails even to see the point of taking a more disinterested view of his own passionate moral involvements. At any rate, his *Ethics* includes nothing of that sort.

Juan Luis Segundo's *The Liberation of Theology* (1976) goes a bit further in sketching an approach to ethics that he believes is consistent with his distinctive view of faith and ideologies. Ethics, like theology, must be relative to the situation in which faith with its absolute claims is working through ideologies. (Cf. McCann, 1981d) Thus ideologies constitute the relative frameworks in which ethical reflection may proceed. Segundo's ethical reflection, nevertheless, turns out to be remarkably thin. He asserts, on the one hand, that "Christian morality is precisely *a morality of ends*" (1976: 171), and, on the other hand, that "by very definition, the end justifies the means." (Ibid.) Since "a 'means'...is precisely that and nothing more, [it] cannot have any justification in itself."

In order to illustrate the practical consequences of this approach to ethics, Segundo discusses the problem of violence. His argument proceeds on both phenomenological and exegetical grounds. Phenomenologically, he contends that violence must be understood within the existing "economy of energy." Violence, in other words, is a necessary dimension of any decisive human thought or action. Therefore it is absurd to link "love" with nonviolence and "egoism" with its opposite. Violence can be a means to either end, and is justified to the extent that the intended end is justified (1976: 161) Exegetically, he argues that since Jesus' own thoughts and actions often were violent, we cannot interpret his praxis as somehow exempt from the economy of energy. (Ibid.: 164) What Jesus' teaching finally implies is what human reason already reveals: "use the least amount of violence compatible with truly effective love." (Ibid.: 166) Segundo, of course, is not interested in working out the specific exegetical warrants for this principle of proportionality. For in his view, "all the remarks we find in the Bible about violence or nonviolence are *ideologies*." (Ibid.) They may illumine the Christian community's current situation, thus helping to fill "the void between faith and concrete historical realities"; but in no sense may they be taken as moral principles for guiding Christian social action.

Far from opening up the frontier joining practical theology and Christian social ethics, Segundo's position actually forecloses the space necessary for "ethics in a more limited sense." If it is true that, by definition, the end justifies the means, and if the critique and reconstruction of ends is a function of the ideologies that faith adopts, then ethical reflection makes no essential or integral contribution to practical religious discourse. In Segundo's theory, it seems, genuine moral perplexities regarding the appropriateness of certain means to certain ends simply cannot arise. Or if they do, they are to be treated as confusions or distortions to be cleared up in the process of "deutero-learning." Nevertheless, as his discussion of violence suggests, Segundo's reductionism is not carried through consistently. While the norm of proportionality governing the use of violence is not presented as a criterion intrinsic to the morality of means, it does raise a question that requires specifically ethical reflection. What warrants the norm of proportionality? It is not logically entailed by Segundo's axiom, "the end justifies the means." If it is a moral norm, and not just a corollary to the "economy of energy," how is it validated? Why should human reason and the teachings of Jesus be followed on this point, in view of the many other points where they are set aside as obsolete ideologies? Unwittingly Segundo demonstrates the need for specifically ethical reflection, even as he attempts to subsume it under the category of ideological discourse.

A rather different approach emerges from Jose Miguez-Bonino's recent work, *Toward a Christian Political Ethics.* (1983) Miguez-Bonino insists that political praxis requires more than a "theological determination of priorities." (1983: 78) It also entails ethical reflection on "the question of transition," that is, on questions of strategy and tactics and the moral guidelines appropriate to them. (Ibid.: 100–115) In contrast to Dussel, Miguez-Bonino sees the practical intent of ethical reflection as a "resource" for social change. (Ibid.: 109) Likewise, his approach differs from Segundo's to the extent that the ethical "question of transition" cannot be disposed of by declaring that the end justifies the means.

While fully aware of the theoretical nature of ethical criteria, Miguez-Bonino upholds the need for a dialectic between abstract ethical principles and the concrete experience of struggle. Such a dialectic ensures that the ethical formulations remain tentative and therefore capable of providing moral guidance without preempting the process of critical reflection within that struggle. As long as this dialectic of ethics and praxis continues, Christian social activists need not fear becoming captive to "both objectivistic procrastination and voluntaristic adventurism" (1983: 107), the twin perils of abstract moral absolutism.

However sketchily presented, Miguez-Bonino recognizes two general moral norms, one concerning ends, the other concerning appropriate means, for political praxis. The question of ends is seen as a reversal of the priorities of "the Constantinian church":

> The true question is not "*What degree of justice (liberation of the poor) is compatible with the maintenance of the existing order?" but "What kind of order, which order is compatible with the exercise of justice (the right of the poor)?* Here alone do we find an adequate point of departure for the theological determination of priorities. The fixed point is "justice, the right of the

> poor." This is the theological premise from which we cannot depart.
>
> (1983: 86)

While this formulation presupposes both a hermeneutic reconstruction of the essence of Christianity (the hope of the Kingdom of God) and a critical social theory interpreting the situation of praxis in Latin America (Ibid.: 54-78), these two operations do not exhaust Miguez-Bonino's agenda for ethical reflection. In view of the concrete ethical dilemmas involved in the exercise of political power, he also proposes a "simple ethical thesis" for testing the appropriateness of means:

> *In carrying out needed structural changes we encounter an inevitable tension between the human costs of their realization and the human costs of their postponement. The basic ethical criterion is the maximizing of universal human possibilities and the minimizing of human costs.*
>
> (1983: 107)

This utilitarian calculus may be applied in both situations of routine political activity and of revolutionary struggle. Thus the traditional criteria of just-war theory, for example, may be used to clarify the ethics of revolutionary violence. (Ibid.: 109) While Miguez-Bonino does not provide a fully developed model for Christian social ethics, he does show how and why practical theology conceived as critical reflection on religious praxis must lead to the threshold of "ethics in a more limited sense."

Miguez-Bonino's sketch is a promising response to critics like James M. Gustafson who rightly judge the work of many practical theologians to be ethically deficient. Miguez-Bonino's position is preferable to Segundo's because he recognizes that normative ethics is different from metaethics. For Miguez-Bonino's dialectic presupposes that Christian moral teaching may still provide distinctive norms for social action, even though these norms can hardly qualify as absolute, in the sense of providing eternally valid principles independent of historical and contextual interpretation. This approach is more sensitive to the complexity of the ethical issues involved in praxis than

Segundo's deutero-learning process with its simplistic discussion of the morality of revolutionary violence. Nevertheless, despite the promise of Miguez-Bonino's proposals, a legacy of ambivalence regarding the role of ethics in praxis remains. Although Miguez-Bonino discerns the threshold of ethical reflection in praxis, he remains rather vague about its theoretical foundations. The logic of our inquiry requires us to ask, "What, then, is the relationship between 'ethics in a more limited sense' and 'critical reflection on religious praxis'?" Rather than chastizing Miguez-Bonino for failing to answer this question fully, we prefer to return to our reformulation of the dialectic of theory and praxis for clues regarding the place of ethics in public discourse.

B. PRAXIS AND ETHICS: THE COMMON GROUND

In our understanding of this dialectic, praxis becomes the struggle to realize a truth-dependent mode of socialization, and theory becomes the genres of public discourse appropriate to this struggle. So we reaffirm Marxism's insight into the unity of theory and praxis, or "the primacy of praxis," but simultaneously we insist that it be formalized and universalized. Within this view of the primacy of praxis, the role of ethics can best be understood by looking once more to Habermas's theory of communicative competence. When the expectations generated in communicative interaction for one reason or another become problematic, questions get asked that require discursive reflection. Among these we located the question of appropriateness raised by regulative speech acts governing the validity claims of various proposals for action. This question of appropriateness formally marks the point of departure for specifically ethical reflection.

While all three of the questions typically raised by speech acts—adequacy, appropriateness, and authenticity—inevitably emerge in praxis, the question of appropriateness represents an irreducibly moral dimension. For in raising this question, the speaker is no longer concerned with problems of strategy and tactics in the narrow sense ("Will it work?"), but with ends and means ("Is it the right thing to do?"). While both questions are implicit in praxis as a truth-dependent mode of socialization, specifically ethical reflection becomes explicit when communicative interaction focuses on the appropriateness of ends and means. The moral question, "Is it the right thing to do?," can only be meaningfully asked and answered when speakers and hearers interact with one another as moral agents.

The theory of communicative competence, moreover, stipulates that such communicative interaction must unfold according to the logic of the ideal speech situation. This counterfactual model defines public discourse as a process in which truth emerges as consensus, that is, as a judgment acknowledged by all participants in the discussion as adequate, appropriate, and authentic. When behavioral norms are under discussion in such an ideal speech situation, all those whose actions may be governed by these norms not only qualify as participants but also must have an equal chance to shape the consensus concerning them. Public discourse thus *in principle* includes an equal chance to make moral judgments and to assess the reasons given for them in ethical argument. Moreover, it also in principle entails a commitment to what ethicists call "the moral point of view," the reasoned supposition that there are patterns of principles which shape human action and which require some form of "logical impartiality," "universalizability," as well as "sociality" in their development. (Cf. Baelz, 1977: 14–27) Commitment to public discourse about the appropriateness of various ends and the means to fulfill them, formally entails a willingness to bind all other participants by one's judgments regarding behavioral norms. The potentially universal scope of participation in public discourse, in short, becomes the ethical criterion of universalizability, or what Habermas calls "the generalizability of interests,"[1] when the consensus in question concerns the moral norms governing praxis.

It will come as no surprise that Habermas's view of generalizable interests exhibits all the limits and possibilities characteristic of his formal procedural model of theory and praxis. On the one hand, it allows him to eliminate any "decisionistic" misconception of the moral point of view which would make it the product of particular acts of faith; on the other hand, it does not allow him to conceive of the moral point of view and its procedures as if they constituted in themselves a universal way of life. Both points must be understood if Habermas's theory of generalizable interests is to remain coherent with the dialectic of theory and praxis.

By arguing that the principle of universalizability is implicit in the basic formal structures of communicative competence, Habermas grounds the moral point of view not upon the values cherished by some particular—and hence inevitably disputed—tradition of moral philosophy, but upon that which is always already presupposed in any successful communication, whether about values or not. Ethics therefore in principle is not optional for praxis. Praxis cannot be praxis without including the moral point of view in a moment of specifically ethical reflection. At the same time, however, such a grounding cannot account for the substantive moral dynamics of any particular tradition of praxis. The interests advanced in such a community's praxis thus will always strive to be generalizable, insofar as the *intention* of generalizability is operative in everything that is said and done about them. But, as we shall see in what follows, in no way does this intention preempt the irreducibly perspectival character of a particular community's praxis and the ideology that sustains it. While interests, in the moral point of view, may be ***generalizable***, rarely, if ever, can they be fully ***generalized***. Nor need they be for Habermas's theory of truth as consensus to be operative in specifically ethical reflection. Thus while ethics remains indispensable for praxis as a truth-dependent mode of socialization, the fact that such modes are irreducibly plural and perspectival means that the specifically ethical reflection occurring within them is inevitably historical and contextual.

Let us move beyond these preliminaries to show how generalizable interests are actually operative in the process of forming a true consensus about praxis. To assert and defend the appropriateness of any action or policy is to imply, if not make explicit, that the action or policy in question represents "the *common* interest ascertained *without deception*." (Habermas, 1975:108) Public discourse, among other things, seeks to validate this claim. It is, as Habermas insists, a cognitive claim, and one with both descriptive and normative dimensions:

> The interest [will prove to be] common [if] the constraint-free consensus permits only what *all* can want; it [will prove to be]

> free of deception [when] even the interpretations of needs in which *each individual* must be able to recognize what he wants become the object of discursive will-formation.
>
> (Ibid.)

How does this definition of generalizable interests secure the basis for ethical reflection in public discourse? Public discourse concerning potentially generalizable interests contains two logically distinct forms of inquiry: critical self-reflection and ethical reflection, the former to test for authenticity, the latter to test for appropriateness. Both forms of reflection are joined in a culture's "interpretation of needs." By "needs" Habermas means what an individual or a group feels is required to sustain their way of life. Needs may be experienced as "wants" or they may go as yet unrecognized. In either case, they have a history. To make them "the object of discursive will-formation" is, in effect, to enter the process of critical self-reflection in the most basic sense. It is to bring one's own needs to consciousness, in order to submit them to the test of reflective criticism.

Reflective criticism of this sort may be triggered, for example, by allowing ourselves to be personally confronted by the critique of "nuclearism" launched by Robert J. Lifton and Richard Falk in *Indefensible Weapons* (1982). Their psychological and ideological "counterdiscourse" may force us to admit that our tendency to "stop worrying and start learning to live with The Bomb" is itself symptomatic of a process of psychic numbing that has had profound consequences in shaping our actual way of life as a way of death. Discursive will-formation implies that we can, both as individuals and as a society, become aware of this process and seek to overcome the distortions in our culture that result from it. Critical self-reflection, in this example, consciousness-raising about how the ideology of "nuclearism" creates many of our previously taken-for-granted "needs" and represses others, will prove to be free of deception when each person is satisfied that this critique truly enhances his or her capacities for authentic development.

The question raised by "what *all* can want," on the other hand, concerns the distinctively ethical dimension. Just as we argued that formal criteria of appropriateness and authenticity are logically distinct, so here we contend that ethics is logically distinct from consciousness-raising, though the two remain dialectically related. To return to our example of the criticism of nuclearism: If I can only be liberated from bondage to the processes of psychic numbing by working to change the culture of society as a whole, my need for authentic development inevitably raises the question of what is appropriately in the "*common* interest." For it may well be that the policies I propose to eliminate nuclearism will conflict with this nation's authentic need to defend itself against unjust aggression. Furthermore, this nation's interest in security may conflict with humanity's authentic need to avoid a nuclear holocaust. From such conflicts arise the moral dilemmas involved in evaluating policies of nuclear deterrence, arms control, and disarmament. (Cf. Geyer, 1982) Critical self-reflection thus passes over into specifically ethical reflection, as the authentic needs of various groups submit to the ethical test for generalizable interests.

Conflicts of interest, in short, give rise to specifically ethical reflection. In contrast to a pragmatism, which advocates compromise on the assumption that no interest can make valid generalizable claims, Habermas argues that conflicts of interest may derive precisely from such competing claims. If they do, then compromise is clearly inappropriate. Alternatively, he proposes that public discourse use the ethical criterion implicit in the formal characteristics of the ideal-speech situation. A truly generalizable interest thus emerges from the following question:

> How would the members of a social system, at a given stage in the development of productive forces, have collectively and bindingly interpreted their needs (and which norms would they have accepted as justified) if they could and would have decided on organization of social intercourse through discursive will-formation, with adequate knowledge of the limiting conditions and functional imperatives of their society?
>
> (1975: 113)

If a particular interest can be justified as one that would have been honored under these conditions by all the participants in public discourse, it qualifies as in the "common interest." As a truly generalizable interest, it overrides any particular interests that fail to meet this test. It cannot justifiably be compromised.

In this schema social injustice is defined as "the suppression of generalizable interests." (Ibid.) So Habermas provides a basis for defining the moral norm of justice in a manner formally analogous to the distinction between communicative competence and systematically distorted communication. Injustice is defined, neither as a refusal to honor any particular tradition's concrete historical ideal, nor as an acquiescence in the compromises that inevitably occur in social praxis, but as the failure to act on what could and would have been regarded as a truly generalizable interest. Conversely, social justice is done when generalizable interests are enforced as a matter of public policy.

Note, however, that any moral content elaborated under this formal definition of justice and injustice must be contextual and not absolute. First, there is no list of generalizable interests apart from the processes of "discursive will-formation," which continually respond to the concrete "limiting conditions and functional imperatives" characteristic of a specific society at a particular moment of its historical development. Second, in line with what we said earlier, a particular community's concrete historical ideal, however perspectival its origins, may be *generalizable.* But it cannot be regarded as *generalized* until it has been persuasively argued as in the "*common* interest" of the society in which the community is situated historically. Just as orthodoxy and orthopraxis cannot be sustained in the dialectic of theory and praxis, so neither of these stipulations will support a moral absolutism in ethics.

Let us illustrate how specifically ethical reflection based on generalizable interests works, by returning to the problem of formulating an appropriate response to the critique of nuclearism. An excellent example of what is involved when religious ideologies attempt specifically ethical reflection in the mode of public discourse was given in the recent pastoral letter of the U.S. National Conference of Catholic Bishops, "The Challenge of Peace: God's Promise and Our Response." Among other things, without explicitly mentioning the Nuclear Freeze movement, the letter urges "immediate, bilateral, verifiable agreements to halt the testing, production and deployment of new nuclear weapons systems." (Cf. *National Catholic Reporter*, June, 17, 1983: 6) While they do not use Habermas's terminology, the bishops clearly argue that such a halt is in the "*common* interest" of the United States as well as humanity as a whole. Their point of departure in making this judgment of appropriateness, not surprisingly, is perspectival. After reviewing the history of Catholic tradition on war and peace, they conclude that Christian witness must utter an unequivocal "No" to nuclear war. Yet they argue their case not just as an authentic application of the essence of Christian witness to the Kingdom of God, but also in terms of its appropriateness to the publicly available criteria of just-war theory. (Cf. Ibid.: 8) Christians, in other words, are not self-deceived in thinking that support for the Nuclear Freeze is consistent with their authentic need to share "the peace of Christ" with the world; nor are they merely seeking to impose their own parochial vision on a pluralistic society whose interests lie elsewhere. Fully aware of the "limiting conditions and functional imperatives" of this society in a disordered but interdependent world (Ibid.: 22–23), the bishops imply that all persons—whether American or not, Catholic or not—would choose to organize their social intercourse without further reliance on the threat of nuclear war. To implement policies consistent with this generalizable interest is to do justice; to resist them is injustice. Be that as it may, our point here is not to argue the substantive merits of this response to the critique of nuclearism, but to show that Habermas's model provides both a formal criterion for ethical reflection beyond critical self-reflection and the outlines of a principal of social justice consistent with it.

While Habermas does not go beyond this polarity to formulate a systematic philosophical ethics, his suggestion does advance the discussion. For it vindicates the principle of universalizability, without adopting any particular moral tradition's explanation of it. (1975: 89) Grounded in the structure of communicative interaction and discourse, universalizability thus is conceived as a criterion of public discourse seeking genuine consensus about the appropriateness of various policies and the validity of the moral norms that warrant them. Yet despite its promise, Habermas's formal ethic needs to be developed further if it is to be fully adequate to the questions implicit in the primacy of praxis. Left as it stands Habermas's ethics of public discourse tends to emphasize reflection on ends to the neglect of reflection on the appropriateness of means.

That Habermas's conception of the role of ethics in praxis must include consideration of means as well as ends, is evident from his critique of Georg Lukacs's apology for "iron discipline" within the Communist Party. If Habermas shared Segundo's metaethical position, namely, that "the end justifies the means" because "a 'means'. . . is precisely that and nothing more" (1976: 171), he would have no moral basis for questioning the appropriateness of an organizational structure whose strategic success and tactical effectiveness have been well documented. Nevertheless, he does reject this form of Communist Party organization, precisely because it preempts the possibility of public discourse in its own operations even as it proclaims itself the "organization of Enlightenment." The question of Communist Party organization is never a question of mere means, but a question of how this means itself embodies the professed end, Enlightenment, of how praxis intends to create a truth-dependent mode of socialization. Habermas's critique of Lukacs implies that the question of means cannot be trivialized by assuming, as Segundo apparently does, that "to will the end is to will the means to it." On the contrary, the formal characteristics of communicative interaction and discourse suggest that the question of means is never "precisely that and nothing more."

Indeed, with a little imagination we can foresee concrete situations of praxis in which moral perplexity about the means chosen to carry out a certain policy may also lead to a reassessment of that policy as a morally appropriate end. This is especially likely in a model of public discourse that allows unrestricted scope for critical questioning. Were we to adopt the Catholic bishops' "No" to nuclearism as an appropriately generalizable interest for our disordered but interdependent world, we would still have to follow them into something like their painstaking analysis of nuclear deterrence and its alternatives.

However universalizable their consensus about the need to avoid nuclear war, the appropriate means to this end are not made clear simply by affirming the end. Inasmuch as nuclear deterrence may plausibly be regarded as such a means, the bishops grant it a "strictly conditional moral acceptance." (*National Catholic Reporter*, June 17,

1983: 19) What makes this acceptance conditional is that it can be revoked any time deterrence ceases to serve this end. Were the possession of nuclear weapons themselves to be seen as destabilizing, for example, because they appeared "to be useful primarily in a first-strike" (Ibid.), they would no longer be a deterrent, but an inducement to nuclear war. Once that verdict on the nature and intent of these weapons were made, the bishops would either revoke their strictly conditional acceptance of the means, or be compelled to revise their conception of the end, our generalizable interest in seeking peace and disarmament and in preventing nuclear war. In either case, ethical reflection on means and ends is always dialectical. Questions in one area continually reshape our judgments about the other. Public discourse must be capable of addressing questions from both areas if it is to be fully adequate to the primacy of praxis.

Habermas's theory of generalizable interests allows us to locate ethical reflection in the formal dialectic of theory and praxis. No more and no less. Like the theory of communicative competence such an understanding of ethical reflection is strictly formal, and in this lies both its distinctive contribution and its necessary limitation. Like other formal or procedural theories of public morality the theory of generalizable interests does not provide us with a compelling vision of the good society and the possibilities for authentic selfhood within it. Such visions are always perspectival: they are formulated hermeneutically and articulated systematically in the various praxeological models of the human aspirations characteristic of religious and secular ideologies. Far from being a "rational" substitute for these, Habermas's theory merely reveals what is logically entailed in all of them. It rules out no particular perspective prior to public discourse, save those by definition that would deny the distinction between strategic action and communicative interaction, or those that assume that all visions are simply reflections of an all-pervasive will-to-power. By insisting that ideologies make cognitively testable moral claims, and by showing how such claims may be understood and adjudicated, Habermas establishes the place of ethical reflection in praxis without predetermining the conclusions that such reflection may lead to. We arrive once more at the threshold of "ethics in a more limited sense," only this time without ambivalence. What Habermas contributes that the Latin American liberation theologians lack is a comprehensively formal understanding of the dialectic of theory and praxis. Having clarified the logic of ethical inquiry in praxis, we may now return to a generic analysis in order to see how this inquiry unfolds in the related genres of practical theology and Christian social ethics. Encouraged by Habermas's theory, we see every advantage in setting aside the legacy of ambivalence in favor of a more constructive relationship of mutual dependence.

C. TWO GENRES OF PUBLIC DISCOURSE: PRACTICAL THEOLOGY AND CHRISTIAN SOCIAL ETHICS

Christian social ethicists, for a number of generations, have been reflecting theologically on the questions raised by Christian social praxis, questions ranging from the nature of the relationship of Church and State to the distinctively Christian agenda, if any, for social change. This is the case not only within Protestant communities where theologians like Walter Rauschenbusch, Reinhold and H. Richard Niebuhr helped create a distinctively American tradition in Christian social ethics (Cf. Gustafson, 1971: 23–82), but also in the Catholic community where exceptional thinkers like Orestes Brownson, John A. Ryan, and John Courtney Murray have anticipated many of the elements of an emerging "American strategic theology." (Cf. Coleman, 1982: 71–107) In both traditions, tacitly or otherwise ethicists strove to fulfill the relevant standards of public discourse, insofar as they understood them. For their inquiries addressed the difficult ethical questions involving Christianity's generalizable interests in an increasingly secular pluralistic society.

Characteristic of both traditions has been a sense of vocation according to which the social ethicist is "to make particular moral judgments about particular social proposals and to suggest optional courses of moral action which might be judged morally approvable." (Gustafson, 1974: 187) Such particular judgments, typically, have been worked out contextually, that is, from within an ideological framework that, whatever its concrete shape, was a functional equivalent to critical reflection on religious praxis. Nevertheless, the vocation of making particular judgments and providing the ethical warrants for them has meant that the genre of Christian social ethics, despite its similarities with practical theology, has been governed by a different agenda of ethical reflection. This difference of perspective accounts for the typical strengths and limitations of both genres. While practical theology runs the risk of moving from theology to politics without going through a stage of more careful ethical reflection, Christian social ethics tends to blunt prophetic criticism with a "premature acceptance of the institutional frameworks within which particular issues are raised." (Gustafson, 1974: 187)

James Gustafson has made one of the very few attempts to develop an account of the genre of Christian social ethics on the basis of this distinctive sense of vocation. He lists "four base points for Christian moral discourse": (1) situational or social analysis, (2) fundamental theological affirmations, (3) moral principles, and (4) a conception of Christian existence. (1971: 117–25) If we focus on the second and fourth of these base points, it seems clear that Gustafson has blurred the distinction between practical theology and Christian social ethics. Certainly there is no crime involved in this, for inventive combinations are the hallmark of successful practical discourse. Our purpose, however, is to tend the fences which both join and separate the genres. Given the ethicist's concern with making particular judgments about particular social proposals, *in practice* the first and third base points will usually be stressed. The distinctive agenda for Christian social ethics thus can be reformulated: In light of situational analysis, moral principles function to make explicit the ethical implications of fundamental theological affirmations and to structure conceptions of Christian existence, so that specific moral guidelines appropriate to particular courses of action are forthcoming.[2]

The complementarity of the two genres emerges when we turn to the one genuine area of overlapping activity—the production of a set of "middle axioms" for shaping concrete religious praxis. Gustafson locates the middle axioms approach, outlined originally by J.H. Oldham and developed by John C. Bennett, within the contextualist understanding of the genre of Christian social ethics which we have just described. (Gustafson, 1971: 114) Inspired by the Social Gospel's attempt to "give relevance and point to the Christian ethic," Oldham described middle axioms as "attempts to define the directions in which, in a particular state of society, Christian faith must express itself." (Oldham, 1937: 193) What Oldham had in mind was some kind of provisional statement that would bridge the gap between "a living fellowship with God" and "movements for the establishment of social justice and the advancement of the common good." (Ibid.: 220) While there are a host of theological considerations informing Oldham's approach to middle axioms, Bennett's focus highlighted their status as mediating principles. (Cf. McCann, 1981c: 75–77) Middle axioms formally are "more concrete than a universal ethical principle and less specific than a program that includes legislation and political strategy." (Bennett, 1946: 77)

Bennett illuminated this concept of a middle axiom by offering a timely example: the Federal Council of Churches' "critical but definite support for the San Francisco Charter and the United Nations organization." "Notice the progression," Bennett remarks:

> guiding principles about which there could be no disagreement; a middle axiom which had behind it a substantial consensus but which related Christian decision to a concrete reality, the United Nations, about which there could be a considerable debate, especially if one belonged to a neutral or enemy nation; and finally support of a particular program which was even more ambiguous and about which there was less agreement. Christians must move from one to three or to some equivalent of three, but as they do so the degree of authority that can be claimed in the name of Christian ethics becomes weaker with each step.
>
> (1946: 79)

Middle axioms thus occur at the intersection of two mediations. The first, an explicit one, mediates between abstract formulations of "guiding principles" and ethical reflections on a concrete "particular program." Equally important is the second, implicit mediation between particular communities of faith and society as a whole. Here each community's concrete agenda for Christian social action judges and is judged by the political arena where consensus is sought regarding matters of public policy. At the first pole in each mediation there is authoritative agreement within and among ideological communities, but only about matters of general principle; at the second, there is the concreteness of specific action guidelines, but insofar as these are necessarily prudential they remain controversial and weaker in their degree of authority. Consistent with Oldham's sense of them as an attempt to discern the signs of the times (1937: 223), Bennett argued that middle axioms allow for a degree of provisional guidance in formulating social goals without preempting the particular moral judgments that Christians—both as individual citizens and as participants in a community of faith—are required to make.

Given the complexity of this kind of mediation, it is not surprising that critics of the middle axioms approach have questioned its theoretical coherence as well as its practical effectiveness. Paul Ramsey, for example, doubted that ethical analysis would exhaust itself with the formulation of middle axioms. "What stands between a 'universal ethical principle' and a 'middle axiom,' " he asked, "or between one of these and specific plans for action? Surely, not another 'middle axiom.' " (1950: 350) Fear of this logical abyss, coupled with growing skepticism regarding the competence of Christian social ethicists to formulate particular moral judgments led Ralph Potter to reject not only middle axioms but also the broadly contextual understanding of Christian social ethics that he once espoused. (Cf. Potter, 1969: 23–4) Instead of continuing to work within his own version of the four base points, Potter now proposed concentrating on "what makes Christian social ethics *ethics* . . . the analysis of patterns of thinking about right and wrong, good and bad, just and unjust." (Potter, 1972: 113) In effect Potter rejected the traditional sense of vocation that included moral advocacy in favor of a professional division of labor in which ethical analysis alone was the distinctive task of the Christian social ethicist. (Cf. Stassen, 1977) Striving to overcome the taint of "dilettantism" in Christian social ethics, Potter unwittingly compounded the confusion about middle axioms. By defining his starting point as "the immediate, specific, existential perplexities of those who, perhaps already in receipt of broad guidelines and middle axioms, still do not know what to do to perform the appropriate action," he covertly reintroduced middle axioms into his definition of ethical analysis. (1972: 105) If Christians are already in receipt of middle axioms, where do they come from, and how are they formulated and tested?

At this point Habermas's theory of generalizable interests may be of some use. We contend that, regardless of the terms in which they are couched, *middle axioms are an attempt to formulate generalizable interests in Christian moral discourse.* Furthermore, given the complexity of the questions involved in validating generalizable interests, *middle axioms are the responsibility of both practical theology and Christian social ethics,* according to the complementarity of their perspectives. In short, we propose that practical theology should be regarded as a form of macroethical analysis which typically terminates in the formulation of a true consensus about middle axioms; whereas Christian social ethics should be regarded as a form of microethical analysis in which middle axioms function as practical hypotheses constantly open to revision on the basis of the particular moral judgments on the social practices and actions warranted by these hypotheses. Ethical reflection occurs in both genres, but it moves from different levels of generality towards the common task of formulating middle axioms.

In what sense does any given middle axiom exhibit the formal characteristics of a generalizable interest? Let us return to Bennett's example, Christian support for the San Francisco Charter and the proposed United Nations organization. Inasmuch as a generalizable interest involves both individual and common interests, we must suppose that the Federal Council of Churches' recommendation involved two cognitively testable validity claims: (1) that such support embodies the Christian communities' authentic need to witness to the ideals of justice and peace at that particular historic moment; (2) that such support can also be recommended to American society as a whole, insofar as the Council regards it as opening up possibilities for a global "organization of social intercourse" that all would affirm if all were to participate in discursive will-formation about it. The first claim, we contend, involves the critical hermeneutics of practical theology: A middle axiom, insofar as it discerns the signs of the times, functions as the practical corollary mediating whatever ethical implications are evident in any restatement of the essence of Christianity. Such hermeneutical judgments are the source of what Bennett referred to as "guiding principles about which there could be no disagreement" within the particular religious community. The second claim, which presupposes translating these judgments into the praxeological models of moral responsibility and cultural synthesis already described, submits the guiding principles to the test of universalizability. As a result, what this hermeneutic process discerns, in fact, will represent the generalizable interest whether society as a whole is fully aware of that hermeneutic process or not. It claims recognition as a viable social goal, as a live option for a particular culture and not as a private vision inspiring the commitments of only one religious community.

If Bennett's example seems vacuous, recall the historic moment in which the Federal Council made its recommendations. At stake was the framework in which the postwar world was to be organized by the victorious Allies. To give "critical but definite support to the United Nations" meant that, in the view of the Council, Christian witness could not be content merely to pray for peace, or to acquiesce either in a return to the isolationism of prewar American foreign policy or in a new division of the world into militarily based hegemonies, such as those which actually resulted from the Cold War. To discern the Christian hope for peace in the emerging United Nations organization was to envision a cultural synthesis in which the rule of international law would ultimately prevail; it was to accept moral responsibility for a process that might radically transform the existing nation-state sovereignty system. This middle axiom thus was more controversial and concretely political than theological generalities about the role of Christian witness in post-war reconciliation, and yet not so detailed as concrete policies would have to be regarding the appropriate political and legal procedures for identifying and adjudicating the conflicting interests among nations. A more recent example, like the Catholic bishops' stance on nuclear deterrence, would disclose a similarly complex pattern of cognitively testable validity claims regarding a generalizable interest. What is left to us now is to understand how these claims may be distributed within the complementary genres of practical theology and Christian social ethics.

While both genres involve middle axioms, practical theology seeks to rationalize them in terms of a praxeological model, whereas

Christian social ethics seeks to analyze the moral dilemmas involved in their implementation. As a form of macroethical analysis, practical theology is primarily concerned with the hermeneutic questions raised by Christian social praxis. A fully developed model of practical theology, however, will pursue these questions until three interrelated practical judgments are made: (1) a determination of the essence of Christianity; (2) an objectification of this essence into praxeological models capable of orienting both self and society in the direction of ethical responsibility and cultural synthesis; and (3) a normative restatement of this essence as a middle axiom for guiding Christian social praxis, that is, a moral discernment of the signs of the times capable of generating action-guiding principles for society as a whole. (See Figure 6.1) Such middle axioms must be formulated as generalizable interests, and be capable of validating that claim in public discourse. In short, practical theology's agenda for specifically ethical reflection is complete with the formulation of a valid middle axiom. This final operation brings us to the threshold of Christian social ethics without preempting the agenda that will be pursued in that genre.

Figure 6.1

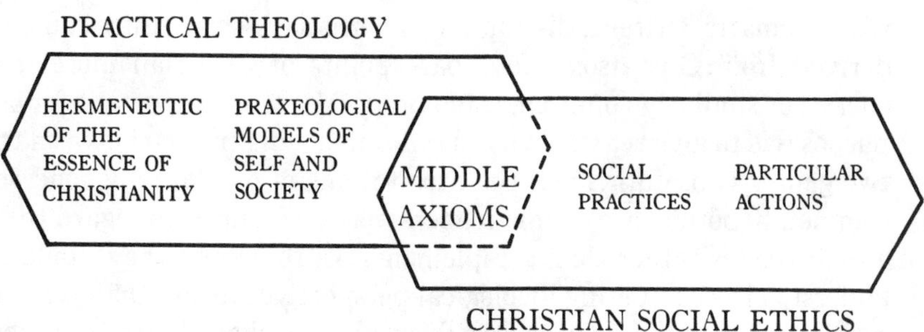

While a comprehensive account of Christian social ethics is beyond the scope of this book, we must clarify the role of middle axioms in that genre in order to make our thesis persuasive. Bennett and Gustafson are surely correct in viewing middle axioms as the agenda setters for Christian social ethics. Gustafson has accurately described them as "anchors and compasses" for Christian moral discourse. (1971: 114) Nevertheless, we also agree with Ramsey and Potter that this agenda is hardly exhausted by a formulation of Christianity's generalizable interests. In Christian social ethics "*how* we do *what* we do," as Ramsey points out, "is as important as our goals." (Ibid.) Potter, in other words, is essentially correct in noting that Christian social ethics focuses on the perplexities of those who are "already in receipt of broad guidelines and middle axioms." (1972: 105) We differ with Potter, however, on two important points: first, we see no reason to think that this focus rules out an advocacy role for Christian social ethicists; second, we insist on this critical role precisely because Christian social ethicists are never merely in receipt of middle axioms, but always actively engaged in testing them against the concrete problems of implementation that constitute Christian social praxis. As we argued in the previous section of this chapter, simply pursuing the ethical question of means and ends will inevitably raise issues that may require a re-thinking of the middle axioms which guide our actions. The threshold between practical theology and Christian social ethics opens in both directions.

This account of the relationship between the two genres is necessarily schematic. Criteria distinctive of Christian social ethics could be derived from Gustafson's four base points of Christian moral discourse, or similarly comprehensive proposals. More important for our purposes is to give reasons why maintaining a distinction between the two genres is useful. Given the broad range of overlapping concerns common to both genres, some readers may be inclined to regard them as substitutes rather than complements. In that case, they would be understood as competing ideological perspectives rather than collaborating genres of public discourse. However, we share Potter's distress over the dilettantism that ensues from well-meaning attempts to cover too broad an agenda. If this agenda is more fruitfully approached by respecting the distinction between the two genres, practical theology will avoid dilettantism by concentrating on what is involved in *the practical intent* of religious ideologies in a pluralistic society; while Christian social ethics will do the same by addressing the moral dilemmas that inevitably emerge as religious communities seek to *implement that intent* in and for society as a whole. In order to illustrate the advantages of this proposal, let us conclude with a case study in which collaboration between the two genres might help to resolve an ideological conflict between two would-be middle axioms.

D. SOCIALISM VS. CAPITALISM: ANOTHER MISPLACED DEBATE

One of the more recent signs of the times is the reopening of substantive debate on the choice between socialism and capitalism among theologians in this country. Robert Benne's important work, *The Ethic of Democratic Capitalism* (1981), for example, challenges the remarkable degree of consensus among the new generation of practical theologians in opting for some sort of socialism, preferably democratic socialism. Although Benne himself once accepted this consensus, he now finds he must dissent on the basis of what he shares with the others, namely, a sense of the crucial role political economy plays in interpreting social praxis. (Benne, 1981: 1–18) His dissent comes at a time when other theologians, often decisively influenced by Latin American liberation theology, are rediscovering a "radical imperative" for socialism. (Cf. Bennett, 1975; Coleman, 1982: 102) In either case, opting for either capitalism or socialism means doing the kind of critical reflection we have defined as practical theology. In what follows we will discuss two extremes in this debate, the case for democratic capitalism made by Michael Novak and the decision for socialism defended by Gustavo Gutierrez. Neither is finally persuasive, we will argue, because both develop arguments that are curiously incomplete. Failing to acknowledge the generic distinction between practical theology and Christian social ethics, both Novak and Gutierrez stumble over the problem of generalizable interests and their implementation. Consistent with the framework of public discourse proposed here, we will conclude by showing how this debate might fruitfully be recast.

The comparison between Novak and Gutierrez seems apt, not simply because each represents an extreme in unguarded enthusiasm for the options advocated. More to the point, each in his own way is determined to do theology as critical reflection on religious praxis, and each, again in his own way, sees political economy playing a decisive role in sorting out the ideological dimensions of the debate. Given the structure of their arguments, we conclude that their options, democratic capitalism and revolutionary socialism, are intended as middle axioms, the conflicting action-guidelines that emerge from two substantively different practical theologies.

Let us begin with their understanding of theology as some sort of critical reflection on praxis. Gutierrez's *A Theology of Liberation* (1973) is groundbreaking not only because it formulates so many of the basic categories of the new practical theology, but also because it seeks to show how these are methodologically required by a Marxist interpretation of the primacy of praxis. (Gutierrez, 1973: 6–15) What is not clear is the praxis orientation of Novak's *The Spirit of Democratic Capitalism.* (1982) While Novak eschews the terminology of praxis, a similar program is implicit in his advocacy of "the Anglo-American sense of *practice*, the experimental method, pragmatism, and self-reform" (Novak, 1982: 290), as the appropriate mode of theological reflection. No one, at this stage of the discussion, should doubt the affinities linking the methodologies of Marxism and American pragmatism. (Cf. Bernstein, 1971)

Within these comparable methodological assumptions, both develop a critical hermeneutic of the essence of Christianity mediated by some form of critical social theory. In Novak's perspective the study of political economy leads him to criticize the social teachings of the modern papacy as obsolete because they are based on the model of a static feudal society. It also encourages him to approach the question of justice no longer in terms of equitable distribution, but in terms of the problem of "producing wealth and creating economic development." (Novak, 1982: 24) In Novak's hermeneutics the ideals of democratic capitalism and the aspirations of Judaism and Christianity become the common components of a cultural synthesis because, among other things, a theology of "creativity" is fundamental to both. (Ibid.: 246)

Gutierrez's reading of Latin American political economy is equally decisive. In light of Cardoso and Faletto's economic analysis of Latin American "underdevelopment" as the necessary consequence of North American capitalist "development," Gutierrez repudiates the reformist politics of the Christian Democrats and their religious justification in the ideology of "New Christendom." (Gutierrez, 1973: 81–92) Dependency, or the unjustifiable economic domination of the "center" over the "periphery," can only be overcome through liberation, concretely envisioned as revolutionary socialism. Hermeneutically, Gutierrez links the political demand for liberation with the vision of "Christ the Liberator" which conveys the essence of Christianity. (Ibid.: 175–8)

While neither practical theologian totally identifies his concrete historical ideal with the Kingdom of God, the relationship between them tends to be negative in Novak's theology and positive in Gutierrez's. Thus while Novak emphasizes divine transcendence over all political and economic systems, he also declares that without democratic capitalism Christianity "would be poorer and less free." (1982: 336) Gutierrez, by contrast, so closely connects the dynamics of liberation and salvation that the one "'Christofinalized' history" must include the struggle for revolutionary socialism. (1973: 172–78)

Novak's argument is implicit in the trinitarian terms by which he defines democratic capitalism: "a democratic polity, an economy based on markets and incentives, and a moral-cultural system which is pluralistic and, in the largest sense, liberal." (Novak, 1982: 14) Out of this triad a set of ideals emerges which, he believes, are not incompatible with the theology of traditional Christianity. These he sketches in terms of six critical correlations or analogies: (1) The pluralism-in-unity evident in the triadic structure of democratic capitalism is another vestigial sign of the Trinitarian nature of the Divine Life: the key to both is the problem of "how to build human community without damage to human individuality." (Ibid.: 338) (2) Democratic capitalism's realistic approach to the limits, weaknesses, irrationalities, and evil forces in human nature resonates well with what Novak takes to be the point of the mystery of the Incarnation, namely, that in redeeming the world, "God did not overpower history but respected its constraints." (Ibid.: 340) (3) The Christian ethos conceived under the sign of Grace opens up possibilities for ennobling our natural appetite for competition. (4) An elective affinity binds the Christian doctrine of original sin to a social system that paradoxically transforms private vices into public virtues. (5) Whatever its historic embodiment in various Christian communities, the concept of separation of Church and State entails the autonomy of political and economic systems, which only democratic capitalism has respected. (6) Properly understood, the theological virtue of charity presupposes a vision of material and spiritual bounty that corresponds to the creative aspirations of democratic capitalism. Taken together, Novak's analogies suggest that to have understood the Judeo-Christian vision is "to glimpse a world in which the political economy of democratic capitalism makes sense." (Ibid.: 355)

By contrast, Gutierrez's argument depends upon a different type of analogy that responds more immediately to the requirements of social transformation and to the figural significance of religious narratives but less directly to the doctrinal traditions of Judeo-Christianity. The key, of course, remains his distinctive interpretation of Latin America's Christofinalized history. Within this hermeneutical framework salvation history as depicted in the Bible becomes the source of historical analogies linking God's salvific activity with contemporary struggles for liberation. The Exodus becomes paradigmatic because it reveals God's political solidarity with the oppressed. (Gutierrez, 1973: 159) Everything else from Creation to the Second Coming of Christ is seen in terms of this paradigm of revelation. Because political economy shows that international capitalism can do nothing more than increase the misery of the oppressed, it is clear that God's solidarity is with those who struggle for revolutionary socialism. This point is confirmed throughout this work, as the analogy between salvation history and liberating praxis is developed in a series of mutually illuminating rhetorical transferences. (Cf. McCann, 1981a: 186–93) Given the fact that Gutierrez's type of analogy is more concerned with praxis than with theology, it is not surprising that he spends even less time describing his model of revolutionary socialism than does Novak in denouncing it. Beyond demanding an end to neocolonialism and asserting Latin America's right to self-determination,

Gutierrez does little to clarify the political, economic, and moral-cultural structures essential to this concrete historical ideal.

Despite the lack of perfect symmetry, we believe that Novak and Gutierrez are doing essentially the same thing: formulating a middle axiom for Christian social praxis that is both "more concrete than a universal ethical principle and less specific than a program that includes legislation and political strategy." (Bennett, 1946: 77) Because they are developing their middle axioms as practical theologians, we can appeal to our account of middle axioms to explain why the debate between these thinkers miscarries. Bluntly stated, the problem with the middle axioms of Novak and Gutierrez is that neither is developed explicitly as a generalizable interest. Even with their diverging emphases on theory and praxis, Novak and Gutierrez both unwittingly restrict themselves to arguing for the authenticity of their concrete historical ideals. Were they to make explicit the question of appropriateness, that is, whether either ideal is in their society's generalizable interest, their arguments would have to move toward the threshold of ethics in a way that neither of them seems inclined to do.

If Novak were to present democratic capitalism as a truly generalizable interest, he would have to show that it represents "the *common* interest ascertained *without deception*." (Habermas, 1975: 108) Specifically, he would have to show that the members of a social system would ratify his choice given "adequate knowledge of the limiting conditions and functional imperatives of their society." An argument fulfilling these formal conditions could not rest content with reasserting the merits of economic liberty or with denouncing the failures of Soviet-styled experiments in all three dimensions of his triadic model of society. It would have to address the problem of economic justice more rigorously, either by arguing that the current inequalities generated by the system are in the common interest or by showing how they can be rectified without changing the basic structures of the system. Given Novak's negative correlation linking democratic capitalism and Christianity, i.e., that they are *not incompatible* when properly understood, his theological analogies must be supported by an ethical analysis that begins with the question of generalizability. Had he done this, however, his case would look less like an apology for the *status quo* and more like a program for genuine reform. A fully developed middle axiom of democratic capitalism would have led him, in our estimation, toward Christian social ethics in the manner of Robert Benne's attempt to synthesize Reinhold Niebuhr's Christian realism and John Rawls's theory of justice. (Cf. Benne, 1981: 181–262)

By the same token, if Gutierrez were to show why revolutionary socialism does represent the generalizable interest in Latin America, he would not rest his case so heavily on the alleged failure of the "decade of development." (Gutierrez, 1973: 82–84) Beyond reasserting the merits of economic justice, he would have to address the problem of how economic progress is possible under conditions of radical social change. His model would have to be specific enough to show why it promises changes sufficiently plausible to convince the members of the Latin American social system that revolutionary socialism is in the common interest. Latin American aspirations for liberation may be authentic, but can Gutierrez show why they may be fulfilled appropriately only in the praxis of socialist revolution? Were he to take the question of generalizable interests seriously, he would have to construct an ethical analysis of the social costs involved, similar to the one outlined by José Miguez-Bonino. (1983: 107) His argument, then, would look less like a utopian dream and more like a mediating principle capable of setting a viable social goal for Christian social praxis in Latin America.

This analysis suggests that there can be no shortcircuiting of the key moment of ethical reflection in developing a middle axiom. We have suggested how the criterion of generalizable interest provides a framework for discussing middle axioms, and what sorts of questions would arise if the ethical dimension of those axioms were examined. Such questions, however, take us beyond the genre of practical theology and into the genre of Christian social ethics. For just as the former formulates middle axioms from within a "macro" analysis of the social system as a whole, so the latter reflects upon them within a "micro" analysis of specific moral dilemmas typically generated by the given system or any activity constituted by it. Let us conclude this chapter by showing how both "macro" and "micro" perspectives may be related in a more fruitful approach to debate over capitalism and socialism.

For the sake of our analysis of these perspectives, we will assume that Novak's democratic capitalism is a plausible, albeit incomplete, model for a practical theology. Insofar as it provides a *prima facie* legitimation of democratic capitalism, it not only addresses the agenda for practical theology but also may serve as the point of departure for Christian social ethics. In other words, the praxis inspired by Novak's theology and his middle axiom inevitably will generate perplexities calling for further ethical analysis in specialized areas, for example, in business ethics and in political ethics. In the context of Novak's practical theology, we can expect Christian social ethics to concern itself with problems like ethical investment strategies, wage scale differentials in multinational corporations, political lobbying, tax policy, affirmative action, and whistle blowing. Christian social ethics in the context of a practical theology legitimating democratic capitalism, in short, will tend to concentrate on defining the meaning and ethical implications of corporate social responsibility for the interrelated political, economic, and cultural subsystems. For this to be a truly dialectical process, however, problems arising at either the macro or the micro level of analysis must be capable of generating radical criticism of the middle axiom operative in both. Novak's middle axiom, for example, might fail either because practical theology is finally unable to accept the adequacy of his theological analogies or the appropriateness of an uninhibited pursuit of economic self-interest. Or it might fail because in case after case Christian social ethics finds it impossible to work out an agenda for corporate social responsibility in a manner consistent with the ethos of democratic capitalism. Our point is simply that the debate over capitalism will remain misplaced so long as either of these levels is emphasized to the exclusion of the other, or neglected to the detriment of the other.

In order to illustrate further the relationship between these levels of analysis, Gutierrez's revolutionary socialism will also be considered a plausible model of practical theology. Insofar as it provides a *prima facie* legitimation of revolutionary socialism, it, too, completes the agenda of practical theology and may serve as the point of departure for Christian social ethics. Only in this context the moral perplexities will be different from those generated by the previous middle axiom. Ethical analysis will tend to focus on the problem of revolutionary violence, for, as Gutierrez himself insists (1973: 48), it would be naive to think that revolutionary socialism can be established in any other way. Christian social ethics in this context will focus on the problem of means and ends. It will have to formulate guidelines for making the transition from the one social system to the other. It may, as Miguez-Bonino suggests, adapt traditional Christian teachings concerning just wars to the strategies of guerrilla warfare and the tactics of political terrorism. Or failing that, it may give reasons why such teachings are inoperative. (Cf. Gunnemann, 1979) Here, too, a dialectical relationship between the macro and the micro levels of analysis must be capable of initiating radical criticism of the middle axiom at either level. Thus, Gutierrez's middle axiom may fail because practical theology is unable to confirm the theological adequacy of a dualistic world-view that sees the whole of humanity either as oppressed or as oppressors. But it may also fail because in case after case Christian social ethics finds that the means and the end are irreconcilable or, to return to Miguez-Bonino's criterion, because the human costs of realizing social change outweigh the human costs of its postponement. (1983: 107) Our point is simply that the debate over revolutionary socialism will remain misplaced so long as the ethical questions raised in critical reflection on praxis receive anything less than fully discursive treatment.

The sheer complexity of the issues raised in this misplaced debate, finally, should suggest the wisdom of recognizing two distinct but related genres of public discourse. Those who would address all these issues in a single comprehensive genre will continue to run the serious risk of dilettantism. Those who, like Potter, would eliminate this risk by reducing Christian social ethics to a formal exercise in clarifying the logic of moral argument unwittingly abandon the ideal of public discourse in an area of our common life that is most in need of it. A more discerning and hopeful response, we believe, is to take up these complex questions as they emerge from Christian social praxis, allowing their specific character to determine when we should resort to one or the other of these two genres of public discourse.

NOTES

1. Habermas's concept of generalizable interests must be distinguished both from the "quasi-transcendental interests" governing the cognitive anthropology of *Knowledge and Human Interests* (1971a) and from basic material needs and wants. Generalizable interests refer to a range of possible social practices and policies that a given society at a given moment in its history could accept as in "the common interest ascertained without deception." Public education, parliamentary democracy, a federal income tax, nuclear deterrence, and the like are possible candidates for generalizable interests. The three "quasi-transcendental," knowledge-constitutive interests, by contrast, define the necessary, if not sufficient, conditions for theory to emerge from the global situation of praxis. Such "quasi-transcendental" interests could never be wholly embodied in any set of social practices and policies but may, indeed must, serve as regulative ideals of public discourse seeking consensus about generalizable interests.
2. Gustafson's position tends to conflate the two genres for a number of reasons: (1) He is more inclined to point out the ethical deficiencies of practical theologians than to suspect that their work has a different practical intent from his own. (2) Furthermore, he is less impressed than we by the complex hermeneutic structure of practical theology. (3) Nor is he willing to commit himself as deeply as we do to the centrality of the problem of theory and praxis in theological ethics. Because of our differences with Gustafson on points (2) and (3) we insist upon the distinctive and limited role of practical theology. Our agreement with him on point (1), however, leads us to suggest that practical theology and Christian social ethics not only can but must work in tandem to shape the terrain of praxis.

CHAPTER SEVEN

ART AND ACT: PRACTICAL THEOLOGY AS PERFORMANCE

> *Passionate partisans cannot seem to find convincing ways of talking about their beliefs. The "connection" between "the prose and the passion" . . . is lost. Or, as Cicero would have put it, "wisdom" (and action guided by wisdom) no longer seems to have any connection with "eloquence." Arguments for our beliefs or actions have become "mere rhetoric" or propaganda or rationalization. Passionate commitment has lost its connection with the provision of good reasons, and reason has been reduced to logical calculation and proof about whatever does not matter enough to engage commitment.*
>
> (Booth, 1974: xi)

> *The function of ideology is to make an autonomous politics possible by providing the authoritative concepts that render it meaningful, the suasive images by means of which it can be sensibly grasped.*
>
> (Geertz, 1973a: 218)

Like any authors, we bear within us the image of an "implied reader." As the work matures, the more distinct and clear becomes the voice of the implied reader. Only in our case the implied reader is appropriately dual—unidentical twins. One reader is sympathetic but skeptical. The other stiffens in principled opposition. They deserve a hearing.

The Sympathetic Skeptic:

I admit that the field of practical theology too often resembles more a wilderness of strident and discordant calls and claims than a community committed to the rule of discourse. Perhaps Booth is right after all. We do seem to inhabit "a kind of international Hyde Park" in which "no one contributor tries to understand and perhaps support the affirmations of any other contributor." (1974: x-xi) Your elaborate scheme, and it certainly seems that to me, for imposing order upon this babble is, therefore, tempting—and I use the term advisedly. Structural elements. Criteria. Warrants. Mediations. Perhaps they could do the trick.

But I must protest the abstractness of it all. Your siren call would certainly doom a vital, if contentious, crew to shipwreck. When I look at what has actually gone on in the name of practical theology, I see a wild proliferation of forms of expression. The proliferation, in fact, is proportional to the vitality of the religious movement for social change. Think back to the Social Gospel: Washington Gladden's or Charles Sheldon's Social Gospel novels. Walter Rauschenbusch's *Prayers for the Social Awakening*. Francis Peabody's analysis of the social teachings of Jesus. Richard Ely's Christian economics. Focus on more recent movements and exemplars. Where do Reinhold Niebuhr's occasional essays in *Radical Religion* or *Christianity and Crisis* fit into your scheme? Or James Cone's personal evocation of the liberation intentionality of the Black spiritual? Even the combined theological and historical approach of Rosemary Ruether's *New Woman/New Earth* seems to lack one or two of your structural elements.

Would you orchestrate these voices or silence them? I, for one, would mourn the loss of any one of these tailored expressions of theological concern for Christian praxis.

Principled Opponent:

I will be short and blunt. The Sympathetic Skeptic unfortunately misperceives the real political damage of your entire operation. The *poiesis* of practical theologians which that critic admires is directly proportional to their involvement in actual struggles for liberation. The more that theology is of the people, the more it will break with abstruse forms of theological expression. Your project would abort this process. It threatens to coopt practical theology, to make it a monopoly of academic theologians.

> The forms of discourse which you ape, the commitment to criteria, warrants, critical reflection—the works—are the stock in trade of theologians whose home is the university. Habermas's "truth-dependent mode of socialization" which you so admire actually promotes an imperialism of the academic mind. Just as classical rhetoric excluded slaves from participation in public discourse, your appeal to Habermas's ideal speech situation as a norm for all speech acts excludes the public itself from the business of practical theology. (Cf. McGuire, 1982: 161) The result of such an endeavor can only be a paralysis of the will to act. Qualification after incessant qualification leading nowhere. We need more of *The Gospel of Solentiname*. We do not need McCann and Strain.

The objections raised by the Sympathetic Skeptic and the Principled Opponent actually restate the question of theory and praxis at the level of performance. If practical theology is itself conceived as a form of literary praxis delicately balanced on the axis of rhetoric and reflection, how can the theoretical labors outlined in the preceding chapters help but frustrate its practical purposes, namely, to precipitate crisis, to persuade, to evoke decision and action?

We have already rejected any attempt to bifurcate theory and praxis and we argued that they are dialectically related. In response to both our Sympathetic Skeptic and our Principled Opponent, we will analyze the workings of this same dialectic. Only now we will clarify it in terms of the literary praxis specific to practical theologies, a praxis in which as "stylized symbolic acts" they execute dramatic enactments for particular audiences, in the hope of evoking strategic responses to particular social contexts. (Wise, 1980: 145, 166, 170–72; Bennett, 1975: 127)

Our thesis is that the practice of practical theology consists of two dialectically related moments. The first we referred to as "constructing the model." The second, which we will consider at present, we term "performing the vision." Practical theologies originate in specific initiatives that seek to dramatize a vision illuminating the political implications of religious commitments. While each initiative necessarily resonates to a specific moment of kairos, *clusters* of such "occasional performances" inevitably imply a model—a formal organization of each of the essential elements of theology-as-ideology that we have specified. To construct the model is to clarify and consolidate the vision.

To argue this thesis we will discuss, first, the relationship of the genre of practical theology to the wild proliferation of various subgenres referred to by the Sympathetic Skeptic. We will reject the suggestion that the formal construction of models of practical theology preempts the creative expression of the theologian attuned to the demands of the occasion. Second, in order to develop a contrast with our own position, we will analyze several inadequate ways of interpreting the role of rhetoric within practical theologies. Third, we will present our own understanding of this role by analyzing practical theologies as forms of literary praxis designed not only to address particular audiences but to create certain kinds of community. Fourth, we will illustrate our analysis by discussing three examples of "performing the vision." Finally, we will argue that there must be criteria governing these rhetorical performances if they are to foster a truth-dependent mode of socialization and that the attempt to meet these criteria leads necessarily to the construction of a model of practical theology.

A. FUNCTIONAL SPECIALIZATIONS AND BLURRED GENRES

We agree completely with our Sympathetic Skeptic that the wild proliferation of forms of theological expression is characteristic of religious movements seeking to transform the course of history. To further the establishment of its Holy Commonwealth, American Puritans invented a richly imaginative variety of forms of literary praxis. (Walzer, 1969: 1–2) In addition to the Jeremiad, the Puritans used elegies and journals, hagiographies and histories to shape a community's vision, to send it on its errand. (Bercovitch, 1974: 7–9) Such inventiveness in the performance of their vision set a pattern for all religiously based social movements in North America. In proposing our distinction between the moments of construction and performance, we intend not to silence, but to orchestrate this profusion of voices.

Admittedly, most of what is generated as religious discourse with a practical intent does not constitute a model of practical theology in the fullest sense. The diverse elements which constitute practical theology are only rarely fused in a single work. What we call the Social Gospel or Christian Realism or Liberation *model* of practical theology is most frequently an abstraction, the distillate of numerous important works. No apology need be offered for this fact. We have argued, after all, that practical theology is necessarily a collaborative enterprise. If numerous exemplars of fully constructed models existed as individual works, then our thesis would be superfluous.

Be that as it may, the wild proliferation that our skeptical friend cherishes may not be so chaotic as it seems. We argued that the three other major genres of theological discourse (Foundational, Historical, and Systematic) reappear within the genre of Practical Theology as functional specializations. Much of the theological discourse that falls into this pattern makes a necessarily limited contribution. So works like J. B. Metz's *Faith in History and Society* (1980) or Charles Davis's *Theology and Political Society* (1980) address not all foundational issues but those especially pertinent to a practical theology. The essays by feminist historians in *Religion and Sexism: Images of Woman in the Jewish and Christian Traditions* (Ruether, 1974) perform only part of the task of a critical hermeneutic, namely, the shattering of the oppressive elements in the received tradition. A work like James Cone's *The Spirituals and the Blues*, on the other hand, is a masterful retrieval of an alternative past. But it is more. Cone's artistry brings out the process of self-formation involved in critical hermeneutics: "I . . . write about the spirituals and the blues," sings Cone, "because *I am the blues* and *my life is a spiritual*. Without them I cannot be." (1972: 7)

Even a single author can develop several works which perform separate functions. So Walter Rauschenbusch's acclaimed *Theology for the Social Gospel* provides the systematic underpinnings for not only his own theological endeavor but for the Social Gospel movement as a whole. (1945: 1) In *Christianizing the Social Order* (1912), however, Rauschenbusch offers public policy pronouncements based on the sort of mediation between the genres of practical theology and Christian social ethics that we have discussed.

To be sure, we cannot cram the totality of that wild proliferation into these few tidy categories of public discourse. Many forms of theological expression do not sort themselves out in clearly recognizable functional specializations. Where would we place a Social Gospel novel, say, *If Christ Came to Chicago* (Stead, 1964), or Reinhold Niebuhr's autobiographical reflections in "Ten Years That Shook My World" (1939), Daniel Berrigan's poems, or Dorothy Day's *Catholic Worker* column, "On Pilgrimage"? It can hardly be claimed that any one of these examples operates at the level of primary religious discourse. Rather, traditional genres, far removed from the functions of model-construction, artfully advance the dialectic of theory and praxis. But despite their "occasional" character, these subgenres tacitly presuppose a coherent religious ideology and, in each case, the outlines of a specific model soon become evident. Commitment to communicative competence need not censor the proliferation of genres of practical discourse. It only requires that persons or communities confronted with ideological pluralism at some point render their implicit models explicit and give reasons for their adequacy, appropriateness, and authenticity.

Another sign of ferment within the realm of practical discourse is the presence of what Clifford Geertz calls "blurred genres." In a situation "at once fluid, plural, uncentered, and ineradicably untidy," writers freely create new hybrids from old forms. (1980: 166–67) Paul Tillich's classic response to the age of anxiety, *The Courage to Be* (1952), successfully blurred the lines between foundational, historical, systematic, and practical theology. Mary Daly's opening salvo for a feminist theology, *Beyond God the Father* (1973), did the same. (Cf. Ruland, 1978: 211–212) In both cases the hybrid character of the work advanced the underlying practical intent. Yet even though it may produce works of classic expressivity, ferment alone cannot create the degree of coherence necessary for an ideological movement to institutionalize itself. Within a blurred field of discourse sharpen your focus. Constructing a model of practical theology, ideal type though it may be, does just that: proliferation, functional specialization, blurring of genres, and reduction of confusion through the construction of models. All are aspects of practical theological discourse.

B. RHETORIC AND REFLECTION

If we can imagine that our Sympathetic Skeptic has at least paused for reflection, we cannot expect as much of our Principled Opponent. Rightly so. We have not dealt directly with the question that this implied reader put to us. Let us sharpen this confrontation by examining a recent exchange between two theologians vitally concerned with the theology of liberation.

Schubert Ogden opened the debate in his *Faith and Freedom* by arguing that liberation theology muddles the distinction between witness and theology. Apparently plagued by a disease endemic in the history of theology, liberation theology rationalizes a specific form of praxis rather than critically reflecting upon its validity. "The vast majority of theologies have been, in effect if hardly in intention, Christian ideologies, in the precise sense of rationalizing the prior claims of the Christian witness instead of critically inquiring as to their meaning and truth." (1979: 33–34, 118–23) The very commitments that should be reflectively grounded become criteria of theological discourse.

Dorothee Soelle has responded by rejecting Ogden's polarization of witness and theology. She admits that liberation theology seeks to recover the power and passion of the language of witness. But she denies that this involves an abandonment of critical reflection. "Is there a possible third way," she asks, "between a theoretical objective talk that excludes passion, self-expression, and the call to struggle, and a merely personal immediate talk which excludes rationality and objectivity?" (1981: 10–11) Appealing to Bultmann's existential interpretation as a precedent, Soelle argues that it is, indeed, possible to be both existential—that is, "praxis-oriented" in testing concepts by the functional criteria of their power to liberate—and reflective in a way that would satisfy Ogden's dual criteria of appropriateness to the Christian witness and intelligibility to human existence. (Soelle, 1981: 11–13)

Ogden, in effect, rejects Soelle's "possible third way," by maintaining that her existential interpretation is just another example of witness and its rationalization. While much discourse can be critically reflective, only "theology proper" can establish when and if witness and its interpretation are appropriate and intelligible. (1981b: 17) For only "theology proper" is committed to "*understanding* the meaning of the Christian witness and to *assessing* its truth. . . . " (Italics ours.) Such a theology, in Ogden's view, breaks not with authentic witness but with the rationalization of witness. (1981a: 131–32)

Clearly, the Principled Opponent has sized us up as partisans of Ogden's brand of proper theological discourse. This, we believe, is a serious misreading of our intentions. If anything, we are closer to Soelle in her search for alternatives to false polarities. The dialectic of theory and praxis worked out in the paired operations of performing the vision and constructing the model represents the "third way" that Soelle calls for but scarcely describes.[1]

We have several objections to Ogden's position. (1) His emphasis upon understanding and assessment as the task of theology proper gives pride of place to foundational and systematic theology. The potential contributions of theology to praxis, in Ogden's estimation, are only *indirect.* (1979: 123) Practical theology as a distinct genre with its own intentionality and mode of discourse fades into the background.[2]

(2) Clearly, Ogden's interpretation of critical reflection is not the form of discourse which we discussed in Chapter Three. We see little evidence of a dialectic of theory and praxis in his formulation of the *process* of theological reflection. Ogden's position, while intended to establish theology as public discourse, presupposes a particularly abstract concept of critical reflection. By legitimating only a narrow band of discourse as "theology proper," Ogden falls prey to the very modernist and scientistic fallacies that, ostensibly, he wishes to overcome.

(3) Ogden's lack of attention to the proper functions and operations of distinct theological genres can be diagnosed as a misreading of the nature and function of practical discourse. We have already argued, following Alvin Gouldner, that ideology is a form of mixed discourse.

It mixes ideals with interests, locutionary with illocutionary acts, the rhetoric of rational persuasion with equally rhetorical appeals for decision and commitment. To construe it as a simple rationalization of predetermined interests is to misconstrue it. While the epistemic, functional, and genetic distortions of ideologies exhibit that genre's tendency to occlude critical reflexivity, ideologies also generate a form of immanent criticism. That process, an internal dialectic between generalizable ideals and the particular interests which advocate them, is surely a sophisticated form of critical reflexivity. (Cf. Gouldner, 1976: 30, 33–35, 38, 45–46, 84–85, 213–14, 219–23) In light of our analysis of the structural elements common to ideologies and practical theologies, any dismissal of either as a mere rationalization of prior commitments, in turn, must also be dismissed as simply a bad argument. *The Communist Manifesto*, to cite our earlier example, does more than rationalize the witness of the Workingmen's movement. In its own rhetorical fashion it advances the arguments presented in Marx's more analytical works. We may be neither moved nor convinced by its appeals, but we cannot dismiss it as a failure of critical reflection.

Our disagreements with Ogden must not obscure the fact that, in our estimation, Soelle fails to provide the "third way." However, elements of such an alternative can be inferred from the way she juxtaposes in that same essay the Biblical figural narratives of Exodus and Sinai to the figural narratives of contemporary advertising media. The Levi's commercial, "Thou Shalt Have No Other Jeans Before Me," epitomizes for her a consumer society devoid of all authentic awareness of religious transcendence. Settled in Egypt, we no longer dream of a Promised Land. (Soelle, 1981: 5–6, 8–9)

This line of argument can hardly be reduced to what Ogden means by witness. Indeed, Soelle stages the clash of figural narratives with their opposing visions of self and history in order to provoke critical reflection on the stark prospects threatening all authentic modes of being human. Provocations like hers, designed to break the hypnotic spell of a consumer society, implicitly claim to be at once more adequate, appropriate, and authentic than typically abstract forms of reflection. A rhetoric of crisis is most fitting, in short, for a time of crisis. Yet Soelle never transforms her vision of crisis into an ideological model. She refuses to use the rhetoric of critical discourse which she deploys in her attack upon Ogden to explicate her own position. Failing to fuse the rhetoric of crisis with the rhetoric of critical discourse, Soelle never moves out on the third way.

The distinction we have proposed between performing the vision and constructing the model provides an alternative to the sterile confrontation between Ogden and Soelle. Emphasizing the rhetoric of crisis, those who perform the vision transcend even as they internalize the sheer immediacy of witness and the cry of pure anguish. Stressing the rhetoric of critical discourse, those who construct the model move beyond narrow definitions of rationality to a genuine dialectic of theory and praxis. As paired moments, performance and construction *together* point toward a "third way."

Obviously this proposal needs both clarification and confirmation. At its heart lies a new understanding of the relationship of rhetoric and reflection. The commonplace distinction between the two—which Ogden, for one, apparently assumes—ultimately derives from Socrates' attack upon the sophists and Plato's upon the poets. In Stanley Fish's rendition of this tradition, there are basically two modes of literary presentation: "rhetorical" and "dialectical." Rhetorical modes of presentation work within the audience's preconceptions about the truth. They confirm the reader's expectations, canonize the community's values; they lead along familiar paths to a goal which harbors no surprises. Dialectical modes, on the contrary, shatter preconceptions, confound expectations, challenge canons. They force the reader to blaze new paths to unfamiliar goals. (1972: 1–2, 15, 19)

To those addicted to binary oppositions, Fish's commonplaces themselves satisfy. But another tradition insists upon the pervasiveness of rhetoric in all human discourse. (Frye, 1957: 331, 350) Philosophers point to the *fusion* of rhetorical and dialectical modes in specifically philosophical discourse. (Mackey, 1971: xii) Rhetoricians insist upon the inescapability of rhetoric in the structuring and restructuring of all social relationships, by which alone we come to be and to think. (McGuire, 1982: 164; Booth, 1974: 134)

> But if all men make each other in symbolic exchange, then by implication they *should* make each other, and it is an inescapable value in their lives that it is good to do it well. . . . The supreme purpose of persuasion in this view could not be to talk someone else into a preconceived view; rather it must be to engage in mutual inquiry or exploration. In such a world, our rhetorical purpose must always be to perform as well as possible in the same primal symbolic dance which makes us able to dance at all.
>
> (Booth, 1974: 137)

Reflection, here, clarifies and structures rhetorical acts.

The first tradition unwittingly confirms our preference for the second. Its very polarization of rhetoric and dialectic is itself a master stroke of rhetoric. More importantly, if dialectic—read, critical discourse—is necessary for a "truth-dependent mode of socialization," rhetoric, as Booth and others have argued, is indispensable to any mode of socialization.[8] Plato's *Republic* is a perfect case in point. Critical discourse may be the key to the liberation of the Prisoners of the Cave. But the very myth of the Cave, covertly associated with Homer's underworld, is a rhetorical device designed to alter fundamental understandings of the nature of society. (Cf. Bloom, 1968: 408) But to return to our chief purpose here, the second tradition can explain the actual discourse of practical theologians—with its mixture of the rhetoric of crisis and the rhetoric of critical discourse—in a way that does not arbitrarily undercut their claims to adequacy, appropriateness, and authenticity. Indeed, this second tradition may also enable us to meet the lingering objections of our Principled Opponent.

C. ART, ACT, AND AUDIENCE

Attention to the rhetorical dimension of practical theologies requires us to explain their construction and performance in terms of the audiences to which they are addressed. (Booth, 1974: xiii; Perelmann and Olbrechts-Tyteca, 1969: 5, 19) Following Booth, we could say that practical theology is a symbolic construction (an art) which makes (acts upon) a particular group (an audience) in a certain way. But who is that audience; what kind of act may be assigned this uniqely creative role; and how are both represented in the form of the work?

Let us move indirectly to answer these questions. We mentioned in our objections to Fish and, implicitly, to Ogden that in philospphy, and a fortiori in theology, rhetorical strategies are fused with dialectical or reflective considerations.[4] Moreover, as we have argued throughout this book, the audiences for whom practical theologies are created are plural but specific. Practical theologies are primarily addressed to those for whom the concern to transform the polis is intrinsically connected to their concern with the Ultimate. For this group, the possibility of participating in a religious community committed to some form of praxis remains a live option.

But what is the task of practical theology with regard to this potential community? If, as Geertz argues, ideologies make "autonomous politics" possible through their "authoritative concepts and suasive images" (1973: 218) and if, as we argued in Chapter Three, the concept of praxis is intelligible only in dialectical relation to critical theory, then a religious community existing in and for a specific form of praxis can sustain itself only on the basis of some more or less explicit practical theology. To be sure, practical theologies arise out of the actual struggles of human beings grasped by the power of God and moved by the agony of human suffering. Nevertheless, the transition *from struggle to praxis* is sparked by an ideology. A practical theology, like its secular counterparts, is neither the reflex of praxis, as some liberation theologians would have it, nor the rationalization of commitment, as Ogden would have it. It does more than convince its audience of the adequacy and appropriateness of a particular cultural synthesis; it seeks to persuade its audience that the praxis inspired by this synthesis is a momentous and compelling choice, the expression of personal and communal authenticity.

We see this concern to reach a *potential* religious community committed to the transformation of society in Walter Rauschenbusch's classic of the American Social Gospel movement, *Christianity and the Social Crisis*. Rauschenbusch envisions no less than a transformation of "the common mind of the Christian Church in America," a mind which lacks "any solid convictions or any permanent basis of action" and which, therefore, stands perplexed before the "imperious call of the future." Out of this transformation Rauschenbusch hopes to bring into being "a new apostolate to meet the new needs in a new harvest-time of history." (1964: xxiii, 414–16) Steeped in the rhetoric of crisis, the work is meant to convince an audience of Protestant Christians that the challenge they face is social as well as religious: Apart from the intervention of religious praxis "the whole social movement may prove abortive, and the New Era may die before it comes to birth." Apart from the practical transformation of the common convictions of Christians, Protestantism risks more than the loss of the loyalty of the working classes, it risks losing its holiness and mission. "There will be a permanent eclipse of the light of life among us." (1964: xxi, 316, 331, 342)

The formal characteristics of public discourse commit practical theology of two secondary audiences as well. We have argued that, like ideology, practical theology is a form of counter-discourse. As such, practical theologies are committed to public debate. To be specific, a practical theology is addressed secondarily to all those for whom the destiny of the polis is a matter of ethical concern, to those whose practical commitments require them to enter the arena of ideological debate where the appropriate direction of the needed social transformation will be decided. A practical theology will seek to convince this group that the crisis which the polis faces is, in the final analysis, religious in character and that, consequently, only a form of praxis which pursues ultimate transformation can respond adequately to that crisis. In the charged atmosphere of ideological debate, conviction implies commitment.

Writing in the crisis-ridden year of 1933, Paul Tillich vainly tried to stem the rising tide of Nazism by challenging the the German public to make an authentic commitment to socialism. "The socialist decision is a decision *of* socialism and a decision *for* socialism. . . . " (Tillich, 1977: xxxi) While eschewing specifically theological language in order to communicate directly with the German public, Tillich nevertheless clearly insisted that the religious dimension formed the "subsoil" out of which the socialist principle emerges. Through his articulation of this principle, he hoped to enable socialism "to understand itself in terms of its own roots, and that means, religiously, on the basis of its own prophetic element to take up a relationship with the prophetic elements in the history of Western religion." (Ibid.: xxxvi, 146) However futile the immediate outcome of Tillich's appeal to his fellow citizens, no more vivid example of practical theology's claim upon this secondary audience exists than his classic, *The Socialist Decision*.

Finally, as theological discourse, practical theology implicitly addresses those for whom ultimate concern is intrinsically connected to the pursuit of ultimate meaning and truth. It seeks to convince this group of sundry theologians that ultimate truth is never fully accessible apart from the realization of its transformative power and that the religious praxis which is the correlate of any ultimate concern necessarily expresses itself politically. In short, while ultimately only the truth liberates, only the truth which liberates can ultimately be true. Here, too, practical theology's claim transcends the level of mere understanding. Juan Luis Segundo, for example, interprets his task as no less than the liberation of theology. Inevitably such a work aims to change the theologian as well as the theology. Its rhetoric is designed to shatter the context, to end the situation where "everyone mouths the words, only to go on as before." (Segundo, 1976: 4–6) Neither of practical theology's secondary audiences can be allowed to ignore the challenge of transformative praxis.

D. PERFORMING THE VISION

The degree to which the rhetoric of crisis is joined to rational argumentation in theologians like Rauschenbusch, Tillich, and Segundo, whom we ordinarily think of as primarily engaged in model-construction, is striking. But this only confirms our thesis concerning the dialectical relationship between performing the vision and constructing the model involved in any fully developed practical theology. Just as the demands of public discourse precipitate a shift from the moment of performance to the moment of construction, so the demands of socialization trigger a similar shift in the opposite direction. Those who perform the vision demonstrate that the ultimate purpose of a practical theology is not merely to address an audience but to create a community. Attuned to audience and occasion, these performers, as much as any Kierkegaard, invent new forms or pirate old forms of persuasion. In this section, we will test our thesis by analyzing three examples of religious literary praxis: the "Easy Essays" of Peter Maurin, the "Letter from a Birmingham Jail" of Dr. Martin Luther King, and the aphorisms of J. B. Metz. We will also describe the modes of socialization which flow from these forms of literary praxis.

1. *The Not-So-Easy Essays of Peter Maurin* Peter Maurin was the French-born anarchist and agitator, poet and philosopher, who with Dorothy Day established the Catholic Worker movement in America. The prototype of Catholic radicalism in North America, the Catholic Worker movement fused communitarianism with the corporal works of mercy, nonviolent direct action with ideological debate. To promote its commitment to Catholic personalism, in the midst of the Great Depression the movement published its paper, the *Catholic Worker*, as a self-styled alternative to the ideology promoted in the communist *Daily Worker*. Maurin's "Easy Essays" were the centerpiece of each edition.

The Catholic Worker believes
in the gentle personalism
of traditional Catholicism.
The Catholic Worker believes
in the personal obligation
of looking after
the needs of our brother.
The Catholic Worker believes
in the daily practice
of the Works of Mercy.
The Catholic Worker believes
in Houses of Hospitality
for the immediate relief
of those who are in need.
The Catholic Worker believes
in the establishment
of Farming Communes
where each one works
according to his ability

and gets
according to his need.
The Catholic Worker believes
in creating a new society
within the shell of the old
with the philosophy of the new,
which is not a new philosophy
but a very old philosophy,
a philosophy so old
that it looks like new.

(Maurin, 1949: 59)

Suiting his essays to the occasion, Maurin used verse form and the repetition of catchy phrases to insinuate his message in the ears of his hearers. "He believed in repeating," said Dorothy Day, "in driving his point home by consistent repetition, like the dropping of water on the stones which were our hearts." (Day in Maurin, 1949: v) Maurin spoke, or rather chanted, his essays at roundtable discussions sponsored by the *Catholic Worker*, at college lectures and even in the fields of the farming commune. In Union Square he proclaimed the virtues of the "green revolution" versus the "red revolution," to the uncomprehending ears of socialist ideologues. (Day, 1952: 167–68; 1963: 6–9, 26, 44)

Maurin thought of his rhetorical style as "indoctrination" (Day, 1952: 168), but if so the *Easy Essays* are a strange form of it. On one level, their artful simplicity corresponded to the simplicity of the anarchistic personalism which was Maurin's social theory. The ideal society for which he labored had been anticipated, proleptically, in the age of the Irish monks:

and it was
in the so called Dark Ages
which were not so dark,
when the Irish
were the light.
But we are now living
in a real Dark Age,
and one of the reasons why

the modern age
is so dark,
is because
too few Irish
have the light.

(Maurin, 1949: 163)

To convey the ideal harmony of that not-Dark age, Maurin uses the simple device of repeating a single syllable over and over.

The Irish Scholars established
agricultural centers
all over Europe
Where they combined
cult—
that is to say liturgy,
with culture—
that is to say literature,
with cultivation—
that is to say agriculture.

(Ibid.)

The hypnotic refrain—*cult*, *cult*ure, *cult*ivation—itself theoretically established Maurin's integral vision. Maurin, of course, was more concerned with performing his vision than with articulating the organismic model implicit in it. Yet the theory was there. He was convinced that there could be no revolution without a theory of revolution. (Day, 1952: 191; 1963: 7)

Maurin's simplicity can be as deceptive as his indoctrination was disruptive. He plays with slogans, hypnotic refrains, and repetitions in order to plant conceptual time bombs.

If the Catholic Church
is not today
the dominant social dynamic force,
it is because Catholic scholars
have failed to blow the dynamite
of the Church. Catholic scholars
have taken the dynamite

of the Church,
have wrapped it up
in nice phraseology,
placed it in a hermetic container
and sat on the lid.
It is about time
to blow the lid off
so the Catholic Church
may again become
the dominant social dynamic force.

(Maurin, 1949: 3)

This all sounds fairly innocuous. Until the bomb goes off. Dynamite. Catholic Church. Catholic Church *and* dynamite? He can't be serious! As in the parables of Jesus, metaphoric juxtaposition here creates mental revolutions. The more outrageous the juxtaposition, the greater the revolution. The essays, indeed, may have been easy, but the sayings were hard. (Cf. Day, 1963: 15) What Maurin said of the New Testament in a quotation from Robert Louis Stevenson could be said as well of his own writings:

These are hard words
but the hard words of a book
were the only reason
why the book was written.

(Ibid.: 26)

While his rhetoric of the "green revolution" was focused upon an audience of ideologues and his scathing references to "Catholic scholars," upon theologians, Maurin's primary target was the American Catholic Church as a whole. The easiness of the essays reflected an intent to reach the masses of Catholics. Yet Maurin knew that such hard sayings could only be acknowledged by a committed few. From these few Maurin sought to create a regenerative core. In contemporary terminology Maurin's essays were designed to create "basic communities" within the larger religious organism. The Catholic Worker movement was to function as an eschatological witness within the mystical Body of Christ. Living by the hard sayings of the Sermon on the Mount, Catholic Worker cells scattered across the country would embody the simplicity of the Christian life—cult, culture, cultivation—for Catholics strangled by the complexity as well as the injustices of the industrial age.

2. *Paul and Martin Bound in Jail* Of all the forms of literary praxis which arose out of the American civil rights movement of the 1960s, one document reached classic status almost immediately, Martin Luther King's "Letter from a Birmingham Jail." The text is a masterly rhetorical performance. While it was written as an "occasional piece," a response to a public statement by eight clergymen from Alabama attacking the use of nonviolent direct action in Birmingham to promote social change, it nevertheless clearly delineates key elements of a practical theology. It develops a theology of history by fusing aspects of American civil religion with a liberal Christian vision of the coming of the Kingdom; it presents King's theory of the relationship of natural or eternal law to civil law and thus outlines the basis of his Christian social ethics. It presents the strategy and tactics of nonviolent direct action as a form of praxis congruent with those ethical principles. For these ideas alone the Letter is justly famous. Yet we would argue that the Letter cannot be fully understood except as a form of literary praxis. Without understanding the form, we cannot fathom the depths of its transformative impact.

Why a letter? Martin Luther King, imprisoned for acts of civil disobedience in Birmingham, was at a rhetorical disadvantage with the middle class, moderate, white, religious leadership which, in the persons of the eight clergymen who had publicly condemned him, was his primary audience. The choice of the letter form of discourse immediately transforms that disadvantageous situation into a rhetorical wedge. By writing a letter, King associates himself with a tradition of imprisoned witnesses to the Kingdom stretching from Paul to Bonhoeffer. Indeed, King explicitly associates himself with Paul in his first argument defending his right to be an itinerant advocate of racial justice. "Just as the apostle Paul left his village of Tarsus and carried the gospel of Jesus Christ to the far corners of the Greco-Roman world, so am I compelled to carry the gospel of freedom beyond my home town." (1963: 77)

Letters, according to Amos Wilder, are the closest form of written discourse to oral speech. The letter "like direct oral address has an implicit dialogue character." (1971: 31) King responds to his accusers' public statement with a personal address. Borrowing from Martin Buber, King argues that the real injustice of segregation is that it "substitutes an 'I-it' relationship for an 'I-thou' relationship and ends up relegating persons to the status of things." (King, 1963: 82) The aim of nonviolent direct action, to the contrary, is always to restore a situation of dialogue.

> The purpose of our direct-action program is to create a situation so crisis-packed that it will inevitably open the door to negotiation. I, therefore, concur with you in your call for negotiation. Too long has our beloved Southland been bogged down in a tragic effort to live in monologue rather than dialogue.
>
> (Ibid.: 80)

The letter form as literary praxis, in other words, transforms King's relationship with his immediate audience in a manner consistent with the ultimate aims of nonviolent praxis. Ideological warfare here yields to the ethical imperatives of personal address.

In form and content King's letter comes close to a classic literary genre—the Apologetic Letter which Paul adopted in his Epistle to the Galatians. Such a letter presupposes a court of law which it transposes into written discourse. Its combination of statements of the case, reviews of pertinent facts, arguments, rebuttals, and exhortations places the implied readers in the position of a jury. (Betz, 1979: 12–24) There is a magnificent irony to King's choice of this rhetorical form. To his audience, King's presence in jail, psychologically if not legally, is prima facie evidence that he is guilty as charged of promoting violence and lawlessness. Yet King dares to seat his accusers in the jury box. Placed in this rhetorical context, the arguments concerning the supremacy of a higher, natural, and eternal law over civil law, and the advocacy of civil disobedience as a religious imperative are bound to receive serious deliberation. (King, 1963: 82–84) The dialectic of form and content itself conveys the dialectic of theory and praxis.

In King's, as in Paul's, hands, apology gives way to admonishment; the accused becomes the accuser. Just as Kierkegaard chose the letter form in order to create an ethical imperative in *Either/Or*, so King finds in personal address the rhetorical means to bring the Southern white moderate and the Southern churches to a day of judgment. (Cf. Mackey, 1974: 81) In apocalyptic tones reminiscent of the letters to the seven churches in the Book of Revelation, King castigates white moderates and the white churches for their failure to act. The moderates, the lukewarm who prefer the negative peace of order to the positive peace of justice are held directly responsible for the impending crisis of racial warfare. (King, 1963: 84–86) The churches, for their part, are condemned for being thermometers of public opinion rather than thermostats of public values. Upon them rests the judgment of God. If they cannot recapture the extremism of Jesus, Paul, and Luther, they will be cast aside as irrelevant social clubs. Yet the failure of both the moderates and the churches to meet the test of the present crisis will not curtail God's future. A people who have endured slavery will not be stopped by current intransigence. (Ibid.: 88–93) Like Paul and Silas bound in jail, those who hold on to the plow, the praxis that liberates, will not be forsaken.

Despite the development of these apocalyptic overtones within King's rhetoric of crisis, the form of address is still that of an *open* letter. Far from dismissing the white moderates and the Southern religious leaders out of hand, King makes clear his desire to create a coalition of religious denominations and liberal Americans. The content of the letter with its argument based on an eternal law and upon appeals to both a common Judeo-Christian tradition and to American civil religion reflects this openness, this pursuit of coalition politics. It is designed to provide the basis not for anything like a basic community but for a broad network of communities committed to the praxis of dialogue and nonviolent direct action. As with Paul, King's disappointment is itself a rhetorical strategy in the service of hope. Castigation leaves the door open for conversion. The tepid may catch fire; the thermometer may change into a thermostat.

3. *Aphoristic Language and the Apocalyptic Imagination* Performing the vision through the invention of modes of literary praxis is characteristic not just of those involved in the daily struggles of a religious community. Even professional theologians find themselves incorporating this dialectical moment into the construction of their

models of practical theology. A case in point is J. B. Metz. In Chapter Ten of *Faith in History and Society*, Metz suddenly deviates from the theologian's work of laying the foundations for practical theology to offer thirty-five "noncontemporaneous theses on the apocalyptic view." (1980: 169–79) But what a strange set of theses! They offer no demonstrations, no discursive validation. Viewed in terms of the canons of scholarship, they look like gratuitous assertions.

What are they doing here, buried in the middle of Metz's erudite presentation? We suggest two clues and an example to help understand this uncommon moment of performance. The first clue is an external comparison. Metz's chapter bears striking resemblance to Walter Benjamin's "Theses on the Philosophy of History." (1968) The format and style are identical and so is the dominant theme—theological or philosophical reflections radically challenging the modern conception of time. But Benjamin's work itself is modelled upon Marx's *Theses on Feuerbach* (1967: 400–402) and, in turn, upon Feuerbach's *Preliminary Theses on the Reform of Philosophy*. (1972: 152–76) In each of these works, the titles notwithstanding, the authors present not so much theses to be proved as chains of related aphorisms designed to blast holes in the prison of thought. Marx's famous Eleventh thesis, "The philosophers have only *interpreted* the world; the point is, to *change* it," is not a proposition for scholarly debate. It is an explosion which alters the topography—the terms, the context, and the character—of public discourse.

A second clue, this one internal. If we had to choose one thesis which compresses the meaning of the thirty-five, we would pick the sixth: "The shortest definition of religion: interruption (*Unterbrechung*)." (1980: 171) Here too we find not a thesis but an aphorism. Nevertheless few of Metz's "theses" explode with the packed precision of this utterance. Yet it is the clue we need. If we look carefully enough, we find that the theses, at least the ones which work, are generally fragments of discourse emitted from this aphoristic core. An example:

> Thesis XX Taking everything into consideration, is it possible to look forward to the end of time? Or has the expectation of an end of time become no more than the expression of a mythical

> eschatology, because time itself has become a homogeneous continuum that is without surprises, a bad infinity in which anything can happen? Anything, that is, except one thing: that moment which becomes the "gate through which the Messiah enters history" . . . and because of this surprising moment would time be found for time?
>
> (Ibid.: 174–75)

In this thesis the illusion of ordered discourse, every bit as much as the rhythms of Maurin's chanted essays, conceals as it implants its explosive device: anything can happen, except that which absolutely matters.

In his recent work on the sayings of Jesus, John Dominic Crossan contrasts aphorisms with discursive modes of presentation. Those who write in the aphoristic as in the proverbial mode refuse to provide explanations, elaborate or otherwise, for their authoritative insights.

> Proverb gives no reason since none is necessary; it is the summation of the wisdom of the past. Aphorism, on the other hand, gives no reason because none is possible; it is the formulation of the wisdom of the future. Proverb is the last word, aphorism is the first word.
>
> (1983: 25)

Where the commonplace tradition on rhetorical modes links critical reflection to discursive reasoning, Crossan, like Francis Bacon, believes that critical reflection *by the reader* is more likely to be occasioned through an aphorism. If symbols give rise to thought, aphorisms provoke thought. Or simply provoke. As Bacon put it: "Aphorisms, representing a knowledge broken, do invite men to enquire further; whereas Methods, carrying the shew of a total, do secure men, as if they were at furthest." (Francis Bacon as cited by Crossan, 1983: 14, cf. 13–18) The aphorism provokes because it contradicts. What traditional wisdom enshrines as commonplace, aphorism destroys. What discursive reason establishes with unshakable authority, aphorism collapses like a house of cards. (Ibid.: 5–7)

Why then does Metz shift from the discursive to the aphoristic mode? Quite simply, to shatter our commonplace understanding of the evolutionary procession of time. "The logic of evolution is the rule of death over history and in the end, everything makes as little difference to it as death." (1980: 173) In their relentless opposition to this logic of death, religion and the apocalyptic imagination amount to the same: Both look to inter-ruption. Metz breaks the flow of ordered discourse to break up our sense of the ordered flow of time. Break-up. Break-in. Inter-ruption. Buried within fragments of theological discourse, Metz's aphorisms trap and surprise their audience into rediscovering an apocalyptic sense of discontinuity. "Thesis XXI: 'It is time for it to be time; it is time.' (Paul Celan)" (Ibid.: 175)

The temptation here is to dismiss Metz's "noncontemporaneous theses" as simply idiosyncratic. What exactly does Metz have in mind besides provoking thought, or simply provoking? Can his literary praxis be part of any mode of socialization? Socialization of whom and for what? We believe that Metz's aphoristic theses are addressed to academic theologians who enter into ideological debate primarily with other intellectuals. Communities of intellectuals are the bearers of a culture's ruling paradigm.

Because a culture's paradigm establishes the limits of what can count as rational discourse and rational behavior, it establishes a field within which any viable ideology must operate. What counts as rational in the technocratic paradigms of Western culture, in Metz's estimation, is fatally irrational. It is not sufficient to blast a hole in this prison house of thought. Within what Alvin Gouldner, among others, calls the New Class, Metz seeks to create a community of intellectual subversives sharing a religious vision of apocalyptic hope. (Cf. Gouldner, 1979) From the point of view of the present this community may seem to be committed to a purely negative dialectic. From the point of view of an anticipated future, however, the aphoristic rhetoric of this community is now broadcasting the seeds of a new ruling paradigm.

E. PERFORMING THE VISION AND CONSTRUCTING THE MODEL

In previous chapters we stressed that ideologies, in contrast to forms of propaganda, intend to convince as well as persuade. Here we have stressed the importance of a rhetoric of persuasion to create various types of communities of religious praxis. We have suggested that ideologies imply a rhetoric of crisis as well as a rhetoric of critical discourse. Beyond the task of constructing an ideological model, there is the more fluid, expressive moment in the execution of an ideology which we call performing the vision. We do not intend, however, to polarize practical theological discourse. These various rhetorics and moments of execution are dialectically related. A rhetoric of crisis must be a rhetoric of critical discourse. In a truth-dependent mode of socialization persuasive rhetoric is governed by the canons of communicative competence. These rules for rhetorical acts enable us to form our convictions in concert. Persuasion becomes propaganda when they are violated.

Rule #1: *Rhetorical performance and forms of literary praxis are justifiable only if their implicit claims can be validated.*

This rule is based on two premises. First, any illocutionary act—an assertion, a command, or a promise—communicates more than a subjective preference. It makes implicit claims about the nature of reality, whose adequacy may be tested. (Habermas, 1979: 63–64) "Workers of the world unite," is more than the expression of Marx's revolutionary wish. It claims that: a) all workers form a homogeneous group based on their common interests; b) a union of workers is historically possible; c) union is the precondition of each individual worker's fulfillment; and d) union is unambiguously imperative because workers have no stake in the prevailing form of political economy. In fact, Marx's theory takes elaborate pains to justify precisely these propositions. Even the rhetorical flourish of the phrase "nothing to lose but your chains," in Marx's estimation, is warranted. A safer more literal expression, "Nothing to lose but your jobs," would be inadequate precisely because it would not convey the totality of alienation—of each self from itself, from other selves, from the fruits of its labor, and from nature—under capitalism. Only rhetorical extravagance can express adequately the Marxist claim, a claim which can be rationally and empirically tested.

The second premise simply restates our commitment to a truth-dependent mode of socialization. Bluntly put, there are no noble lies.

Praxis depends upon intelligent commitment. It is the antithesis of mob action. However noble the intended end, rhetoric based upon unwarranted claims is a case of systematically distorted communication. Whatever else it accomplishes, systematically distorted communication invariably either reinforces old patterns of domination or creates new ones. Lacking a situation of crisis, resorting to rhetorical extravagances similar to Marx's would hardly be justifiable.

Rule #2: *The form of literary praxis invented should cohere with the vision which it presents.*

At one level this rule is simply a criterion of effectiveness. This chapter has been built on the premise that form is more than the vehicle of content. In light of certain master examples of practical theological discourse, we have shown that where form and content mutually interact the power of the work to transform as well as to elucidate is enhanced. (Cf. Wilder, 1971: xxiii-xxiv)

At a deeper level, however, this rule embodies the criterion of appropriateness. The vision of the commonweal must be reflected in the rhetorical acts that create the particular community. We discovered earlier that Martin Luther King's choice of the form of an open letter was ethically appropriate to the theory and praxis of nonviolence expressed in the letter. If, as King suggests, nonviolence is grounded in a dialogical understanding of the human person, a dogmatic rhetoric would have violated that vision. This criterion, it appears to us, would place stringent ethical limitations on both the media politics of advanced industrial societies and upon the rhetoric of popular movements. A truly democratic community cannot be created through a rhetoric of manipulation. Both in terms of effectiveness and appropriateness the dialectic of form and content confirms our analysis of the dialectic of theory and praxis.

Rule #3: *Modes of literary praxis and rhetorical strategies are limited by the imperative to preserve the public realm which makes them possible.*

The criterion of authenticity applied to speech acts generally refers to the trustworthiness of the speaker. But in cases of systematic distortion in the communication of an ideology the first persons to be deceived may frequently be the speakers themselves. We need a more reliable index of authenticity in rhetoric than our intuitions regarding a speaker's sincerity.

The limit-cases of a psychotic or an absolute skeptic can lead us toward an appreciation of the conditions necessary for authentic rhetoric. A psychotic's speech is inauthentic because it creates a closed system, an impenetrable world of private meaning. An absolute skeptic's speech is also inauthentic because it must communicate the impossibility of any genuine communication. In both cases the public character of speech acts in principle is undermined.

We have argued all along that both ideology and practical theology are forms of public discourse. They exist where the world of the matter-of-fact has collapsed, where models of reality and for action must be invented. This invention, as the preeminently political act, can only be accomplished through symbolic interaction. Such interaction, like all forms of human action, depends upon a public space where ideological models can be presented, visions performed, and alternatives debated. (Cf. Booth, 1974: 137) Rhetoric which undermines the public realm by triggering behavior while precluding a genuinely political response ultimately threatens to destroy our very humanity.

> If it is good for men to attend to each other's reasons—and we all know that it is, because without such attending none of us could come to be and questions of value could not even be asked—it is also good to work for whatever conditions make such mutual inquiry possible. *Whatever imposes belief without personal engagement becomes inferior to whatever makes mutual exchange more likely.*
>
> (Booth, 1974: 137. Italics ours.)

Viewed in this light the polemical infighting of the Young Hegelians or Marx and Engel's attacks upon the utopian socialists must be repudiated as inferior rhetorics verging towards systematic distortion of communication. While a rhetoric of manipulation will tend to transform the public into an anonymous mass, a rhetoric of persuasion will seek to constitute the public as responsive and responsible.

Rule #4: *As public performers, practical theologians must stand ready to construct the model implicit in their visions and performances.*

We believe that the commitment to discourse in the public, political arena carries with it the need, at various critical junctures, to construct theological models. Occasionally, a practical theologian will be confronted by those who say: "We are moved to the brink of commitment by your rhetoric but we draw back because we are not convinced that what you say is true." At this point the claims to adequacy, appropriateness, and authenticity implicit in the practical theologian's vision will have to be redeemed. This is particularly the case when practical theologians address themselves to their two secondary audiences—those whose commitment to the polis urges them to ideological debate and those whose ultimate concern inspires them to a pursuit of ultimate truth. The attempt to convince one's audience in either of these arenas will entail reaching agreement upon common elements, criteria, and warrants.

If on the basis of these rules our Principled Opponent concludes that we are after all siding with Ogden, then so be it. We have argued that we do not find Ogden's distinction between theology as rationalization and theology as critical reflection helpful in dealing with practical theologies. We have tried to show what Ogden himself recognizes, namely that discursive modes of reasoning possess no monopoly on critical reflection. (Cf. Ogden, 1981b: 17) Various rhetorical but nondiscursive strategies can be very successful in promoting critical reflection. Moreover, canons of communicative competence applied to the rhetorical acts of performing the vision encourage critical reflexivity in this dialectical moment of executing an ideology. But in the moment which we have called constructing the model discursive acts are indispensable. Here, too, however, our position is slightly different from Ogden's. Our commitment to criteria and to discursive validation depends upon a prior recognition. We construct models knowing full well that they are always only models. In other words, deliberate model construction is the quantum leap of imagination that makes possible the critical reflection which Ogden desires. Apart from this supposition even our rhetoric of critical discourse threatens to become not merely rationalization but systematically distorted communication.

Performance and Construction. Each moment in the dialectical execution of an ideology is incomplete without the other. Each passes over into the other. In most cases, the different moments of the dialectic of performance and construction will be accomplished by different authors or at least in different works. On rare occasions, however, an author manages to both perform a vision and construct a model. The work as performance responds to the demands of the occasion and the needs of the audience. The work as construction executes the formal tasks of a practical theology. Such works fuse reflection and rhetoric, art and action. When this occurs, and, we would hazard, *only* when this occurs, a classic of the genre of practical theology is born.

Walter Rauschenbusch's *Christianity and the Social Crisis* (1964), Paul Tillich's *The Socialist Decision* (1977), Gustavo Gutierrez's *A Theology of Liberation* (1973), without such classic performances and constructions we would never even be able to define the genre of practical theology. (Cf. Strain, 1978: 538–40) In each case the artful fusion of the rhetoric of crisis with the rhetoric of critical discourse gives the lie to those who misunderstand the relationship of rhetoric, in all of its guises, to reflection. To insist upon one rhetoric, one mode of discourse, would be to drain not practical theology but all theology of its life. (Cf. Booth, 1974: 187) Without the art, the thought and the act could not be joined. Without the art, the act would never mold an audience.

NOTES

1. We most emphatically do not agree with Soelle's labeling of Ogden's position as "a frontal attack from the right on any form of liberation theology." (Soelle, 1981: 13) Ogden, in Soelle's terms, is not only wrong; he is beyond the pale. This charge is both unwarranted and subversive of the public discourse that Soelle herself chooses to engage in.

2. We are puzzled why Ogden in this entire discussion neglects the distinctions between systematic theology and practical theology which he developed in his essay, "What is Theology?" (1972) If he had utilized that work, we do not see how he could have used the label "theology proper" when referring to the specific functions of systematic theology in his debate with Soelle.
3. Habermas's lack of attention to the role of rhetoric in socialization processes is a serious flaw in his theory of communicative competence. Only the rhetoric of critical discourse appears to have a place in the ideal speech situation. So we must side with Booth rather than with Habermas at this juncture. In Section E we will clarify how the rhetorical acts involved in performing the vision are subject to the criteria of a truth-dependent mode of socialization.
4. Nowhere is this more apparent than in the writings of Sören Kierkegaard. Kierkegaard's authorship, in fact, is the modern paradigm of religious reflection as itself a mode of praxis. (Cf. Crites, 1972; and Mackey, 1971) It has become fashionable among some recent practical theologians to launch their enterprise by criticizing the individualism of Kierkegaard's literary praxis. This valid criticism should not blind us to certain affinities linking the *rhetorical strategy* of an author like Kierkegaard with those pursued by numerous practical theologians. Insofar as practical theologies seek not to rationalize but to convince, not simply to witness but to persuade, they themselves are forms of literary praxis.

CHAPTER EIGHT

AN INVITATION: PRACTICAL THEOLOGY AS PUBLIC DISCOURSE

We face a crisis that is new in history. We would do well to face it with a new cleanliness of imagination, in the realization that internecine strife, beyond some inevitable human measure, is a luxury we can no longer afford. Serious issues confront us on all . . . levels of public argument. Perhaps the time has come when we should endeavor to dissolve the structure of war that underlies the pluralistic society, and erect the more civilized structure of the dialogue. . . . The pattern would not be that of ignorant armies clashing by night but of informed men locked together in argument in the full light of a new dialectical day.

(Murray, 1958: 41)

There is no assumption here . . . that all truly reasonable men will always finally agree. On the contrary, it is assumed that reasonable men of differing interests, experiences, and vocabulary will disagree about some questions to which reason, nevertheless, must apply. Consequently they not only can but must, by virtue of their common problems, search for meeting places where they can stand together and explore their differences about the choices life presents.

(Booth, 1974: 111)

Throughout this book we have tried to clear a public space in which rival practical theologies along with their secular counterparts might meet in fair and forthright contest. But clearing such a space required us to unearth certain misconceptions, prejudices, and unwarranted claims about the nature of practical theology and to eliminate any rigging of the contest, any privileged refuge from the rule of reason. What we have achieved, we believe, is a generic definition of practical theology, a specification of the rules governing its enterprise, and a complex set of criteria for adjudicating the contest among rival models addressing its tasks.

We will now review the ordered set of propositions, argued previously, which constitute our definition of practical theology. We will underline exactly what agreement on these propositions entails regarding the way practical theologies are created, expressed, and defended, and regarding the kinds of claims that may be made on their behalf. We submit, finally, that agreement on these issues neither predetermines the outcome of any contest nor precludes fundamental disagreement about which concrete models of religious praxis Christian communities may actually adopt.

Here, then, is our definition of practical theology:

Practical theology is:

1. *A distinct genre of theological discourse*
2. *formally analogous to secular ideology.*
3. *It is grounded in a dialectic of theory and praxis*
4. *and works from a critical construction of the essence of a religious tradition*
5. *to create distinct theological models of self and history.*
6. *With the help of other genres of public discourse it leads to social policy formation, decision, and action*
7. *and establishes a mode of socialization*
8. *that is truth-dependent.*

Let us review each of these interlocking statements for what they entail about the nature and tasks of practical theology:

1. *A distinct genre of theological discourse. . . .* We accept David Tracy's and Schubert Ogden's understanding of theology in general as divided by a variety of focal questions, modes of inquiry, and implied audiences. But we also insist that these distinguishing factors become effective only within distinct forms of discourse. A formal structure, a genre, like a mode of economic production, puts theological reflection to work in a distinctively organized and directed manner.

Agreement here requires a commitment not just to theological pluralism but also to theological polyphony. No single genre of theological discourse can be labeled "theology proper." Paradigms do not arise out of any single genre. Rather they exist, if at all, as deep structures underlying all theological and humanistic disciplines in a particular historical epoch. Further, a commitment to polyphony means developing an ear for polyphony. Each genre has its own timbre and range, its own purpose and standards of excellence.

2. . . . *formally analogous to secular ideology.* While we compared practical theologies to other forms of religious practical discourse like the Jeremiad, our principal objective was to establish the formal similarities between practical theologies and modern ideologies understood in a nonpejorative fashion. The following chart summarizes our argument. (Figure 8.1) Only in one respect do ideologies and practical theologies differ: the latter develop models which explicitly refer to Ultimate Reality and seek nothing less than an ultimate transformation through religious praxis. This basic intentionality, of course, must be understood as qualifying each of the similarities between ideologies and practical theologies which we have elaborated.

Agreement on this proposition entails several corollaries. We will mention three: a) Practical theologies, as kin to secular ideologies, cannot lay claim to some privileged plateau of sacred discourse. Practical theologies are thrown, willy nilly, into the same arena of public debate as their secular counterparts. Any practical theology will have to argue the adequacy, appropriateness and authenticity of its own model of cultural transformation. It will also have to defend the basic assumption governing religious praxis, namely, that only a process of ultimate transformation can produce true social change. b) Practical theologies, therefore, do more than shape the consciousness of the religiously committed. They seek, as does any ideology, to transform the consciousness of the public at large. Vying with other ideologies, they must recommend positive cultural syntheses. They cannot simply engage in a negative dialectic towards the other available ideologies, as if that stance did not necessarily imply a commitment to seek specific alternatives. c) Practical theologies are not immune to the diseases which infect their ideological kin. The single most effective preventive medicine is to view *any* practical theology as only a model. Model-theory allows practical theologians to preserve the space of public discourse which the pathological deformations of ideology would otherwise destroy.

3. *It is grounded in a dialectic of theory and praxis.* With its perspectival understanding of truth, model-theory makes us suspicious of any orthodoxy or orthopraxis. More importantly, as was

Figure 8.1 Common Traits of Ideologies and Practical Theologies

1. Context	Characteristic of modern cultures
2. Motivation	Dialectic of ideals and interests
3. Foundation	Dialectic of theory and praxis
4. Structure	Synchronic Normative images Explanatory theories Diachronic Critical retrievals Utopian projections
5. Public Stance	Apology Critique
6. Rhetoric	Rhetoric of crisis Rhetoric of critical discourse
7. Product	Models of cultural reality which form the basis for social policy formation, decision, and action
8. Impact	Create communities committed to a determinate form of praxis; establish a truth-dependent mode of socialization
9. Pathology	Epistemic, functional, and genetic deformations
10. Criteria	Comprehensive criteria of adequacy, appropriateness, and authenticity applied to the structural elements

argued, the very nature of praxis itself requires us to reject formally the dogmatic claims of any position determined a priori, whether theoretically or practically. Praxis emerges only in dialectical relationship with theory. In such a relationship each pole of the dialectic transforms the other pole.

Apart from the rejection of orthodoxy and orthopraxis, the primary implication of the dialectic of theory and praxis is to reinforce our commitment to the public validation of models of practical theology. As symbolically constituted and critically reflected action seeking to inaugurate the truly human good, praxis depends upon speech acts which represent that good with some degree of universalizability. We may and must ask: are these specifically religious representations substantively adequate, normatively appropriate, and authentically expressive of an emancipatory intent for society as a whole?

4. *And works from a critical construction of the essence of a tradition. . . .* We argued that neither religious praxis nor the interest in emancipation ever appears in purely formal terms. The obvious limits to Habermas's analysis of the regulative power of the ideal speech situation led us to insist upon the pivotal role of critical hermeneutics in developing any practical theology. Later we defined hermeneutics as the critical reconstruction of both past and present horizons of meaning, value, and action, and thus placed ourselves in opposition to Gadamer's "hermeneutic of consent." But we also argued against any orthodox or orthopraxic hermeneutics which would canonize some past or present religious form of life as a *norma normans non normata.* As a constructive alternative we revised Troeltsch's approach to determining the essence of a religious tradition, by sharpening his notion of immanent criticism so that in principle it includes ideology-critique.

Beyond the rejection of any norm that has been canonized a priori, the most important implication of this critical hermeneutic is to recognize that the adequacy and appropriateness of cultural interpretation can only be achieved through processes of historical immersion within the full multiplicity of a tradition. The authenticity of critical hermeneutics, however, demands that such processes contribute to the self-transcending formation of persons in community. Hermeneutics as self-justification is profoundly untrue to the dialectical character of any attempt to formulate the essence of a tradition.

5. . . . *to create distinct theological models of self and history.* We then argued that the dialectic of theory and praxis at some stage requires systematic reflection in order to transform the results of critical hermeneutic inquiry into an explicit model of practical theology. Such models correlate a synchronic element (theological anthropology) with a diachronic element (theology of history), derived from some particular conception of religious transcendence or Ultimate Reality.

Figure 8.2 Models of Practical Theology

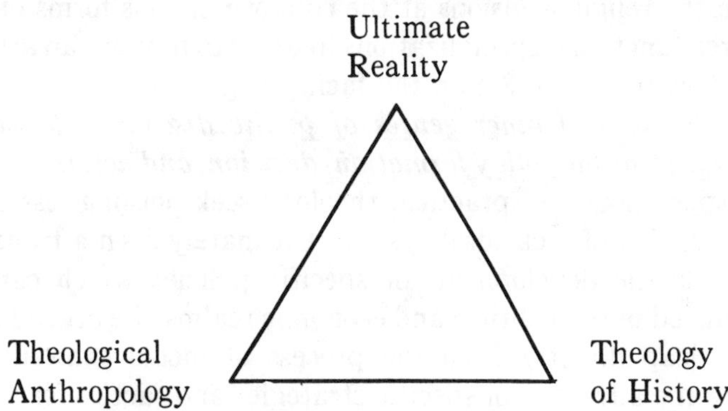

The triangular character of Figure 8.2 nicely indicates the interdependence of these elements. Just as each angle of the triangle varies in direct relationship with the other two angles, so the specific structures of theological anthropology and the theology of history vary, not only in relationship to each other but also in response to a distinctive perspective on Ultimate Reality.

Each element of systematically theological reflection in practical theology also corresponds to competing elements in secular ideologies. So we insisted that practical theologies confront the denial of religious transcendence in secular ideologies and struggle with the issues of autonomy versus theonomy and utopia versus eschatology. Each of these debates was seen as an aspect of the fundamental intention of practical theologies to correlate models of emancipation with models of redemption.

To accept the moment of model-construction in the dialectic of theory and praxis is to reject the notion that practical theology merely reflects the involvements of a religious community. The struggles of such a community become praxis only through the mediation of some explicit model of practical theology. The development or selection of such models is likewise never the result of purely strategic considerations. The integrity of the functional specializations must be respected in the development of the models, and procedures of typological comparison and evaluation must guide the selection of these models. The enterprise of constructing models of practical theology moves from the religious visions at the core of religious forms of life through three functional specializations in order to produce an articulated model, as in Figure 8.3 on the facing page.

6. *With the help of other genres of public discourse, practical theology leads to social policy formation, decision, and action. . . .* Like ideologies, models of practical theology seek nothing less than the transformation of a cultural system. Ultimately such a transformation entails the development of specific policies which can be institutionalized in the political and economic realms. We argued that no one can leap directly from the process of model construction directly into the advocacy of specific strategies and tactics for social change. For highly generalized models of emancipation and redemption cannot dictate either specific social policies or forms of collective action appropriate to them. This does not mean that practical theologians must abdicate responsible advocacy in favor of strategic planners, politicians, and revolutionary leaders. It does imply that the dialectic of theory and praxis requires a *series* of interlocking mediations. One genre of public discourse, in particular, is necessary to effect the transition to specific questions of policy, the genre of Christian social ethics.

The first step in *this* phase of the dialectic of theory and praxis is to create a set of middle axioms. Middle axioms represent both the

Figure 8.3 Constructing a Model of Practical Theology

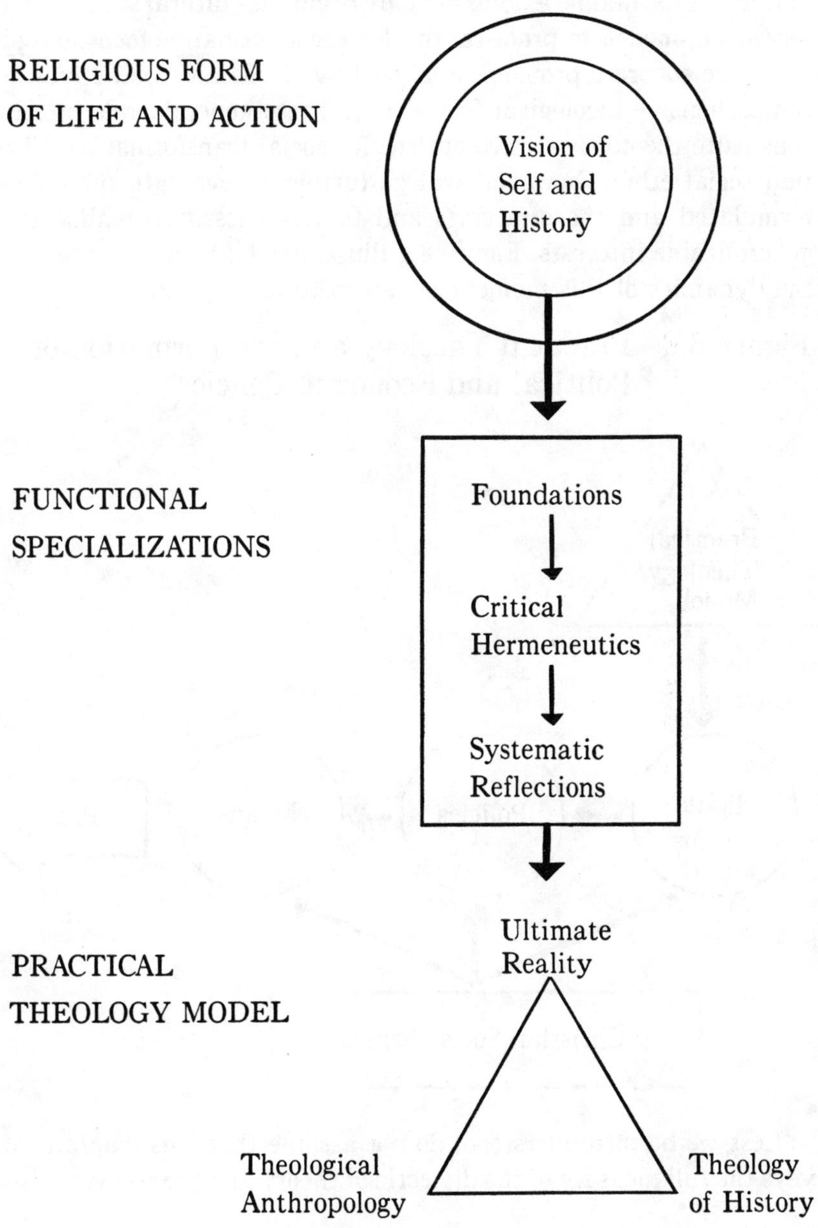

culmination of practical theology and the point of departure for Christian social ethics. By seeking to determine a society's generalizable interests, middle axioms not only bring the cultural syntheses put forward in models of practical theology to a normative focus, but also place the concrete problems analyzed by Christian social ethics in a comprehensive ideological framework. These generalizable interests constitute the culture's live options for social transformation. Christian social ethics, however, will go further to evaluate the policies formulated and the strategies and tactics chosen to realize these generalizable interests. Figure 8.4 illustrates both the structure and the dynamics of this moment of return towards praxis.

Figure 8.4 Practical Theology and the Formation of Political and Economic Policies

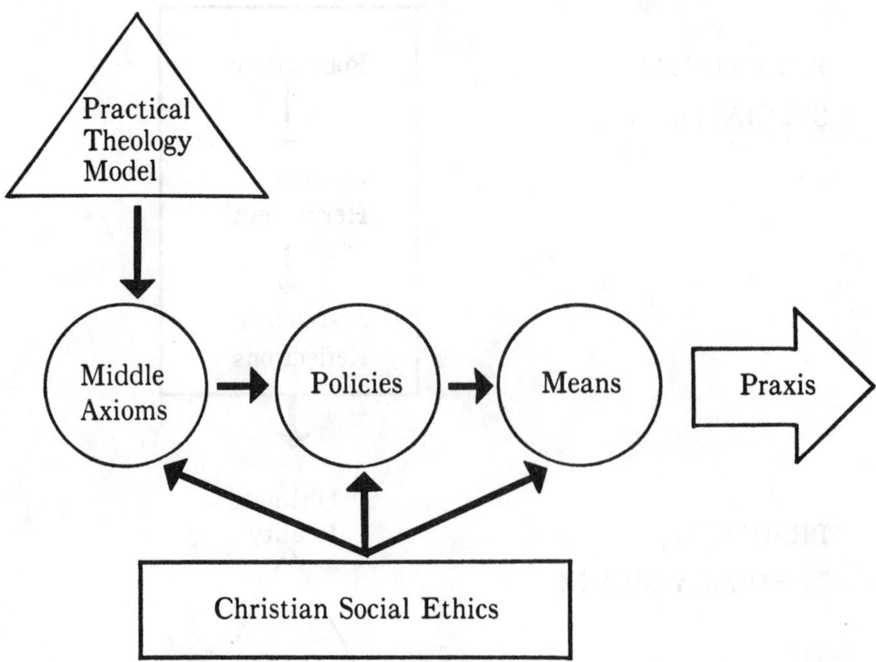

Lest we be misunderstood, do not assume that this diagram conveys the full measure of the dialectic of theory and praxis even within

this moment. It does not indicate how praxis affects theory. A fully explicit diagram would also show all the various feedback loops. The creative breakthroughs and the dead ends, the moral dilemmas and the unforeseen repercussions of praxis, each in turn raise questions about the determination of middle axioms, policies, strategies and tactics. Such questions may force major revisions of both Christian social ethics and practical theology.

To accept our view of middle axioms implies a willingness to engage in more extensive processes of collaboration than most practical theologians have envisioned. Anything less would justify the charge of dilettantism raised by those who have been forced to recognize that the urgency of the need for social change is matched by the complexity of the task.

7. *And establishes a mode of socialization. . . .* Since social policies remain lifeless apart from the groups which carry them forward, practical theologies necessarily seek to create and sustain communities of praxis. As we indicated, practical theologies address themselves to three audiences: religious communities potentially committed to a specific praxis of ultimate transformation, ideological communities, and theological communities. In their attempts to influence such communities, practical theologies employ both the rhetoric of crisis and the rhetoric of critical discourse. Both are combined in the formal operations of constructing the model and in the more fluid, audience-centered subgenres which perform the vision.

Acceptance of these propositions means rejecting any option that makes either rhetoric the exclusively appropriate norm for practical theological discourse. Both rhetorical modes are not only permissible, they are essential to the task of practical theology. Any particular combination of these modes, however, must adhere to the rules of rhetoric derived from the dialectic of theory and praxis.

Chapters Six and Seven, therefore, point to two different but related functions of models of practical theology. We can get a clearer grasp of these functions, namely, the formation of a culture's consciousness and the creation of communities of praxis, if we view culture not as a typical triad but as a tetrahedron of interacting dimensions: Consciousness (the dimension of symbolic interaction or

Figure 8.5 Practical Theology: Consciousness and Community-Formation

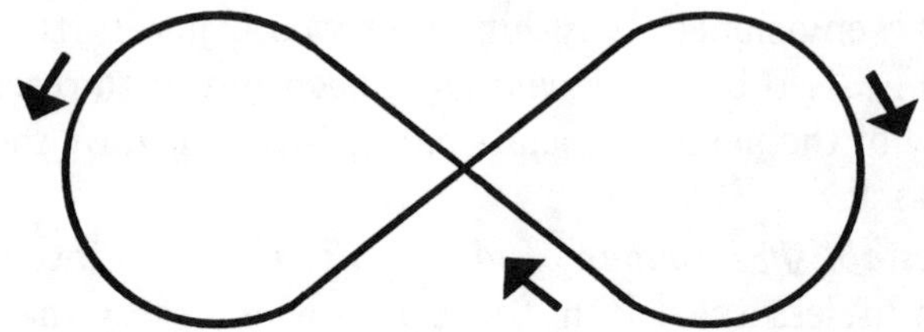

public opinion), Labor (economic dimension), Power (political dimension), and Community (the dimension of primary personal formation):

In terms of our tetrahedonal model of culture, Chapter Six referred to the complex set of operations necessary for the consciousness shaped by practical theologies to establish public policies and priorities for the transformation of the political and economic dimensions of the cultural system. Chapter Seven, on the other hand, focused on the task of providing, in Clifford Geertz's terminology, a matrix for the creation of a particular community's conscience. As forms of literary praxis, practical theologies shape communities even as they address public issues. For within models of practical theology, consciousness and community are reciprocally related. Finally, when the dialectical interplay between performing the vision and constructing the model unfolds successfully, a unique mode of socialization emerges—a truth-dependent mode of socialization.

Figure 8.6 Cultural System

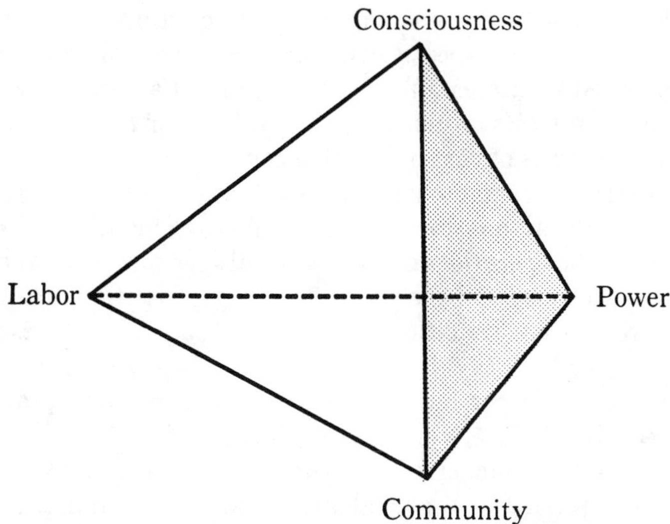

8\. . . . *that is truth-dependent* We argued that all ideologies seek not merely to persuade but to convince. Furthermore, persuasion is contingent upon conviction. In this sense any ideology intends to foster a truth-dependent mode of socialization. Even in their pathological forms ideologies must *appear* to be governed by the norms of adequacy, appropriateness, and authenticity. Propaganda, as systematically distorted communication, apes the forms of a truth-dependent mode of socialization as it subverts them. An authentic ideology, by contrast, really is open to both public validation and transformation according to publicly available criteria.

To state the need for common criteria is one matter; to develop them is another. "Nothing is more controversial among human beings," insists Schubert Ogden, "than just what are to count as the standards or criteria for determining the credibility of their various claims." (1981a: 132) Whatever the general merits of Ogden's remark, it certainly is applicable to practical theologians. We sought to resolve this difficulty by locating the basis for comprehensive judgment in the canons of communicative competence which govern all speech acts. Habermas's important contribution was to link the criteria of communicative competence—adequacy, appropriateness, and authenticity—to the emancipatory interest through the regulative fiction of the ideal speech situation. Ideological discourse which claims to serve the interest in emancipation must anticipate so far as is possible those traits of noncoercive, truth-seeking discourse.

A formal analysis of communicative competence, however, cannot provide criteria for concrete judgments. (Cf. Lonergan, 1958: 277–78) So we derived the actual standards for evaluating models of practical theology from the operations of its functional specializations and from the structural elements of the genre. These concrete standards reflect the comprehensive criteria of adequacy, appropriateness and authenticity.

We can neither enter into the dialectic of theory and praxis nor follow the procedures of constructing models of practical theology without committing ourselves to a complex process of making judgments. The integrity of this evaluative process is a function of its conformity to the mode of discourse and structure characteristic of the genre of practical theology. By contrast, the attempt to stipulate a single norm, say, the criterion of practical effectiveness, simply short-circuits the dialectic of theory and praxis. How do we know that a seemingly effective strategy is adequate, appropriate, and authentic allegiance to the cause of the oppressed? When, as previously discussed, we introduce the feedback loop into the evaluative process, such questions become more complicated but less abstract. Nevertheless, our claim for this truth-dependent mode of socialization finally comes down to a single decisive proposition: While only the truth liberates, only the truth that liberates can be fully adequate, appropriate, and authentic.

The aim of this book, then, has been to clear a public space within which practical theologians of every stripe can stand and debate their differences. Such a space is necessary, we believe, if practical theology is to avoid being transformed into an instrument of war, a weapon in a truth-distorting mode of socialization. Our response to John Courtney Murray's call for dialogue, we hope, will not merely dispel the spectre of "ignorant armies clashing by night." (Murray, 1958: 41) It will also enhance the prospects for a healthy pluralism. Accepting our view of the elements and procedures of practical theology will lead to no false ideological consensus. As Wayne Booth insists, practical theologians will continue to "disagree about some questions to which reason, nevertheless, must apply." (Booth, 1974: 111)

Even public discourse may not resolve all differences. Rational argument may remove some models as inadequate, inappropriate and inauthentic but it may also confirm more than one position. There are numerous valid perspectives. While some perspectival models may be more inclusive than others, it is highly unlikely that any single model will sublate all of its competitors. At this point praxis must have the final word. Is a given model a live option in the sense that some community wills to embody it in a process of ultimate transformation? Will that process generate a new and fruitful religious form of life permeating a cultural system? Again, we forsee no single form of praxis as sublating all others. There are many paths up the same mountain.

The pluralism that we advocate must not be confused with a merely liberal tolerance, with the safe and stultifying consensus which, to paraphrase Metz, allows anything to happen except something which might make a difference. (Cf. 1980: 174–75) Healthy pluralism thrives in the contestation of conflicting perspectives. A genuinely pluralistic society transforms itself by actualizing a variety of live options. Social change moves along several axial directions. Forms of life, grounded in conflicting models for praxis, proliferate, interact, and merge. Within a healthy pluralism survival may become a function of self-transcendence.

That, at least, is our answer to the challenge to practical theology dramatized by Brecht's *Mother Courage and Her Children*. In reasserting the intrinsic connection between religion and politics, practical theologians must not forget the bitter lessons of the Thirty Years War. This generation's attempt to retrieve Christianity's worldly mission need not yield to the illusions of simplistic activism nor to the wizened cynicism embodied in Mother Courage herself. Yet we believe that Brecht's parable may envision our fate, unless those of us committed to critical reflection on religious praxis pursue our tasks with a disciplined sense of intellectual responsibility. Public space, public discourse, reasoned debate. Will any of it actually lead to the creation of more powerful and more relevant models of practical theology? No one knows for certain. We do know, however, that Murray's vision of "a new dialectical day" rises before anyone who would undertake the tasks of practical theology as both an invitation and an imperative. Before that vision we stand gifted and confronted.

WORKS CITED

Alves, Rubem

1973 "Christian Realism: Ideology of the Establishment," *Christianity and Crisis* 33:173–76.

Apel, Karl-Otto

1980 *Towards a Transformation of Philosophy*. Trans. Glyn Adey and David Frisby. London: Routledge and Kegan Paul.

Arendt, Hannah

1958 *The Human Condition*. Garden City, N.Y.: Doubleday and Co.

Assmann, Hugo

1976 *Theology for a Nomad Church*. Introduction by Frederick Herzog. Translated by Paul Burns. Maryknoll, N.Y.: Orbis Books.

Baelz, Peter

1977 *Ethics and Belief*. New York: Seabury Press.

Bailyn, Bernard

1967 *The Ideological Origins of the American Revolution*. Cambridge, Mass.: Belknap Press of the Harvard University Press.

Barbour, Ian G.

1971 *Issues in Science and Religion*. New York: Harper and Row.

1974 *Myths, Models, and Paradigms: A Comparative Study in Science and Religion*. New York: Harper and Row.

Barthes, Roland

1972 *Critical Essays*. Evanston, Ill.: Northwestern University Press.

Beecher, Catherine

1857 *Common Sense Applied to Religion; or the Bible and the People*. New York: Harper and Brothers.

Benjamin, Walter

1968 *Illuminations*. Edited with an introduction by Hannah Arendt. New York: Harcourt, Brace, and World.

Benne, Robert

1981 *The Ethic of Democratic Capitalism: A Moral Reassessment*. Philadelphia: Fortress Press.

Bennett, John C.

1946 *Christian Ethics and Social Policy*. New York: Charles Scribner's Sons.

1975 *The Radical Imperative*. Philadelphia: Westminster Press.

Bercovitch, Sacvan ed.

1974 *The American Puritan Imagination: Essays in Reevaluation*. New York: Cambridge University Press.

1978 *The American Jeremiad*. Madison, Wisc.: University of Wisconsin Press.

Bernstein, Richard J.

1971 *Praxis and Action*. Philadelphia: University of Pennsylvania Press.

1976 *The Restructuring of Social and Political Theory*. New York: Harcourt, Brace, Jovanovich.

Betz, Hans-Dieter

1979 *Galatians: A Commentary on Paul's Letter to the Churches in Galatia*. Philadelphia: Fortress Press.

Bloom, Allan

1968 "Interpretive Essay" in *The Republic of Plato*: 305–436. New York: Basic Books.

Bondurant, Joan

1958 *Conquest of Violence*. Berkeley: University of California Press.

Booth, Wayne

1974 *Modern Dogma and the Rhetoric of Assent*. Chicago: University of Chicago Press.

Brecht, Bertolt

1962 *Mother Courage and Her Children*. Translated by Eric Bentley. London: Methuen and Co. Ltd.

Browning, Don S.

1983 "Pastoral Theology in a Pluralistic Age." In *Practical Theology: The Emerging Field in Theology, Church, and World*: 187–202. Edited by Don S. Browning. New York: Harper and Row.

Burkhart, John E.
1983 "Schleiermacher's Vision for Theology." In *Practical Theology: The Emerging Field in Theology, Church, and World*: 42–57. Edited by Don S. Browning. New York: Harper and Row.

Buss, Martin
1979 "Understanding Communication." In *Encounter With the Text*: 3–44. Edited by Martin Buss. Philadelphia: Fortress Press.

Capps, Walter H.
1976 *Hope Against Hope: Moltmann to Merton in One Theological Decade*. Philadelphia: Fortress Press.

Cherry, Conrad, ed.
1971 *God's New Israel*. Englewood Cliffs, N.J.: Prentice-Hall.

Clebsch, William
1974 "Towards a History of Christianity," *Church History*. 43: 5–16.
1979 *Christianity in European History*. New York: Oxford University Press.

Cobb, John B.
1967 *The Structure of Christian Existence*. Philadelphia: Westminster Press.
1982 *Process Theology as Political Theology*. Philadelphia: Westminster Press.

Coleman, John
1979 "Theology and Philosophy in Public: John Courtney Murray's Unfinished Agenda," *Theological Studies* 40: 701–706.
1982 *An American Strategic Theology*. New York: Paulist Press.

Cone, James H.
1972 *The Spirituals and the Blues*. New York: Seabury Press.
1975 *God of the Oppressed*. New York: Seabury Press.

Cott, Nancy F.
1977 *The Bonds of Womanhood: "Woman's Sphere" in New England, 1780–1835*. New Haven: Yale University Press.

Crites, Stephen
1971 "The Narrative Quality of Experience," *Journal of the American Academy of Religion* 39: 291–311.

1972 "Pseudonymous Authorship as Art and as Act" in *Kierkegaard: A Collection of Critical Essays*: 183–229. Edited by Josiah Thompson. Garden City, N.Y.: Doubleday and Co.

Crossan, John Dominic
1975 *The Dark Interval: Towards a Theology of Story*. Niles, Ill.: Argus Communications.
1983 *In Fragments: The Aphorisms of Jesus*. New York: Harper and Row.

Daly, Mary
1973 *Beyond God the Father*. Boston: Beacon Press.

Davis, Charles
1967 *A Question of Conscience*. London: Hodder and Stoughton.
1980 *Theology and Political Society. The Hulsean Lectures in the University of Cambridge, 1978*. Cambridge: Cambridge University Press.

Day, Dorothy
1952 *The Long Loneliness*. Garden City, N.Y.: Doubleday and Co.
1963 *Loaves and Fishes*. New York: Curtis Books.

Degler, Carl N.
1980 *At Odds: Women and the Family in America from the Revolution to the Present*. New York: Oxford University Press.

Didion, Joan
1979 *The White Album*. New York: Pocket Books.

Douglas, Ann
1977 *The Feminization of American Culture*. New York: Avon Books.

Dumont, Louis
1977 *From Mandeville to Marx: The Genesis and Triumph of Economic Ideology*. Chicago: University of Chicago Press.

Dussel, Enrique
1978 *Ethics and the Theology of Liberation*. Translated by Bernard F. McWilliams, C.SS.R. Maryknoll, N.Y.: Orbis Books.

Ellul, Jacques
1973 "Le Rôle Médiateur de l'Idéologie." In *Demitizzazione e Ideologia, Archivio di Filosofia*, (1973): 336–54.

Epstein, Barbara Leslie

1981 *The Politics of Domesticity: Women, Evangelism and Temperance in Nineteenth Century America.* Middletown, Conn.: Wesleyan University Press.

Fackenheim, Emil

1967 *The Religious Dimension in Hegel's Thought.* Boston: Beacon Press.

Farley, Edward

1983 "Theology and Practice Outside the Clerical Paradigm." In *Practical Theology: The Emerging Field in Theology, Church, and World*: 21–41. Edited by Don S. Browning. New York: Harper and Row.

Feuerbach, Ludwig

1972 *The Fiery Brook: Selected Writings of Ludwig Feuerbach.* Translated by Zawar Hanfi. Garden City, N.Y.: Doubleday and Co.

Fierro, Alfredo

1977 *The Militant Gospel: A Critical Introduction to Political Theologies.* Translated by John Drury. Maryknoll, N.Y.: Orbis Books.

Fish, Stanley E.

1972 *Self-Consuming Artifacts: The Experience of Seventeenth Century Literature.* Berkeley: University of California Press.

Fowler, Alastair

1971 "The Life and Death of Literary Forms," *New Literary History* 2: 199–216.

Freire, Paulo

1970 *Pedagogy of the Oppressed.* Translated by Myra Bergman Ramos. New York: Seabury Press.

Frye, Northrop

1957 *Anatomy of Criticism.* Princeton: Princeton University Press.

Fulbright, J. William

1971 "The Arrogance of Power." In *God's New Israel: Religious Interpretations of American Destiny*: 332–46. Edited by Conrad Cherry. Englewood Cliffs, N.J.: Prentice-Hall.

Fuller, Margaret

1971 *Woman in the Nineteenth Century*. New York: W.W. Norton.

Gadamer, Hans-Georg

1971 "Replik." In *Hermeneutik und Ideologiekritik*: 283–317. Edited by Jürgen Habermas et. al. Frankfurt am Main: Suhrkamp.

Gallie, W.B.

1964 *Philosophy and Historical Understanding*. New York: Schocken Books.

Geertz, Clifford

1973a "Ideology as a Cultural System." In *The Interpretation of Cultures*: 193–233. New York: Basic Books.

1973b "Religion as a Cultural System." In *The Interpretation of Cultures*: 87–125. New York: Basic Books.

1980 "Blurred Genres: The Refiguration of Social Thought." *The American Scholar* 49: 165–79.

Geuss, Raymond

1981 *The Idea of a Critical Theory: Habermas and the Frankfurt School*. Cambridge: Cambridge University Press.

Geyer, Alan

1982 *The Idea of Disarmament: Rethinking the Unthinkable*. Elgin, Ill.: Brethren Press.

Gilkey, Langdon

1976 *Reaping the Whirlwind*. New York: Seabury Press.

1981 *Society and the Sacred*. New York: Crossroad Books.

Girnus, Wilhelm

1973 "On the Problem of Ideology and Literature," *New Literary History* 4: 483–500.

Gouldner, Alvin W.

1976 *The Dialectic of Ideology and Technology: The Origins, Grammar, and Future of Ideology*. New York: Seabury Press.

1979 *The Future of Intellectuals and the Rise of the New Class*. New York: Seabury Press.

Gunnemann, Jon

1979 *The Moral Meaning of Revolution*. New Haven: Yale University Press.

Gustafson, James M.

1971 *Christian Ethics and the Community.* Philadelphia: Pilgrim Press.

1974 *Theology and Christian Ethics.* Philadelphia: Pilgrim Press.

1975 *Can Ethics Be Christian?* Chicago: University of Chicago Press.

1978 *Protestant and Roman Catholic Ethics.* Chicago: University of Chicago Press.

1981 *Ethics from a Theocentric Perspective, Volume One: Theology and Ethics.* Chicago: University of Chicago Press.

Gutierrez, Gustavo

1973 *A Theology of Liberation.* Translated and edited by Sister Caridad Inda and John Eagleson. Maryknoll, N.Y.: Orbis Books.

Habermas, Jürgen

1970 *Toward a Rational Society.* Translated by Jeremy J. Shapiro. Boston: Beacon Press.

1971a *Knowledge and Human Interests.* Translated by Jeremy J. Shapiro. Boston: Beacon Press.

1971b "Vorbereitende Bemerkungen zu einer Theorie der kommunikativen Kompetenz." In *Theorie der Gesellschaft oder Sozialtechnologie: Was leistet die Systemforschung?*: 101–141. Frankfurt am Main: Suhrkamp.

1971c "Die Universalitätsanspruch der Hermeneutik." In *Hermeneutik und Ideologiekritik*: 120–59. Edited by Jürgen Habermas et. al. Frankfurt am Main: Suhrkamp.

1973 *Theory and Practice.* Translated by John Viertel. Boston: Beacon Press.

1975 *Legitimation Crisis.* Translated with an Introduction by Thomas McCarthy. Boston: Beacon Press.

1979 *Communication and the Evolution of Society.* Translated with an Introduction by Thomas McCarthy. Boston: Beacon Press.

1982 "A Reply to My Critics." In *Habermas: Critical Debates*: 219–283. Edited by John B. Thompson and David Held. Cambridge, Mass.: M.I.T. Press.

Harned, David

1973 *Faith and Virtue.* Philadelphia: Pilgrim Press.

Harrison, Beverly Wildung

1975 "Challenging the Western Paradigm: The 'Theology in Americas' Conference." *Christianity and Crisis* 35: 251–54.

Harvey, Van A.
1966 *The Historian and the Believer.* New York: MacMillan.

Hegel, G.W.F.
1953 *Reason in History: a General Introduction to the Philosophy of History.* Translated by Robert S. Hartman. Indianapolis: Bobbs-Merrill.
1977 *Phenomenology of Spirit.* Translated by A.V. Miller. New York: Oxford University Press.

Hennelly, Alfred T.
1979 *Theologies in Conflict: The Challenge of Juan Luis Segundo.* Maryknoll, N.Y.: Orbis Books.

Hirsch, E.D., Jr.
1967 *Validity in Interpretation.* New Haven: Yale University Press.

James, William
1967 *The Writings of William James.* Edited by John J. McDermott. New York: Random House.

Kant, Immanuel
1963 "What Is Enlightenment?" In *Kant: On History*: 3–10. Edited with an Introduction by Lewis White Beck. Indianapolis: Bobbs-Merrill.

Kermode, Frank
1967 *The Sense of An Ending.* New York: Oxford University Press.

King, Martin Luther
1963 *Why We Can't Wait.* New York: New American Library.

Kuhn, Thomas S.
1970 *The Structure of Scientific Revolutions.* Second Edition. Chicago: University of Chicago Press.

Küng, Hans
1968 *Truthfulness: The Future of the Church.* Translated by Edward Quinn. London: Sheed and Ward.

Lamb, Matthew
1976 "The Theory-Praxis Relationship in Contemporary Christian Theologies," *Proceedngs of the Catholic Theological Society of America* 31: 149–78.

1982 *Solidarity With Victims: Toward a Theology of Social Transformation*. New York: Crossroad Books.

Lichtheim, George
1967 *The Concept of Ideology and Other Essays*. New York: Random House.

Lifton, Robert J., and Falk, Richard
1982 *Indefensible Weapons: The Political and Psychological Case Against Nuclearism*. New York: Basic Books.

Little, H. Ganse
1966 "Ernst Troeltsch and the Scope of Historicism," *Journal of Religion* 46: 343–64.
1968 "Ernst Troeltsch on History, Decision, and Responsibility," *Journal of Religion* 48: 201–34.

Lobkowicz, Nicholas
1967 *Theory and Practice: History of a Concept from Aristotle to Marx*. Notre Dame, Ind.: University of Notre Dame Press.

Lonergan, Bernard
1958 *Insight*. New York: Harper and Row.
1972 *Method in Theology*. New York: Herder and Herder.

Lukacs, Georg
1971 "Towards a Methodology of the Problem of Organization." In *History and Class Consciousness: Studies in Marxist Dialectics*: 295–342. Translated by Rodney Livingstone. Cambridge, Mass.: M.I.T. Press.

McCann, Dennis P.
1976 "Ernst Troeltsch's Essay on 'Socialism'," *Journal of Religious Ethics* 4/1: 159–80.
1981a *Christian Realism and Liberation Theology: Practical Theologies in Creative Conflict*. Maryknoll, N.Y.: Orbis Books.
1981b "Habermas and the Theologians." *Religious Studies Review* 7:14–21.
1981c "A Second Look at Middle Axioms," *The Annual of the Society of Christian Ethics, 1981*: 73–96.
1981d "Political Ideologies and Practical Theology: Is There a Difference?" *Union Seminary Quarterly Review* 36: 243–257.

McCarthy, Thomas

1978 *The Critical Theory of Jürgen Habermas.* Cambridge, Mass.: M.I.T. Press.

1982 "Rationality and Relativism: Habermas's 'Overcoming' of Hermeneutics." In *Habermas: Critical Debates*: 57–78. Edited by John B. Thompson and David Held. Cambridge, Mass.: M.I.T. Press.

McElwain, Hugh T.

1983 *Theology of Limits and the Limits of Theology: Reflections on Language, Environment and Death.* Lanham, Md.: University Press of America.

McGuire, Michael

1982 "The Structure of Rhetoric," *Philosophy and Rhetoric* 15: 149–67.

MacIntyre, Alasdair

1981 *After Virtue: A Study in Moral Theory.* Notre Dame, Ind.: University of Notre Dame Press.

Mackey, Louis

1971 *Kierkegaard: A Kind of Poet.* Philadelphia: University of Pennsylvania Press.

McLaughlin, Eleanor L.

1975 "The Christian Past: Does it Hold a Future for Women?" *Anglican Theological Review* 57: 36–56.

Mannheim, Karl

1936 *Ideology and Utopia: An Introduction to the Sociology of Knowledge.* Translated by Louis Wirth and Edward Shils. New York: Harcourt, Brace and World.

Manuel, Frank E. and Manuel, Fritzie P.

1979 *Utopian Thought in the Western World.* Cambridge, Mass.: Harvard University Press.

Marx, Karl

1967 *The Writings of the Young Marx on Philosophy and Society.* Translated and edited by Loyd D. Easton and Kurt H. Guddat. Garden City, N.Y.: Doubleday and Co.

1977 *Critique of Hegel's "Philosophy of Right."* Translated by Annette Jolin and Joseph O'Malley. Edited with an introduction and notes by Joseph O'Malley. London: Cambridge University Press.

Marx, Karl and Engels, Frederick

1947 *The German Ideology.* New York: International Publishers.

1959 *Basic Writings on Politics and Philosophy.* Edited by Lewis S. Feuer. Garden City, N.Y.: Doubleday and Co.

1964 *On Religion.* Introduction by Reinhold Niebuhr. New York: Schocken Books.

Maurin, Peter

1949 *Catholic Radicalism: Phrased Essays for the Green Revolution.* New York: Catholic Worker Books.

Metz, Johannes B.

1969 *Theology of the World.* Translated by William Glen Doepel. New York: Herder and Herder.

1980 *Faith in History and Society.* Translated by David Smith. New York: Seabury Press.

Miguez-Bonino, José

1983 *Toward a Christian Political Ethics.* Philadelphia: Fortress Press.

Miller, Perry

1956 *Errand into the Wilderness.* New York: Harper and Row.

Miller, Perry and Johnson, Thomas, eds.

1963 *The Puritans Vol. I.* New York: Harper and Row.

Mink, Louis O.

1974 "History and Fiction as Modes of Comprehension." In *New Directions in Literary History*: 107–24. Edited by Ralph Cohen. Baltimore: Johns Hopkins University Press.

1981 "Everyman His or Her Own Annalist." *Critical Inquiry* 7:771–83.

Misgeld, Dieter

1976 "Critical Theory and Hermeneutics: The Debate Between Habermas and Gadamer." In *On Critical Theory*: 164–83. Edited by John O'Neill. New York: Seabury Press.

Moltmann, Jürgen

1967 *Theology of Hope.* Translated by James W. Leitch. London: SCM Press.

1974 *Man: Christian Anthropology in the Conflicts of the Present.* Translated by John Sturdy. Philadelphia: Fortress Press.

Murray, John Courtney

1958 "America's Four Conspiracies." In *Religion in America*: 12–41. Edited by John Cogley. New York: Meridian Books.

National Conference of Catholic Bishops

1983 "The Challenge of Peace: God's Promise and Our Response," *The National Catholic Reporter* (June 17, 1983) 19: 5–28.

Niebuhr, H. Richard

1937 *The Kingdom of God in America.* New York: Harper and Row.

1951 *Christ and Culture.* New York: Harper and Row.

1963 *The Responsible Self: An Essay in Christian Philosophy.* Introduction by James M. Gustafson. New York: Harper and Row.

Niebuhr, Reinhold

1939 "Ten Years That Shook My World," *The Christian Century* 56: 542–46.

1953 *Christian Realism and Political Problems.* New York: Charles Scribner's Sons.

1958 "Walter Rauschenbusch in Historical Perspective," *Religion in Life* 27: 527–36.

1962 *The Irony of American History.* New York: Charles Scribner's Sons.

1964 *The Nature and Destiny of Man.* 2 vols. New York: Charles Scribner's Sons.

1979 *An Interpretation of Christian Ethics.* New York: Seabury Press. (Reprint of 1935 edition).

Nielsen, Kai

1973 *Ethics Without God.* Buffalo, N.Y.: Prometheus Books.

Norman, Edward

1979 *Christianity and the World Order.* New York: Oxford University Press.

Novak, Michael

1982 *The Spirit of Democratic Capitalism.* New York: American Enterprise Institute/Simon and Schuster.

Ogden, Schubert

1972 "What Is Theology?" *Journal of Religion* 52: 22–40.

1979 *Faith and Freedom: Toward a Theology of Liberation.* Nashville: Abingdon Press.

1981a "The Concept of a Theology of Liberation: Must a Christian Theology Today Be So Conceived?" In *The Challenge of Liberation Theology: A First World Response*: 127–40. Edited by Brian Mahan and L. Dale Richesin. Maryknoll, N.Y.: Orbis Books.

1981b "Response to Dorothee Soelle." In *The Challenge of Liberation Theology: A First World Response*: 17–20. Edited by Brian Mahan and L. Dale Richesin. Maryknoll, N.Y.: Orbis Books.

Olafson, Frederick

1979 *The Dialectic of Action: A Philosophical Interpretation of History and the Humanities.* Chicago: University of Chicago Press.

Oldham, J.H.

1937 "The Function of the Church in Society." In *The Church and its Function in Society*: 91–238. By W.A. Visser 'T Hooft and J.H. Oldham. Chicago: Willett, Clark and Company.

Ollman, Bertell

1971 *Alienation: Marx's Concept of Man in Capitalist Society.* Cambridge: Cambridge University Press.

Overend, Trond

1975 "Alienation: A Conceptual Analysis," *Philosophy and Phenomenological Research* 35: 301–22.

Pannenberg, Wolfhart

1976 *Theology and the Philosophy of Science.* Translated by Francis McDonagh. Philadelphia: Westminster Press.

Perelmann, Chaim and Olbrechts-Tyteca, L.

1969 *The New Rhetoric.* Notre Dame, Ind.: University of Notre Dame Press.

Petersen, Norman

1974 "On the Notion of Genre in Via's 'Parable and Example Story,' " *Semeia* 1: 134–81.

Polak, Frederik

1966 "Utopia and Cultural Renewal." In *Utopias and Utopian Thought*: 281–95. Edited by Frank E. Manuel. Boston: Beacon Press.

Potter, Ralph B., Jr.

1969 *War and Moral Discourse*. Richmond, Va.: John Knox Press.

1972 "The Logic of Moral Argument." In *Toward a Discipline of Social Ethics: Essays in Honor of Walter George Muelder*: 93–114. Edited by Paul Deats. Boston: Boston University Press.

Raboteau, Albert J.

1978 *Slave Religion*. New York: Oxford University Press.

Ramsey, Paul

1950 *Basic Christian Ethics*. New York: Charles Scribner's Sons.

Rauschenbusch, Walter

1912 *Christianizing the Social Order*. New York: Macmillan.

1945 *A Theology for the Social Gospel*. New York: Abingdon Press.

1964 *Christianity and the Social Crisis*. New York: Harper and Row.

Rawls, John

1971 *A Theory of Justice*. Cambridge: The Belknap Press of Harvard University Press.

Ricoeur, Paul

1973a "The Hermeneutical Function of Distanciation," *Philosophy Today* 17: 129–41.

1973b "The Task of the Political Educator," *Philosophy Today* 17: 142–52.

1974 "Science et Idéologie," *Revue Philosophique de Louvain* 72: 328–55.

1978 "The Narrative Function," *Semeia* 13: 177–202.

1980 "Narrative Time," *Critical Inquiry* 7: 169–190.

1981 *Hermeneutics and the Human Sciences*. Edited and translated by John B. Thompson. Cambridge: Cambridge University Press.

Robb, Carol S.

1979 "Ethical Procedures of Gutierrez and Alves." In *The American Society of Christian Ethics 1979: Selected Papers*: 75–93. Edited by Max Stackhouse. Waterloo, Ontario: The Council on the Study of Religion.

Ruether, Rosemary Radford

1974 *Religion and Sexism: Images of Women in the Jewish and Christian Traditions.* New York: Simon and Schuster.

1975 *New Woman New Earth: Sexist Ideologies and Human Liberation.* New York: Seabury Press.

Ruland, Vernon

1978 "Understanding the Rhetoric of Theologians." In *The Poetics of Faith: Essays Offered to Amos Niven Wilder. Part Two: Imagination, Rhetoric, and the Disclosure of Faith.* Edited by William A. Beardslee. *Semeia* 13: 203–24.

Rupp, George

1974 *Christologies and Cultures: Toward a Typology of Religious Worldviews.* The Hague: Mouton.

Samuelson, Paul A.

1980 *Economics.* Eleventh Edition. New York: McGraw-Hill.

Schroyer, Trent

1973 *The Critique of Domination.* Boston: Beacon Press.

Schüssler-Fiorenza, Elisabeth

1981 "Toward a Feminist Biblical Hermeneutics: Biblical Interpretation and Liberation Theology." In *The Challenge of Liberation Theology: A First World Response*: 91–112. Edited by Brian Mahan and L. Dale Richesin. Maryknoll, N.Y.: Orbis Books.

1983 *In Memory of Her: A Feminist Theological Reconstruction of Christian Origins.* New York: Crossroad Books.

Segundo, Juan Luis

1976 *The Liberation of Theology.* Translated by John Drury. Maryknoll, N.Y.: Orbis Books.

1979 "Capitalism Versus Socialism: Crux Theologica." In *Frontiers of Theology in Latin America*: 240–59. Edited by Rosino Gibellini. Maryknoll, N.Y.: Orbis Books.

Seliger, Martin

1977 *The Marxist Concept of Ideology: A Critical Essay.* Cambridge: Cambridge University Press.

Shklar, Judith

1966 "The Political Theory of Utopia: From Melancholy to Nostalgia." In *Utopias and Utopian Thought*: 101–15. Edited by Frank Manuel. Boston: Beacon Press.

Sklar, Kathryn Kish

1973 *Catherine Beecher: A Study in American Domesticity*. New Haven, Conn.: Yale University Press.

Soelle, Dorothee

1981 " 'Thou Shalt Have No Other Jeans Before Me' (Levi's Advertisement, Early Seventies): The Need for Liberation in a Consumerist Society." In *The Challenge of Liberation Theology: A First World Response*: 4–16. Edited by Brian Mahan and L. Dale Richesin. Maryknoll, N.Y.: Orbis Books.

Stassen, Glen ed.

1977 *The Journal of Religious Ethics. Vol. 5, No. 1.* Missoula, Mont.: Scholars Press.

Stead, William T.

1964 *If Christ Came to Chicago*. New York: Living Books Inc. (Reprint of 1894 edition).

Strain, Charles R.

1976 "Bruno Bauer's Theory of Alienation During the Critical Years, 1839–1843." Unpublished Ph.D. Dissertation. University of Chicago.

1977 "Ideology and Alienation: Theses on the Interpretation and Evaluation of Theologies of Liberation," *Journal of the American Academy of Religion* 45: 473–90.

1978 "Toward a Generic Analysis of a Classic of the Social Gospel: An Essay-Review of Walter Rauschenbusch, *Christianity and the Social Crisis*," *Journal of the American Academy of Religion* 46: 525–543.

Streng, Frederick J., Lloyd, Charles L., Jr., and Allen, Jay T.
1973 *Ways of Being Religious.* Englewood Cliffs, N.J.: Prentice-Hall.

Taylor, Charles
1975 *Hegel.* Cambridge: Cambridge University Press.

Tillich, Paul
1952 *The Courage to Be.* London: Collins.
1955 *Biblical Religion and the Search for Ultimate Reality.* Chicago: University of Chicago Press.
1957 *The Protestant Era.* Abridged Edition. Chicago: University of Chicago Press.
1971 *Political Expectation.* Edited by James Luther Adams. New York: Harper and Row.
1977 *The Socialist Decision.* Translated by Franklin Sherman. New York: Harper and Row.

Todorov, Tzvetan
1975 *The Fantastic: A Structural Approach to a Literary Genre.* Translated by Richard Howard. Ithaca, N.Y.: Cornell University Press.

Tracy, David
1974 "Religious Language as Limit Language," *Theology Digest* 22: 291–307.
1975 *Blessed Rage for Order: The New Pluralism in Theology.* New York: Seabury Press.
1981 *The Analogical Imagination: Christian Theology and the Culture of Pluralism.* New York: Crossroad Books.

Troeltsch, Ernst
1957 *Christian Thought: Its History and Application.* Edited by Baron von Hügel. New York: Meridian Books.
1960 *The Social Teachings of the Christian Churches.* 2 vols. Translated by Olive Wyon. New York: Harper and Row.
1961 *Gesammelte Schriften, Dritter Band. Der Historismus und seine Probleme.* Aalen: Scientia Verlag. Reprint of Tübingen: J.C. B. Mohr (Paul Siebeck) 1922 edition.
1971 *The Absoluteness of Christianity and the History of Religions.* Translated by David Reid. Richmond, Va.: John Knox Press.
1977 "What Does 'Essence of Christianity' Mean?" In *Writings on Theology and Religion.* Translated and edited by Robert Morgan and Michael Pye. Atlanta: John Knox Press.

Turner, Victor

1974 *Dramas, Fields, and Metaphors: Symbolic Action in Human Society*. Ithaca, N.Y.: Cornell University Press.

1980 "Social Dramas and the Stories About Them," *Critical Inquiry* 7: 141–68.

Walzer, Michael

1969 *The Revolution of the Saints: A Study of the Origins of Radical Politics*. New York: Atheneum.

Warren, Robert Penn

1946 *All the King's Men*. New York: Bantam Books.

Wellmer, Albrecht

1971 *Critical Theory of Society*. Translated by John Cumming. New York: Herder and Herder.

Welter, Barbara

1974 "The Feminization of American Religion, 1800–1860." In *Clio's Consciousness Raised: New Perspectives on the History of Women*: 137–57. Edited by Mary S. Hartman and Lois Banner. New York: Harper and Row.

White, Hayden

1973 *Metahistory: The Historical Imagination in Nineteenth Century Europe*. Baltimore: Johns Hopkins University Press.

1978 *Tropics of Discourse: Essays in Cultural Criticism*. Baltimore: Johns Hopkins University Press.

Wilder, Amos

1971 *Early Christian Rhetoric: The Language of the Gospel*. Cambridge, Mass.: Harvard University Press.

Wills, Garry

1979 *Inventing America: Jefferson's Declaration of Independence*. New York: Vintage Books.

Wise, Gene

1980 *American Historical Explanations: A Strategy for Grounded Inquiry*. Second edition. Minneapolis: University of Minnesota Press.

INDEX OF NAMES

D

E

F

G

H